The Business of Sports Agents

The Business of Sports Agents

KENNETH L. SHROPSHIRE and
TIMOTHY DAVIS

PENN

University of Pennsylvania Press

Philadelphia

Copyright © 2003 University of Pennsylvania Press
All rights reserved
Printed in the United States of America on acid-free paper

10 9 8 7 6 5 4

Published by
University of Pennsylvania Press
Philadelphia, Pennsylvania 19104-4011

Library of Congress Cataloging-in-Publication Data

Shropshire, Kenneth L.
The business of sports agents / Kenneth L. Shropshire and Timothy Davis.
    p. cm.
    Includes bibliographical references and index.
    ISBN 0-8122-3682-3 (cloth : alk. paper)
    1. Sports agents—United States.   2. Sports—Corrupt practices—United States.   3. College
sports—United States.   I. Davis, Timothy, 1954–   II. Title

GV734.5 .S58 2003
796'.06'9—dc21   2002072534

Contents

Preface

The Business of Sports Agents seriously examines one of the most intriguing professions to develop as sport has become big business entertainment. The sports agent industry has been glamorized by motion picture, television, and journalistic accounts. Who would not want to be the business person behind the all-star athlete? This text is focused on the business and legal aspects that impact sports agents. This book is an outgrowth of a book originally published by one of the current authors, Kenneth Shropshire, in 1990. In the decade that has passed since the publication of that work, *Agents of Opportunity: Sports Agents and Corruption in Collegiate Sports,* much has occurred. This new work reflects that evolution.

The first three chapters of this book describe what is currently taking place in the sports agent industry. Chapters 1 and 2 examine the history of the sports agent industry, its legal foundations, and what it is that agents do. Chapter 3 examines the consolidation occurring among firms in the industry. Chapter 4 begins the book's examination of the problems affecting the sports agent. Focusing on client recruitment, Chapters 5 through 8 examine criminal, ethical, and agent qualification issues. There, particularly in the ethical discussion, many questions yet to be answered by the courts are raised. Chapter 9 looks at long-standing amateurism principles and how they contribute to many of the unethical activities of agents and student athletes. Chapter 10, "Knights of Columbus Rules? Private Sports Agent Regulations," sets forth agent regulations that have been put in place by private organizations such as the NFL. Chapter 11, "The Laws," presents an overview of state laws aimed at regulating agents. This chapter also examines legal action that may be asserted against agents without the aid of these statutes. Chapter 12 addresses the new uniform law that regulates agents. The final chapter evaluates where we currently stand and where the industry is headed.

Many of the relevant statutes may be found at www.NCAA.org and elsewhere on the Internet. That site and others have the capability of regular updates that are truly valuable in this field. It should be noted that the book focuses largely, although not exclusively, on United States–based team sports. This is not intended to suggest that the athlete agent industry does not have international dimensions; it certainly does.

With the emphasis on U.S. team sports, we focus on the four major sports leagues and often list them without reference to others, including, for example, the WNBA. As competition for clients in the non-major leagues increases, many of the issues impacting the major leagues will impact these emerging leagues as well.

A point of style should be noted. The legally correct name for the individual who represents the athlete is "athlete agent," not "sports agent." The individual is the agent for the athlete, not the sport. The term sports agent, however, has developed as probably the most commonly recognized and accepted label, so the terms "athlete agent," "sports agent," and "agent" are used liberally and interchangeably throughout.

Introduction

It didn't seem so wrong. It seemed as though I worked my whole life to get where I am, and at the same time, when it was presented to me, it was like this was the time I could start to get back some of the fruits of my labor.[1]

—*Paul Palmer, former star college football running back, regarding cash payments of more than $5,000 he received from sports agent Norby Walters while a college senior*

Paul Palmer's 1980s dilemma is still with us in this millennium. He is not alone in having received payments that violate National Collegiate Athletic Association (NCAA) rules and, potentially, state and federal laws. Other student athletes have allegedly received inducements such as interest-free loans, automobiles, clothes, concert tickets, airline tickets, insurance policies, and dates with Wilhelmina models.[2] In 2000, an Auburn University basketball star admitted to taking $2,500 from Nate Cebrun, a "runner" for a sports agent. The student athlete, Chris Porter, said that he used that money to pay his mother's mortgage.[3] The interaction with Porter was not Cebrun's first controversial contact with student athletes. In 1994, Cebrun, acting on behalf of certain agents, arranged a shopping spree for Florida State student athletes.[4]

Clearly, the incidents involving Palmer, Cebrun, and student athletes from Auburn and Florida State do not constitute recent phenomena. In 1979, after receiving $1,000 from agent Mike Trope, former University of Maryland football player Steve Atkins told *Sports Illustrated*: "I knew I did something wrong. I didn't want the NCAA to do something to Maryland, but I just needed some money to pay some bills. I didn't want to sign with him [Trope], but I just needed some money to pay some bills."[5]

An illustration from the mid-1990s involved former NFL running back Greg Hill. In responding to the controversy involving agents,

Hill stated: "The guys accepting pay or the guys who want to take pay, that mainly falls on you guys—the NCAA. . . . I think that's your fault because of the strict restrictions on how long guys work and how much [financial aid] guys get. Many families are too poor to give that child money. My mom couldn't give me any money. Sometimes your team has functions where you have to dress up. Some guys don't have suits. I didn't have a suit. I had to wear jeans all of the time."[6]

The views expressed by these student athletes are not unique. From the student athlete perspective, rules perceived as unfair and irrelevant to their life circumstances effectively fail to deter problematic or possibly illegal involvement within the underground economy of college sport.

Athletes point to what they perceive as fundamental inequities in intercollegiate athletics in explaining why collegiate athletes should be paid by the colleges and universities for which they play sports. National Basketball Association (NBA) and former Georgia Tech star Stephon Marbury told the *New York Times*, "When I signed to go to Georgia Tech, we were on ESPN twenty times, instantly. When you make the tournament they just give you money. And then they say a coach can't buy you a winter coat, even if you grew up in the 'hood and you don't have one."[7] Former college basketball star Eldridge Hudson summarized the attitude of at least some athletes in a *Time* magazine cover story more than two decades ago: "Once you get out on the floor, it's a job, and you expect to get paid. If a kid is busting his ass on the court, if somebody wants to buy a car, let him have it."[8]

An affidavit submitted by NFL linebacker Johnny Rutledge regarding payments he allegedly received during his collegiate career at the University of Florida illustrates the improper transactions between student athletes and agents:

Beginning in 1997, my junior year, I began receiving money from Alfred Twitty, who worked for [then sports agent] Tank Black and his company PMI [Professional Marketing Incorporated] in Columbia, S.C. I initially received $200 per month, but in the summer of 1997 I asked for more. Twitty told me then that the usual amount for players like me was $600 per month. I thereafter received $600 per month through December of 1998. On occasion, I would get more than $600, like in December for Christmas and during my birthday month when I got $1,000 in cash.

Twitty began asking me about what car I wanted during my junior year, when it was possible I would consider turning pro. I decided to play my senior year instead. During my last season in 1998, Twitty again asked me what car I wanted. I eventually told him in December of 1998 that I wanted a Mercedes Benz S420.

I understood while I was receiving cash from Twitty that it was being provided by Tank Black. I met Tank Black in Tampa in the summer of 1998 at an event arranged by Twitty. Present were myself, Jevon Kearse, Fred Taylor and others from Tank's agency. At that time, Tank asked me "Is Tweet taking care of you?" I answered in the affirmative. And he told me that if I ever needed anything, I should contact Tweet.

I also talked with Tank during the balance of 1998 when he would call me by telephone and ask how I was doing. On one such call, I told him I needed money to buy furniture. Soon thereafter, Twitty came with the cash (about $700) and Reggie McGrew and I used it to purchase furniture for our apartment.

I was aware that Jevon Kearse and Reggie McGrew were also receiving monthly cash payments from Twitty. On occasion, the entire amount for all three of us would be delivered to one of us. . . .

I knew all along that it was expected by Twitty and Tank Black that I would sign with PMI when I turned pro. I informed them late in the 1998 season that I would do so. The day I signed with PMI—Jan. 4, 1999—I got the car I told Twitty that I wanted, which was a 1999 Mercedes S420 with all of the equipment I had said I wanted.[9]

Additionally, automobiles and cash payments may be supplemented by promises of the even more unsavory, such as drugs or prostitutes. Illustrative is the courtship of former University of Massachusetts basketball star Marcus Camby by agents John Lounsbury and Wesley Spears. This interaction involved the agents supplying Camby with prostitutes, cash payments, stereo equipment, jewelry, and rental cars with the hope that they would represent Camby once he turned pro.[10] In addition, Lounsbury and Spears, who is an attorney, followed another course of action often pursued by agents. They attempted to gain favor with Camby by ingratiating themselves with the athlete's family, friends, and other associates, oftentimes by providing them with gifts. Despite the agents' efforts, Camby signed with neither Lounsbury nor Spears, but with the ProServ athlete representation firm.

Criminally culpable conduct by agents also occurs. In 1987, a federal investigation of agents began after the alleged slashing and beating of an agent's associate by a rival agent. The investigation revealed that agents had threatened to "break the legs" of athletes who would not sign with them.[11] Although there is no evidence to suggest that threats and acts of violence are employed today, other criminal acts are being committed. In 2000, allegations of sophisticated stock market scams and money laundering became the crimes of the day. These criminal activities also contribute to the corrupt image of college sports. Gone are the "good ol' days" of raccoon coats, fight songs, and tailgate parties. Today college sports are often associated with scandal.

Why do agents engage in illegal and unethical conduct? Why do payments by agents to athletes and other improprieties persist? Economists refer to such actions by agents as "opportunism." Oliver Williamson, in his work *Markets and Hierarchies*, defines opportunism as "self-interest seeking with guile."[12] The self-interest of sports agents is the right to receive approximately 2 to 5 percent of multimillion-dollar athlete contracts coupled with up to 30 percent of multimillion-dollar endorsement deals. As a result of this income opportunity, a wide range of techniques have been developed to secure student athletes as clients. For example, payments to athletes have become standard practice for some agents. Agent Jim Abernethy told *USA Today* back in 1987, "Everyone is being paid and signed. If anyone says otherwise, they're really stupid, blind or they're lying."[13] There is no indication that the environment has dramatically improved, as indicated by the following statement: "It is the wild, wild west out there. . . . The things agents are doing to each other, to their clients is worse than I can remember. The reason is pretty simple: there is more big money, but few hard-core punishments to serve as a deterrent to an agent who breaks the rules or breaks the law."[14]

The absence of meaningful improvement is attributable, in part, to heightened competition for getting the rewards of representing an athlete. As will be discussed in greater detail in Chapter 3, the trend toward consolidation of sports agency firms affords the larger firms advantages in securing clients. Thus, structural changes in the industry create the potential for exacerbating problems derived from competition for the limited numbers of athletes. Consolidations have created deep-pocketed representation firms such as SFX Sports (SFX), International Management Group (IMG), Octagon, and Assante Corporation (Assante) that have the resources to spend considerable amounts to obtain and retain athlete clients. SFX reportedly advanced Peter Warrick a $500,000 line of credit as an advance on the bonus he was to receive from the Cincinnati Bengals upon signing his initial contract. The firm spent more in attempting to recapture Warrick as a client when he fired them days following the draft.[15] Competitors are not averse to turning to illegal conduct as a way of leveling what may be perceived as an un-level playing field in their efforts to sign clients. For example, agents Lounsbury and Spears not only spent significant sums of money, but were willing to take risks that exposed them to criminal liability in their respective attempts to sign a representation agreement with Marcus Camby.

Changes occurring in the business of sports agency converge with the uniquely American sacred cow: collegiate amateur sports. Collegiate sport, although slowly evolving, is the last field in the world where athletes are supposed to receive absolutely no direct monetary compensation for their athletic prowess. All the athlete may receive, under NCAA rules, is room, board, tuition, and educational fees. An athlete who requires more is only in limited circumstances allowed to work to earn it or even receive legitimate loans.

This concept of amateurism becomes more problematic when one understands that the Greek amateurism that many perceive American collegiate sports to be founded on may have actually allowed amateur athletes to receive compensation. Classicist David C. Young maintains that amateur athletes in ancient Greece won prizes worth as much as the value of ten years' wages.[16] If this is the case, then why is so much energy exerted to ensure that collegiate athletes receive no compensation? And even if the Greeks were not compensated, why is it so important to retain this limitation today? And what of the fact that many of the athletes generating these huge collegiate athlete dollars are African Americans from lower economic backgrounds? These issues are key elements in the present agent-regulation problem.

What is being done to stop undesirable agent activities? First, state and federal prosecutors are taking action. For example, beginning in 1999, the agent most aggressively pursued by state and federal forces was William "Tank" Black.[17] His premier client was NBA star Vince Carter. Carter fired Black as the details of the evidence alleged against Black unfolded.[18] High-profile prosecutorial action goes back as far as 1989 when sports agents Norby Walters and Lloyd Bloom were convicted and sentenced for racketeering, conspiracy, mail fraud, wire fraud, and extortion after a trial that showcased sports and entertainment figures like then University of Michigan head football coach Bo Schembechler and singer Dionne Warwick. That conviction, ironically, was ultimately overturned. In addition to prosecutorial action, colleges and universities are taking direct action against agents. In 1999, the University of Southern California sued Robert Caron, attorney and unregistered agent, alleging that he improperly induced certain of its student athletes to violate NCAA rules.[19]

Second, twenty-nine states, prior to 2001, had passed or were contemplating some sort of legislation to regulate athlete agents. As addressed in Chapter 11, these laws focus on regulating illegal activities of agents. Unfortunately, legislation that has either been enacted or proposed has done little to ensure agent competency. In fact, except for the higher price tag, registering to be a sports agent is often as simple as obtaining a license to fish: complete a form, pay a fee, and you're a "licensed" sports agent. Florida, for example, is the lone state requiring applicants to pass a competency exam. The number of states that have enacted athlete agent legislation will likely increase with the promulgation of the Uniform Athlete Agents Act in August 2000. A principal goal of this act, which was prepared by the National Conference of Commissioners on Uniform State Laws, is to create uniform standards for regulating athlete agents. Proponents of the act hope that uniform standards will curtail the noncompliance with existing state legislation.

Third, the NCAA is vigorously reviewing existing concepts of amateurism. For example, the NCAA is considering proposals that, if enacted, will significantly redefine its concept of amateurism. One proposed rule will permit athletes who compete as professionals to retain partial eligibility to play in intercollegiate athletics.[20] Under existing NCAA regulations, such an athlete would be permanently banned from participating in that sport at the intercollegiate level.[21] In addition, the sports agent question is an important element in the NCAA's regulatory review process. For example, the NCAA is contemplating steps to address the increasing influence and threat of corruption posed by "street agents,"[22] individuals that serve as the intermediaries between sports agents and athletes before and after they enter college.

What can be done to stop the corruption associated with sports agents in collegiate athletics? Improprieties occur because the opportunity exists to make money. The solution, in broadest terms, is simple: remove the opportunity to prosper by "cheating." Impose sanctions that penalize agents who act improperly. And, perhaps more importantly, eliminate the opportunity to benefit from such conduct by implementing reforms that recognize the economic, social, and structural realities of college sports. This is all, as you will read, much more simply said than done. The reality is that the system may always have major flaws.

Part I
Background

Chapter 1

Historical and Legal Foundations

A Brief History of the Business

The sports agent profession is not a new one. What is new are the high finance and intense competition that pervade the profession. Most attribute the genesis of the athlete agent industry to theatrical promoter, impresario, and showman Charles C. "Cash and Carry" Pyle. Pyle was the agent for many athletes in the early part of this century, most notably the legendary football star Harold "Red" Grange,[1] the "Galloping Ghost," a charter member of the NFL Hall of Fame. It was Pyle who negotiated a $3,000-per-game contract for Grange to play professional football with the Chicago Bears in 1925. In addition, he negotiated for Grange to receive more than $300,000 in movie rights and endorsements including a Red Grange doll, a candy bar, and a cap.[2] Other Pyle sports clients included tennis stars Mary K. Brown and Suzanne Lenglen.[3] Lenglen was the Wimbledon singles champion from 1919 to 1923. She signed with Pyle in 1926 for $50,000 to become the first professional tennis player.[4] Another example of an early sports agent was cartoonist Christy Walsh. Walsh, according to *Sports Illustrated*, advised baseball Hall of Famer Babe Ruth to invest in annuities prior to the stock market crash of 1929.[5]

During the 1960s, the number of sports agents increased and individuals from diverse backgrounds and professions entered the industry. For example, considerable press coverage was given to Hollywood movie producer J. William Hayes, the agent for actor Vince Edwards (television's Ben Casey), when Hayes orchestrated a $1 million "holdout" by Los Angeles Dodgers' pitching superstars Sandy Koufax and Don Drysdale.[6] In a holdout, a technique used to gain leverage in negotiations with a team, the athlete is, in effect, "held out" from playing with a team until the parties negotiate an agreement on the terms of the player contract. The Koufax-Drysdale holdout was precipitated by a demand for a salary of $167,000 per year for each player for three years. This figure represented an amount that was $42,000 more than the salary earned by the highest-paid player of the day, Hall of Famer Willie Mays. As part of their negotiating strategy, Drysdale and Koufax signed with Paramount Pictures to act in a movie if their contract demands were not met.

Yet even in the mid-1960s, the use of an agent by an athlete was a conspicuous enough event to receive coverage in *Time*.[7] Before settling the Dodgers' contract dispute with Drysdale and Koufax, Dodgers' president Walter O'Malley told *Sports Illustrated*, "We can't give in to them. There are too many agents hanging around Hollywood looking for clients."[8] O'Malley's prognostication regarding the future was prescient.

The development of the sports agent as a recognized professional has by no means been smooth. One of the standard anecdotes of the industry, disputed by some, is one told about the legendary coach of the Green Bay Packers, Vince Lombardi. It was time to negotiate center Jim Ringo's contract for the coming year. The player came into the office with a gentleman wearing a suit. When Lombardi asked the player to identify the gentleman, Ringo responded that he had come to help in the contract negotiation. The story has it that Lombardi excused himself, stepped into the next room, and made a phone call. When he returned he informed Ringo that he was negotiating with the wrong team because he had just been traded to Philadelphia.

Lombardi was not alone in his view of agents. Another team executive, Don Klosterman, of what was then the NFL's Houston Oilers, told *Time*, "We spend $200,000 a year in evaluating talents and some uninformed agent is going to tell *us* what a player's worth? They're just parasites, in it for a fast buck."[9] Many believe that Klosterman's blunt and early view was fairly accurate.

Obviously, acceptance of the sports agent by management has come a long way since the days of O'Malley, Lombardi, and Klosterman. It is now more common than not for a player to be represented by an agent. Professors Schubert, Smith, and Trentadue, in their book *Sports Law*, conclude that the evolution of the sports agent profession is not accidental, but simply a natural response to dramatic developments witnessed in the professional sports arena during this century.[10] The authors cite several events that have transpired during this time period to account for the prominent position agents currently have in the sports industry.

First was the demise of the extensive use of reserve and option clauses in standard player contracts through the early 1970s. These clauses bound athletes to teams in perpetuity without an opportunity to have their contracts affected by open-market bidding. Beginning in the mid-1970s, however, courts and arbitrators began to deliver rulings that invalidated the perpetual nature of these clauses. In the 1970s, athletes in the major sports—professional football,[11] basketball[12] and hockey,[13]—successfully asserted that mechanisms such as the draft and reserve clauses constituted improper restraints of trade in that they limited players' ability to market their services freely. In this regard, *Mackey v. National Football League* is illustrative.[14] In this case, the player compensation rule known as the "Rozelle Rule" provided that "when a player's contractual obligation to a team expires and he signs with a different club, the signing club must provide compensation to the player's former team."[15] The court held that the rule constituted an unreasonable restraint of trade in violation of Section 1 of the Sherman Act. In reaching this conclusion the court stated: "[The Rozelle Rule] operates as a perpetual restriction on a player's ability to sell his services in an open market throughout his career."[16] With the opening provided by these favorable court decisions, athletes obtained increased bargaining power.

Second, competition from newly created leagues in football, hockey, and basketball presented athletes with an appealing alternative to participation in the established leagues. Athletes were able to tell owners that they would command fair-market compensation or they would take their services to the rival leagues. This demand led to higher salaries, which were simultaneously enlarged by the voracious appetite of the newly formed leagues to sign players of some fame. Examples include the signing of then collegiate All-American Joe Namath by the upstart American Football League and the later signings of NFL veterans Paul Warfield, Larry Csonka, and Jim Kiick by the rival World Football League for relatively astronomical salaries. Economist Roger Noll of Stanford University wrote in 1988 that interleague competition was an important cause of increases in player salaries. During the National Basketball Association–American Basketball Association wars from 1967 to 1972, the average professional basketball player salary increased from $20,000 to $90,000.[17] During the United States Football League (USFL) and NFL war between 1982 and 1985, the average salary for players rose from $90,000 to $190,000.[18]

Third, the strength of the unions went from informal to the powerful position most hold today. Although the major sports unions have varying degrees of strength, they have all had an impact in increasing player salaries, particularly median salaries. The unions have also been responsible for solidifying the role of agents by leaving the role of salary negotiator to the agents and not retaining it for themselves, as unions traditionally do.

Fourth, tax planning became a necessity for athletes. The higher salaries made it necessary for athletes to obtain professional tax advice. Just as with any other highly compensated individual, it is generally wise for the professional athlete to obtain competent tax advice. The advice that the athlete requires is complicated by the fact that a playing career in most sports averages less than five years. With this in mind, the planner may have to take extra precautions to protect the athlete's earnings.

Fifth, additional sources of revenue began to emerge both for the leagues and for individual players. Media interest in including sports as part of regular television programming expanded very rapidly, pouring enormous amounts of revenue into the leagues. Using the muscle of their bargaining units—players' associations—athletes benefited handsomely from this revenue bonanza. Furthermore, the increase in the degree of media exposure afforded athletes helped to widen their popularity, which resulted in a booming commercial endorsement business for players. Today this exposure includes the personal websites of athletes and other online opportunities. These five elements and the increasing complexity of the clauses required to protect athletes in player contracts caused the demand for agents to increase.

Two agents who might be appropriately referred to as the "modern fathers" of the sports agent industry for team sports were Boston-based agent Bob Woolf and New York–based agent Martin Blackman. The late Bob Woolf's beginnings in the business are chronicled in his 1976 book *Behind Closed Doors*.[19] A former criminal lawyer and college basketball player, Woolf entered the sports agent business in 1964. He maintained that he was the first attorney to specialize in the area and that as of 1976 he had negotiated more than 2,000 contracts. Woolf entered the field by serendipity when professional baseball player Earl Wilson came to his office for standard legal advice following an automobile accident. According to Woolf, "When we talked we discovered we had a lot of attitudes in common. One day we found ourselves discussing methods by which an athlete could defer income and that, I guess, is where the whole thing began."[20] Some of Woolf's most famous clients included Carl Yastrzemski, Jim Plunkett, Julius Erving, and Derek Sanderson.

While Woolf is noted as a pioneer in the representation of athletes in contract negotiations, Martin Blackman is best known for his pioneering negotiation of endorsement deals for athletes. His most famous connection of athletes with products is the series of Miller Lite television commercials featuring retired professional athletes of the "tastes great, less filling" genre. Many point to the early deals put together by Blackman as the foundation for the growth in endorsement contracts today.

Probably the most successful agent of the 1970s was Mike Trope. Trope writes about the successes and tribulations of his career in his autobiographical *Necessary Roughness*, published in 1987.[21] Trope entered the business in 1973 at the age of twenty while still a student at the University of Southern California. Not only did he enter the business at an unusually young age for any profession, but he did so with an unusually prominent client: Johnny Rodgers, the 1972 Heisman Trophy winner. This began an amazing string of signings by Trope of six Heisman Trophy winners and other first-round draft picks in the sport of football. Trope negotiated a $1.6 million contract plus a Rolls Royce for Rodgers from the Canadian Football League's Montreal Alouettes. His other clients included running backs Ricky Bell, Tony Dorsett, and Earl Campbell.[22]

Perhaps it was Trope's success, other agents' jealousy, or simply the truth that accounted for what may have been the first widely circulated stories regarding improprieties by agents in obtaining clients. When anyone young in any business is successful, it is natural to ask how it was done. And whenever there is a young "whiz kid" in any industry, he or she will probably be subject to intense scrutiny. Perhaps this explains why Trope was alleged, among other things, to have made payments to athletes to induce them to sign with him.

In his book Trope readily admits that "some things" occurred. He also makes it clear that he did not consider the rules of the NCAA to be the law of the land and so he had not, in his mind, done anything illegal. Unfortunately, he was only the first of a long line of agents to make this flawed argument. Trope alleges that his competitors started the stories about his illegal activities and maintains that he was not alone in being involved in activities that violated NCAA regulations.

One successful competitor, and one who remained in the business even after Trope retired, is agent Leigh Steinberg, who, like Trope, started out at a relatively young age. While a law student at the University of California at Berkeley, Steinberg developed a relationship with an undergraduate student and star athlete, quarterback Steve Bartkowski. Steinberg was an adviser in Bartkowski's dormitory. Bartkowski became Steinberg's first major client, and at the age of twenty-five, Steinberg negotiated a then-record $650,000 per year contract with the Atlanta Falcons of the NFL.

Steinberg continued to have great success and was noted not only for negotiating what were considered outstanding contracts for his clients, but for being a master of public relations. His unique contracts often required that athletes donate a portion of their professional contract earnings to their colleges or high schools. It was not simply the terms of these contracts that brought Steinberg public notoriety, but numerous positive quotes in the press and appearances on television shows such as "Lifestyles of the Rich and Famous." One of the hottest tickets at the NFL's Super Bowl is a ticket to the annual party hosted by Steinberg. Through such self-promotion, Steinberg manufactured an early reputation as one of the few "honest" agents.

While Steinberg and Trope became successful as individual agents, two other sports agents developed firms that became sports marketing powers: Mark McCormack's IMG in Cleveland and Donald Dell's Washington, D.C.–based ProServ.[23] IMG got its start representing athletes in professional golf. McCormack's first client, in the early 1960s, was Arnold Palmer. Because of the firm's marketing and management successes with Palmer, other golfers soon followed, including Jack Nicklaus and Gary Player. The firm eventually branched out into other sports and other areas of representation. In 1989, it represented such diverse clients as the Wimbledon Tennis Championships and the Vatican.

Donald Dell is an attorney and former captain of the U.S. Davis Cup tennis team. It is understandable, then, that ProServ got its start in tennis. Dell's first client was Arthur Ashe. Building on his success with Ashe, Dell began to represent other tennis players and, like IMG, eventually began to branch out into other team and individual sports. IMG remains a solo player while ProServ is now a part of the Clear Channel SFX corporate empire.

By 1980, other agents had become prominent. Some of them specialized in specific sports, while others represented athletes in several sports. The agent ranks continued to swell, with even boxing promoter Don King becoming certified as an agent by the National Basketball Players Association (NBPA).[24] Beginning in the 1980s, agents began to have their names closely associated with the athletes they represent. If one attends a sports agents' conference or an event where there are potential professional athletes, one can walk away with a wide array of business cards with firm names such as Sports Plus, The Sports Management Group, Superstars, Inc., and Sportstars. The owners of most of these types of firms are part-time agents and full-time stockbrokers, attorneys, accountants, insurance agents, dentists, or members of virtually any other profession. As we have seen, with the increase in the number of individuals in the industry, the hostility between agents has also increased. Some agents jokingly refer to their ongoing battles as "agent wars."

Another event has begun to impact the industry as well: the growth of women's professional sports. For example, agents were quite valuable during the existence of the WNBA's rival, the American Basketball League. They remain so in sorting through offers for their clients to play in Europe, Asia, and South America. Curiously absent from these ranks are significant numbers of female sports agents.

The new millennium has brought about a series of mega mergers of superstar successful agents, such as David Falk and Arn Tellem, joining forces with publicly traded entertainment enterprises such as, in their case, SFX. These mergers only highlight the dominant role that the concept of sports as entertainment has come to play.

Fact has blended with fiction to discredit the business with anecdotes, but not until the 1989 trial of agents Norby Walters and Lloyd Bloom were many of the anecdotal stories confirmed to the public at large. Only agents and athlete clients fully realize how intense the competition has become or what type of recruiting tactics continue today. Many agents who have unsuccessfully tried to recruit clients without making payments or taking other steps in violation of NCAA rules and state laws cannot imagine someone legitimately making a living as a sports agent. Is this the reality or only sour grapes? The chapters that follow examine the consolidation trend among sports agencies in greater detail. Also explored is conduct spurred by competition that led to the convictions of agents Walters and Bloom and, more recently, of "street agent" Myron Piggie and agent Tank Black. We also examine the call for state regulation of agents. Before these matters are addressed, we take a brief look at the principles that provide the legal basis for the athlete/agent relationship. First, however, we need to have an idea of the number of agents and athletes involved in the major professional sports (see Table 1).

TABLE 1
NUMBER OF AGENTS AND PLAYERS, MARCH 2001

	Registered Agents	*Players on Total Roster*
NBA	350 (fewer than 100 are estimated to have a client)	350
NHL	186 (with two applications pending)	750 (690 on active roster)
NFL	1,112 (30 percent have clients currently in league)	1,900
MLB	328 (only includes those who represent a player on 40-man rosters)	1,200 on 40-man rosters; 750 on 25-man rosters

Sources: Telephone interviews with representatives of the players' associations; Mark Fainaru-Wada & Ron Kroichick, *Agents of Influence*, San Francisco Chronicle C1 (March 11, 2001).

The Legal Basis of the Relationship

A great deal of criticism was directed toward Leland Hardy, the agent who negotiated the contract between then–top draft pick and current NFL running back Ricky Williams and the New Orleans Saints. Critics assailed the length and the incentive-laden nature of the contract that resulted in Williams making a base salary far less than a player of his caliber could demand. In defending Hardy against criticism that questioned the agent's competence and negotiation skills, Williams stated as follows: "I'm first and last when it comes to my decisions. . . . I don't work for my agent. My agent works for me. This was my decision and my decision alone. . . . When I got drafted, I told Leland I was going to get the deal done in the next two weeks. So we waited a little while longer . . . and after the course of negotiations [with Saints salary cap expert Terry O'Neil], Leland called and said, 'I'm going to give you some options on contracts to look at,' and when I told him what kind of a deal I wanted, he told me I shouldn't do it."[25] Williams reportedly told Hardy to reject a deal that would have paid him a guaranteed salary of $25.6 million over seven years. Instead, Williams signed a contract that paid him an upfront signing bonus of $8.8 million and required him to meet certain performance objectives in order to earn more than the yearly base salaries ranging from $175,000 to $350,000 for the years 1999 through 2002.[26]

Williams' statement is instructive for two reasons. First, Williams demonstrates an appreciation for the most fundamental principle of the agent's relationship with his principal: ultimate decision making authority rests with the principal. In addition, Williams' statement illustrates that the relationship between sports agents and the athletes whom they represent are governed by the same core concepts that govern other principal/agent relationships. Thus a personnel officer who, acting as an agent, hires an employee for a corporation, and a building leasing manager who, acting as an agent, rents residential or commercial buildings for its owner are bound by the same legal principles relevant to the sports agent's relationship with his or her client.[27]

The agency relationship is defined as "the fiduciary relationship which results from the manifestation of consent by one person to another that the other shall act in his behalf and subject to his contract, and consent by the other so to act."[28] The Restatement (Second) of the Law of Agency also provides definitions of agent and principal. The principal is "the one for whom action is to be taken."[29] In the sports context, the athlete is the principal. The agent is "the one who is to act" for the principal.[30] "The essential nature and character of the

agency relationship is that the principal authorizes his agent to contract on his behalf with one or more third parties."[31]

These definitions tell us that the agency relationship is consensual—
typically expressed in a contract. This is certainly the case in the sports
context where the major sports leagues have developed model contracts for the agent/principal relationship. For example, the National
Football League Players Association (NFLPA) has developed a "Standard Representation Agreement" for mandatory use by agents and
their football-player clients. In addition to provisions governing the
fees to which an agent is entitled, the NFLPA agreement sets forth
general principles including the concept that the "Contract Advisor"
acts "in a fiduciary capacity." The Uniform Athlete Agents Act provides the following definition: " 'Agency contract' means an agreement
in which a student-athlete authorizes a person to negotiate or solicit
on behalf of the student-athlete a professional-sports-services contract
or an endorsement contract."[32]

The above definitions relating to agency also inform us that the
most basic obligations that agents owe to their principals are defined
not only by contract, but by the fiduciary characteristics of the relationship. A fiduciary is defined as "one who acts primarily for the benefit
of another."[33] Consequently, the essence of the principal/agent relationship spawns a fundamental obligation that the "agent owes his
principal the fiduciary duty of undivided loyalty and the duty to act
in good faith at all times. This fiduciary relationship is imposed by law
upon the agent because the very nature of the agency relationship
involves the principal entrusting his fortune, reputation, and legal rights
and responsibilities to his agent whose actions, for better or worse, vi-
tally affect the economic well-being and reputation of the principal."[34]

As alluded to above, Ricky Williams' statement also reflects the basic
notion that it is an agent's duty to carry out the desires of its principal.[35] This certainly makes sense, as the agent acts not to carry on its
own business affairs, but those of the principal.[36] Thus it is the agent's
duty to act in accordance with his or her principal's instructions even
if the agent believes they are unwise. As stated by two commentators,
"An agent has the duty to obey all of his principal's lawful instructions
no matter how arbitrary or capricious any of those instructions seem
to the agent or anyone else. . . . By contrast, if the principal's instructions are illegal, immoral, unethical, or opposed to public policy, as
where the principal instructs his agent to bribe another to obtain business for his principal, the agent has no duty to obey."[37] Moreover, by
acting on its principal's behalf, the agent assumes a duty that it "possesses a degree of skill commensurate with the job to be done and that

he will use such skill with diligence."[38] In exercising this duty of reasonable care and skill, it is important to emphasize that the agent does not guarantee or insure that he or she will achieve the result desired by the client unless the agent has expressly agreed to do so.[39] Rather the agent has fulfilled his or her duty by acting with the care and skill employed by a reasonable person under the same circumstances.[40]

Agent Michael B. Siegel notes the tension created by this agency norm. "I can't play for him [the athlete] and he can't negotiate for me. But I think it's important that a guy [athlete] be in a position so that he can determine whether he wants to go left or right."[41] Siegel knowingly concludes, "if they say they want to go left and I disagree, I will give them every reason why they should go right. If after I lay it out for them and we discuss it and they still want to go left, then it's fine because they have made an educated decision."[42]

Another basic duty of the agent to the principal seems particularly relevant in the sports context. The agent must account to its principal for all of the principal's funds that come into the agent's possession as a part of the agency relationship.[43] Other basic duties that the agent owes to the principal include the duty to comply with the law, the duty to notify the principal of all matters that may affect the principal's interests, and the duty not to delegate the performance to another without the consent of the principal.[44]

Finally, the agent owes a duty of loyalty and good faith to its principal. This duty precludes an agent from acting on behalf of parties adverse to his or her principal.[45] Courts have attempted to incorporate these core concepts into rulings addressing matters ranging from agent malpractice to conflict of interest. Further, as discussed in Chapters 11 and 12, some state legislatures, as well as the recently promulgated Uniform Athlete Agents Act, attempt to explicitly spell out these obligations.

Chapter 2
The Business

"That's what agents are for."

—*Latrell Sprewell of the New York Knicks explaining why he failed to inform his team and teammates about missing a week of practice prior to the 1999–2000 NBA season*

For many people, the life of a sports agent conjures up visions of a Hollywood lifestyle complete with fast cars, fancy clothes, and beautiful women. The motion picture *Jerry Maguire* and the television series *Arli$$* have done much to further glamorize the profession. Some sports agents refer to their profession as "the business," in much the way natives of New York or San Francisco refer to their towns as "the city." Long-time successful agent Leigh Steinberg once described the stereotypical agent as "short and slick, he wears a gold chain around his neck and a diamond ring on his pinky finger; he's armed with a stream of fast talk and a package of promises to fatten his wallet at the expense of the athlete."[1] Statements made in a more recent interview suggest that Steinberg continues to view agents with something that falls short of admiration. "One of the major problems of contemporary agentry is the lack of collegiality. . . . With most agents, they seem to be psychologically incapable of finding the good or acknowledging the strengths of their competitors, and it's really sad. I didn't want my wife to marry me because I convinced her [that] all other men were [jerks]."[2]

It is this flashy and competitive lifestyle that many agents point to as a prime reason for their success in obtaining athlete clients. These images, as will be discussed, have also been largely responsible for the negative perceptions of sports agents.

Who Needs an Agent?

Although sports agents often exude the heady glamour of life in the fast lane, in reality agents attract clients primarily by performing valuable services for athletes who are enmeshed in increasingly complex business activities on and off the field. Agents provide a level of parity in negotiations between athletes and clubs or other entities for whom athletes have contracted to perform. Club management representatives have had years to become expert negotiators, sometimes negotiating dozens of contracts per year. The athlete may have only one opportunity to negotiate a contract in an entire professional career. A sports agent, however, may have negotiated many sports contracts and is often a match for the negotiating experience of the management representative. Even an agent who has not negotiated dozens of contracts in sports may have experience negotiating contracts in other business settings. Rarely does a student athlete possess similar talents.

Reginald Wilkes was a premedical student at Georgia Tech University. When he graduated from college, he had no idea that he would be drafted and subsequently be named the NFL's rookie of the year. Even with his serious academic background, Wilkes recalls, "I don't think I was mentally prepared to choose an agent or negotiate a contract." He adds that it would be difficult for any student fresh out of college to attempt to negotiate a contract without an agent.[3]

A different perspective, however, was offered by then veteran NFL wide receiver Carl Pickens, who defied conventional wisdom by negotiating a contract without any direct form of representation. Following a release from his acrimonious relationship with the Cincinnati Bengals, Pickens signed a five-year deal worth $20 million with the Tennessee Titans. During the negotiation process, Pickens fired his second agent and may have received advice from a third, the agent who represents Tennessee Titans' head coach, Jeff Fisher.[4] In commenting on whether he had anyone review the contract, Pickens stated that he knew what to look for after eight years in the league. "This is my third time going through this situation. . . . I'm the one that has to deal with the deal at the end of the day, so I kind of know what I want. I can come down here and sell myself. I don't need an agent to tell me yea or nay over a contract I can read and understand."[5]

Scholars indicate that the athlete salary negotiation is the classic scenario where the use of an agent is appropriate. In their article "When Should We Use Agents? Direct vs. Representative Negotiation," Jeffrey Z. Rubin and Frank E. A. Sander conclude that it is most appropriate to use an agent "when special expertise is required, when tactical flexibility is deemed important and—most importantly—when direct contact is likely to produce confrontation rather than collaboration."[6]

This is not to say that the use of an agent is mandatory. Until the agent became an accepted part of sports, athletes often negotiated their own contracts with management. They might or might not have the documentation reviewed by an attorney or other knowledgeable third party. Notable recent "self-negotiators" have included Ray Allen of the Milwaukee Bucks, the previously noted Carl Pickens of the Cincinnati Bengals, and Tedy Bruschi, who negotiated a two-year, $3.4-million contract to play for the New England Patriots and who at times consulted with an attorney.[7] Self-negotiators in earlier times were Danny Ainge of the Boston Celtics, Alan Trammell of the Detroit Tigers, and Mike Singletary of the Chicago Bears.[8]

Another recent illustration involves Matt Morris, a pitcher for MLB's St. Louis Cardinals. Morris reportedly dismissed his agent due to uncertainty as to where the "agent's company was going" and handled negotiations himself.[9] Morris reportedly said that Cardinals' general manager Walt Jocketty "sent me a proposal I thought was fair. They've always treated me well, even with my injuries and everything."[10] Morris recognizes that he may have left money on the table by not using an agent, but he remains satisfied with the deal he struck. "I'm sure if I had an agent, he'd be scratching at the door trying to get as much as he could but that's not the person I am and that's not the relationship I want with the club, either."[11] Morris signed a contract that will guarantee him $27 million over a four-year period.

Nevertheless, there are reasons why self-negotiation may not be a good idea. In addition to the need for "expertise" and "tactical flexibility," the avoidance of confrontation is particularly applicable in the sports setting. The athlete must play for the team once the negotiation is complete. It is often necessary in these negotiations for the athlete's representative to sing the praises of the athlete. To counter this, in the paradigm of bargaining, the management representative must discuss the skills the player lacks, whether factual or not. When the goal is to make the athlete a member of the team, both literally and ideologically, it is easier for both parties to negotiate when the player does not actually have to brag, or invite management's criticism.

An intermediate measure between self-representation and employing an agent is to use a family member or close friend for contract negotiation. George Brett is probably the most prominent athlete who took that route.[12] Similarly, hockey's Eric Lindros has been represented by his father. Long-time NBA great Dominique Wilkins had various contracts negotiated by his mother.

Others urge athletes to avoid agents and to have their contracts negotiated or reviewed by lawyers. Edward Garvey, the former executive director of the NFLPA, was one of the most vocal critics of the use of people who call themselves agents. His harshest criticism of agents homed in on the large fee that they charge. Garvey recommended that athletes use attorneys who will charge a standard hourly rate for negotiation services.

Recently, pitcher Brad Radke used an attorney to negotiate his contract with the Minnesota Twins.[13] Former University of Maryland basketball star Steve Francis hired Washington attorney Jeff Fried to provide a range of services.[14] The NBA's Ray Allen received considerable notoriety in 1999 for employing a lawyer to review a contract that he had negotiated with the Milwaukee Bucks basketball franchise. Allen's use of a team of attorneys, whom he reportedly paid up to $500 per hour to review his contract, and his retention of a business manager and accountant, provoked varying reactions.[15] Some heralded Allen's conduct as the beginning of a trend that would contribute to diminishing the power and influence of agents. Others, perhaps unable to be so prescient, nevertheless viewed Allen's decision as a wise business move that allowed him to take control of his affairs, a view shared by Allen: "It was merely a good business decision . . . I don't need an agent. I know how much money I'm going to make. If you're smart, and know what you're doing, you can negotiate what you're worth."[16] Others were quick to caution, however, that Allen's decision was prudent only because of the convergence of a unique set of circumstances—the NBA hard salary cap, and Ray Allen's intelligence, business acumen, and strong family structure.[17] Allen admitted that his decision might not be appropriate for other athletes and in particular in sports other than basketball. For example, an NBA player who would not be awarded the maximum amount permissible under the collective bargaining agreement might be better suited to use an agent who can negotiate and act as a buffer when the player and team disagree on a player's worth.

NBA star Grant Hill is represented by attorney Lon Babby, who has carved out a niche in representing professional athletes in contract negotiations at the litigation-oriented Washington, D.C. firm of Williams & Connolly.[18] Babby's other athlete clients include the NBA's Tim Duncan, Shane Battier, Christian Laettner, Malik Rose, and Andre Miller, the NFL's Raghib Ismail, and several WNBA stars including Chamique Holdsclaw. Although Babby charges $400 or more per hour for his legal services, he asserts that the total cost is considerably less than the standard 2 to 4 percent agent fee typical in the NBA.[19]

Babby charged Hill a reported $100,000 to negotiate his first contract, a six-year, $45-million deal with the Detroit Pistons. The standard 4 percent would have cost Hill $1.8 million.

Nevertheless, according to some agents, charging an hourly fee has disadvantages including hampering the development of both a business and personal relationship between attorney and client. This view is held by attorney agent Leonard Armato, who once represented Shaquille O'Neal of the Los Angeles Lakers. "Some clients prefer to have the knowledge that there's a fixed cost and not worry whether conversations, communications or meetings are work and are billable or were social and not billiable. . . . An hourly fee is much easier when a client puts a contract on your desk and says, 'here, negotiate this deal.' But when you provide a range of services, the relationship between the agent and athlete often runs a range beginning in business and ending in friendship."[20]

Lon Babby believes that another advantage of athlete representation by an attorney is that an attorney attempts to avoid appearing as the "bigger-than-life agent who calls the shots for his clients. 'The player is the brand name that should be known, not the agent's.' "[21]

A related issue involves the advantages that may accrue to an athlete who hires an attorney, whether the attorney acts merely as an agent or in a dual capacity as an attorney and agent. A former professional basketball player is reported to have expressed the following view regarding lawyers who represent athletes: "Lawyers do the same things agents do: they lie, connive, cheat, and hurt athlete clients."[22] Despite the cynicism expressed in this statement, scholars have identified several advantages that can result from an attorney who represents athletes. From the perspective of competence, the education and training necessary to become an attorney arguably prepares them to substantively understand increasingly complicated collective bargaining agreements used by professional sports leagues.[23] Moreover, unlike nonlawyer agents, attorneys representing athletes possess the duty to know the law or consult with others who know the law regarding a broad range of potentially relevant matters that traverse collective bargaining agreements, such as the Americans with Disabilities Act and workers' compensation.[24]

Other potential advantages to attorney representation include:

(1) Attorneys, in contrast to agents, are held to standards, such as the American Bar Association's Model Rules of Professional Conduct, which arguably make them more accountable to their clients. Consequently, athletes who feel their interests have not

been adequately protected by an attorney have greater avenues of recourse available, such as registering complaints with bar associations, in addition to filing malpractice claims;

(2) Information such as formal evaluations may be available to assist an athlete in researching the competence and ethics of an attorney; and,

(3) In contrast to nonlawyers, lawyers are better equipped to avoid conflicts of interest and will be held to higher standards of accountability to avoid conflicts of interest. In instances where an attorney represents more than one athlete client, "[i]f a conflict of interest is present, a lawyer-representative must fully disclose the conflict to the athletes and obtain an acknowledgment of the conflict and an express waiver of the conflict of interest from each athlete."[25]

Notwithstanding the perceived benefits of the alternatives to representation by an agent—no representation, familial representation, and attorney representation—they remain the exception. The most common practice is for the athlete to be represented by an agent. One of the conclusions of a 1977 congressional inquiry into professional sports was that "player agents are now generally accepted as permanent, highly visible, and at times positively beneficial element[s] in the sports labor relations process."[26] Former Senator John Culver stated in another setting, "when performed properly it's about as honorable a thing as you can do so these kids [student athletes] are not exploited."[27]

In the aftermath of Ray Allen's use of an attorney, newspaper headlines asked if agents are an endangered species. In a recent commentary, former basketball star and former agent Len Elmore opined that various factors may converge to radically reduce the prominence and significance of agents.

To bring down the pro sports agent house of cards, players need only to sincerely question "what are we getting for the percentage of gross compensation that we pay to our agents?" In an environment where they must constantly restate their value proposition, a majority of agents are going to be hard-pressed to prove fairly and comparatively how they enhance a player's bottom line or his overall career.

Certainly instances exist where some players feel that a few agents in fact enhance careers, but the grumblings are growing louder than the praise. . . .

The day has come when superstars can meet face-to-face with an activist owner and without an agent reach the basics of an agreement. In the NBA world of "max-out" players, a ceiling is placed on what a free agent can earn. Even in the "never-never" ("as in never leave money on the table") land of Major League Baseball the same remains true. With professional help from a lawyer, accountant or even an economist, a superstar might agree with an owner to only 80 to 90 percent of what an agent could have gotten him, and wind up in no worse position than if an agent did the deal. . . .

Thanks to the most recent collective-bargaining agreement and the millions of marketing dollars it should receive pursuant to it, the National Basketball Players Association is now in a financial position to hire a law firm or two to negotiate individual contracts for far less than the aggregate dollars spent by players for their individual agents. Players could use the savings to contract for all the services agents now propose to provide such as public relations, endorsement opportunities and financial advice. The NCAA and its member institutions would beam with glee because this development would all but erase the headaches caused by agent involvement with high school players and college players with eligibility remaining.[28]

Others involved in the industry share the views expressed by Elmore. In commenting on whether rookies need agents, agent Keith Kreiter stated, "Every contract is just a form agreement. My plummer *[sic]* could negotiate a first-round pick's contract as good as the best negotiator in the county can."[29] Notes another agent, "It used to be that it came down to good negotiation on the part of the agent, . . . but now (with the rookie scale) those skills have been taken away, so that puts the average agent on par with the David Falks and Arn Tellems of the basketball world."[30]

Elmore's comments could represent the future of the industry. However, for now it appears that agents will continue to play a prominent role in representing professional athletes. The phrase "value added" is often employed to explain the enduring prominence of agents who stress that "he or she offers management services as well [as negotiation services], everything from finding a hotel room for a player's mother for when she flew into town to shopping an athlete when trade time looms."[31] Notes another agent, "contract negotiation becomes secondary in a changing sports world accentuated by the merging of sports and entertainment, and by new technologies that create expanding opportunities to exploit the athlete's image for financial gain in contexts extending beyond the sport in which he or she plays." Moreover, agents remain important because of the influence they yield. An example of such influence is that used by David Falk in helping to facilitate the trade that resulted in Stephon Marbury moving from the NBA's Minnesota to its New Jersey franchise.[32]

Agent Bill Strickland comments on the broad scope of an agent's activities: "I have in my career done everything including physically moving a client, that is driving a moving truck and loading and unloading the furniture onto and off of the truck, which was a rare case. . . . [I have handled] prenuptial agreements and rape cases, sued [an athlete's] family members, attended funerals, simply shown support for an athlete, sat with mothers, parents and significant others who may not understand the process going on with a player. I've done a little bit of everything."[33]

Interesting questions regarding the duties of agents have been raised in recent years. As addressed in Chapter 1, some of these questions arose in the context of the representation of Heisman Trophy winner Ricky Williams by agent Leland Hardy.[34] Williams was the fifth player selected in the 1999 NFL draft. More importantly, however, he was the lone draft pick of the New Orleans Saints. The team traded away all other picks as they coveted Williams and this was the only way the team could be assured of selecting him. Most viewed this as an opportunity for Williams, through his agent, to exert tremendous leverage. Not only did the Saints' action show how much they wanted Williams, but the team obtained an additional benefit. Rather than having to negotiate contracts with and pay up to eight new players, it only had to negotiate with and pay one player—Williams—thus the contract to be negotiated had a substantial upside for Williams from a negotiation perspective. But instead of securing a contract with substantial amounts of guaranteed monies, Williams' contract was incentive laden. In essence, Williams, beyond a sizeable signing bonus, would have to earn every dollar above the minimum base salary. Most faulted agent Leland Hardy for this deal. As discussed in Chapter 1, Williams indicated in an interview in the *SportsBusiness Journal* that Hardy had simply structured the deal according to his instructions: "This was my decision and my decision alone."[35] This being the case, Hardy was acting in the role as the agent is traditionally defined. Williams' view of Hardy has apparently changed. In the year 2000, Williams reportedly filed a countersuit against Leland Hardy and Percy Miller (aka Master P) alleging incompetence in Hardy's negotiation of his initial contract with the New Orleans Saints.[36] Williams' countersuit is purportedly in response to a suit in which Miller and Hardy assert that the player failed to pay a $75,000 installment toward the commission arising out of his signing bonus.

The agent concept in sports is similar to that which has long existed in the motion picture, theatrical, television, and music sectors of the entertainment industry, as exemplified by the influential William Morris Agency. The duties that agents undertake in the entertainment industry, however, are often more specific than those of the agent in sports. In the entertainment industry, traditionally it is common for a performer to employ a group of advisers, including an agent, a personal manager, a business manager, and an attorney, in contrast with the athlete who may employ *an* agent.[37] The combined fees for the entertainer's group of advisers have been estimated to equal 30 to 40 percent of the entertainer's gross income.[38] The "agent" in the entertainment industry is loosely defined as the person who finds employment for the entertainer.

Another distinguishing characteristic relates to the nature of regulation. The agent in entertainment has been regulated by state laws for some time. Because of the nature of the entertainment industry, an agent can be regulated only by the laws of New York and California, the states where the entertainment industry is centered. This situation contrasts with that of the sports industry, where an agent may need to conduct business (for example, contract negotiation) in many states. As discussed further in Chapters 5, 11, and 12, this aspect of the sports agent industry has resulted in regulatory problems and influenced the creation of the recently promulgated Uniform Athletes Agents Act in 2000.

This is certainly not to say that all is perfect in the entertainment industry relative to the sports industry. The personal manager in entertainment wears many of the hats the sports agent does. According to the entertainer Kashif, personal managers often enter the business like sports agents, with no experience at all. Kashif quipped that it would not surprise him to hear a personal manager say, "Yesterday I was a garbage man, today I'm a manager." Fortunately, it is a generally recognized practice in the entertainment industry for the personal manager to hire professionals to handle the tasks of the combined team.[39]

Increasingly, sports agents provide services beyond the negotiation of the professional contract.[40] These additional services may include the following: providing advice regarding financial matters such as tax, investment, insurance, and money management; obtaining and negotiating endorsement contracts; medical and physical health and training consultations; legal (including criminal) consultation; post-playing career counseling; counseling players regarding their particular sport; counseling players regarding their media image; and counseling players on matters pertaining to everyday life.[41] All of these services and more are certainly required, in varying degrees, by today's professional athletes.[42] Once the player signs a contract, the agent may continue to have ongoing obligations, depending on the nature of the specific athlete/agent agreement. Some agents are finished with their duties once the player contract is negotiated and simply receive their fee. Others maintain an ongoing relationship, providing certain of the laundry list of functions described above, particularly financial, endorsement, and counseling services.

A negative aspect of the business is what some agents refer to as "babysitting," such as taking the 1:00 A.M. telephone call about the bad game the player had that night. Atlanta-based sport agent and attorney David Ware expands on the related statements of Bill Strickland, "The good agents have to accept that as a part of the business. If you don't like being in the personal service business, it's [being a sports agent] not the business for you. You may not think the 1:00 A.M. phone call from a player is important, but obviously he does."[43] The burdensome nature of this role was expressed by another agent as follows: "An athlete calls you at 12:30 in the morning and says, 'I've got this girl in my hotel room and now my wife's here. What do I do?' Or, 'I've got my shoes in Detroit and I'm in Orlando. What do I do?' It's a full-time service position. Being called an 'agent' is misleading. It's a combination. You're agent, manager, social worker, family counselor, psychologist. All under one hat."[44]

On the other hand, not all agents view this role from a negative perspective. As noted in Chapter 1, some sports agents use their babysitter function as a tool for recruiting players. In this regard, it becomes a part of the value added that an agent can offer in contrast to a player representative such as an attorney, who only negotiates a contract for a player. Thus, they accept the fluid role of agents. Notes agent Larry Fox, agents have evolved into " 'full-service providers,' handling their clients' finances, endorsement and marketing opportunities, and even personal affairs. . . . An agent is wearing many different hats. Contract negotiation is one of the minor roles that an agent performs."[45]

Some athletes do not need such services and consequently do not want to pay for them. NBA player Pat Garrity, in commenting on why he selected attorney Lon Babby to represent him rather than an agent, remarked, "I didn't want someone always checking up on me. . . . I'm a mature person and can take care of a lot of things myself."[46] Others welcome having an agent available to help deal with everyday matters from paying monthly bills to assisting in the purchase of a home.

Not all sports agents can provide all the services an athlete may require. That too causes some confusion in the business. Most people today accept that professionals such as doctors or lawyers specialize in particular areas. You may go to a general practitioner who will refer you to a surgeon to take care of the actual problem you are enduring. Likewise, your tax attorney may refer you to a trial lawyer. There are agents, however, who will attempt to provide services they are not qualified to perform for fear that they will lose their athlete clients by referring them to an expert. This is especially true when the expert is (or is secretly anxious to become) a rival agent.

Full-Service Firms

Some agents maintain that athletes not only want their contract negotiated but want to have the agent manage their income as well. Obviously, this is appropriate when the agent is qualified. In other cases,
however, the agent may not provide adequate service in this capacity.
In fact, the agent may be violating state or federal laws or relevant
codes of ethics if not properly licensed to perform this duty. To
remedy this and similar problems, agents have recognized that special
steps must be taken if they want to provide more than contract
negotiation services. One solution is the full-service sports management firm, the largest and most prominent being Cleveland-based
IMG. There are mega newcomers as well, such as SFX Sports,
Octagon Professional Athlete Representation, and Assante. These full-
service firms provide, under one roof, individuals who negotiate contracts and deal with financial issues, endorsements, and whatever else
athletes might encounter during and even after their careers. In addition, these firms possess the resources that allowed IMG to ploy millions of dollars into the development of a controversial 190-acre sports
academy. The facility gives it a competitive advantage not only against
smaller agencies but also against larger rivals SFX, Octagon, and
Assante, which send their clients to independent training sites with
which they have forged relationships.[47] The newer firms also promise
entrée to the entertainment industry. Many of the most successfully
marketed athletes, such as basketball's Michael Jordan and golf's Arnold Palmer and Tiger Woods, are clients of these firms. Jordan even
remained a client of SFX during his retirement from the NBA.

The key benefits of a full-service agency are twofold. First, the athlete is presumably able to receive the best service possible without having to shop around for various specialists. Second, the agent does not
lose any part of the client's business. In fact, the athlete often pays an
additional fee for any services beyond the initial contract negotiation.
Where the cost of a contract negotiation may range anywhere from a
low of 2 percent to a typical high of 5 percent of the total value of a
contract, often an endorsement will cost the athlete as much as 30 percent of the value of the contract negotiated.

The marketing service a sports agent provides is not just a matter of
pairing an athlete with some product that will pay the price. Although
there is no special license required to be involved in product endorsements, an athlete can be harmed by an inexperienced representative.
David Falk, founder of SFX Sports, observes that "sports marketing is a very specialized business. There is a very broad range of

opportunities."[48] Falk notes that product choice is important and that the agent must be careful in determining "what kind of an athlete is appropriate to be utilized for a particular [product] campaign."

Not only is the product choice important, but so is the type of relationship the athlete has with the product. The athlete/product relationship may range from a one-day appearance at a local automobile dealership to what Falk calls the "autograph relationship" with a product. The autograph relationship is one where a product is named for a particular athlete, such as the Air Jordan athletic shoe manufactured by Nike and named after NBA star Michael Jordan, a long-time Falk client.

The agent must be particularly conscious of client overexposure. There is a view in the sports and entertainment industry that a client who is overexposed, or who appears in the public eye too frequently, will not be able to demand high endorsement dollars. The full-service sports marketing firms pay particular attention to this issue.

By way of example, Octagon used the in-house resources available to its clients in devising a comprehensive marketing plan for the NFL's top pick in 2001, Michael Vick. Octagon's director of media and business development created pre- and post-draft strategies for shaping and marketing Vick's image. These strategies included creating a series of comedic commercials that revolved around Vick and the Heisman Trophy, developing a plan to broaden the scope and extent of public service announcements that Vick would make, controlling media access to Vick, and working with the Atlanta Falcons (the team with which Vick signed) to develop and implement marketing plans for Vick.[49]

Praise for full-service firms is not universal. In fact, it is not difficult to interpret the practice of providing all services under one roof as a classic case of conflict of interest. Reginald Wilkes, the former NFL star, makes the analogy of a union that hires a money-management firm to run a pension fund. It is unlikely that the union would want the same firm also to evaluate the fund's performance, establish investment guidelines, and evaluate those guidelines as well. As Wilkes points out, such a setup "invariably breeds an air of conflict of interest. The full-service agent firms are the exact same thing as far as I'm concerned."[50]

Edward V. King, Jr., a San Francisco–based attorney who has successfully sued several agents for athletes, agrees with this as well. "It's like having all the foxes in the hen house. What you lose with a full service firm is a proper check-and-balance system."[51] Despite this warning, however, even King maintains that often the full-service firm is the best place for the athlete to go.

But the current allure of these mega-firms cannot be overrated. First, the difficulty in competing with these firms is being acknowledged by the large number of smaller, boutique firms merging with them. Second, in many instances this is what the athletes want. An example in 2000 was Vince Carter. Long-time journeyman agent Merle Scott was able to "close the deal" with Carter when Scott announced that he was becoming an employee of IMG. Scott as the solo agent could not match the marketing resources of the worldwide enterprise.[52]

The size and financial resources of the larger firms afford them a very distinct competitive advantage: they routinely forgo charging the commission that they can collect from recent draft picks in the NBA. These firms are willing to take the risk that they will collect more three to four years later when rookie players sign more lucrative contracts. Whether this situation will occur is dependent, of course, on whether the athlete maintains his relationship with the agent firm. The following comments regarding the 2001 NBA draft illustrate how agents hope for larger returns in the near future.

Since almost every first-round pick receives a salary that is 20 percent more than the scale each year, the No. 1 pick in this year's draft likely will make $11.92 million over three seasons. The agent's share would be $158,990, or $52,996 per year. Meanwhile, an agent that negotiated a $11.92 million for a veteran would make some $476,971 on a 4 percent commission from the deal. Therefore, profiting is dependent upon an agent retaining the player until he becomes a free agent. "It's my understanding that most agents don't charge for rookie contracts," said agent Lon Babby . . . "but in return, there is some kind of moral imperative that the player will be around for his free agent contract," Babby said in the ESPN.com report, "and that the agent will be appropriately paid for that."[53]

In the NBA, turnover has been relatively low. In other words, athletes tend to maintain their relationships with the agents who initially represented them. Forgoing the fee is a luxury that agents operating independently or in small firms may find difficult to afford.

The willingness of larger sports agencies to forgo rookie fees also supports the idea that for many firms the commission is of secondary importance. "The real action, the chance to earn double-digit commissions, is in moving an athlete into promotional opportunities elsewhere—sneaker and movie deals."[54]

One other impact these mega-mergers are having is a negative one on the number of agents, particularly African Americans and females, who are able to enter or continue successfully in the agent business. As one former African American agent said in returning to the full-time practice of law in 2001, "It was difficult enough battling one on one with agents, particularly the white ones who might play the race card, but how can my two man operation possibly compete against Fortune 500 companies?"

Another alternative available to the athlete who wants agent services that go beyond contract negotiations is to pull together his or her own team of professionals. If the athlete is able to retain the appropriate mix of professionals, a natural check-and-balance system is established. Each professional necessarily has some overlap with the others as well as the opportunity to review portions of their work in an unbiased manner. The athlete in this situation may, for example, hire an attorney to negotiate the player contract, an accountant to handle finances, an investment firm to handle investments, and one of the sports marketing firms to handle endorsements.

Conclusion

With this historical and business foundation established, the next chapter focuses on the consolidation that has been occurring in the industry over the last several years. Although the initial flurry of mergers and acquisitions has subsided, the end result will have a lasting impact on the business.

Chapter 3
Consolidation
An Evolving Industry

The last ten years have been marked by an evolution, influenced significantly by consolidation, of the athlete agent industry. Taking steps to create their own full-service sports agent firms, SFX Sports (SFX), Assante Corporation (Assante), and Interpublic Group's Octagon have followed the lead of industry pioneer IMG in planning for the evolution of sports into a component of the larger entertainment industry. As was mentioned in the last chapter, some smaller athlete representation firms believe that consolidation is necessary for them to be able to compete successfully in this changing marketplace. In 2001, however, there was evidence of how fragile some of these newly formed relationships can be, as lawsuits and departures were not an uncommon event for some of these relationships.

As previously noted, an agent's main source of revenue was once derived from the fees his or her clients paid to them for contract negotiation services. During the period when Bob Woolf entered the industry, the most lucrative contracts that athletes signed were with the teams for which they played. While the number of agents increased dramatically in the 1970s, so did players' salaries, the number of players desiring representation, and the number of athletes engaged in professional sports. The increase in the total amount of revenues available to sports agents led to increased prosperity for those already in the industry, and increased appeal for those desiring to join it.

With the standardization of agent fees by player unions and the imposition of salary caps by professional leagues, revenues available to sports agents from contract negotiation have plateaued. The NFL has maximized the agents' cut at 3 percent of a player's salary, a salary which is usually not even guaranteed.[1] Moreover, competition among agents often pushes that 3 percent number downward. Salary caps instituted by the NFL, NBA, and NHL, with degrees of variation, have capped the total amount available for players' salaries in each league. Another factor that has contributed to a decrease in potential revenues for agents is the modest increase in the pool of athletes. During the

1990s, the number of athletes on teams in the NBA, NHL, NFL, and MLB increased by only 16.7 percent, or 1.6 percent annually.[2]

Although the overall number of people seriously considering themselves agents has probably decreased over the past ten years, competition remains fierce. Woolf estimated in 1989 that 11,000 agents worked in the United States, far more than the number of professional athletes.[3] Today, the field has narrowed considerably. As the table in Chapter 1 reveals, in 2001 there were 1,900 players in the NFL and 1,112 certified agents. In Major League Baseball there were 1,200 players on the 40-man roster and 750 on the 25-man roster and only 328 certified agents. In the NHL, there were 690 active players and 186 certified agents and the NBA had roughly one agent for each of its 350 players.[4]

Increased competition in this market has forced agents to find ways in addition to salary contract negotiation to increase their revenues. Agents desiring to grow their practices have done so by either trying to increase their portion of the pie or the pie itself. To increase the pie, agents, for example, negotiate contracts with businesses desiring endorsers. Agents also offer athletic training, financial services, legal services, medical consultations, and postcareer development services to their clients.[5] Financial services include tax planning, financial planning, money management, investments, estate planning, incorporating the client, and income tax planning and preparation. The more services a firm offers, the larger the amount of fees it can collect from its clients. In response to a question about how agents will make their money in the future given the convergence of factors (for example, increased competition, players associations, and collective bargaining agreements), David Falk said, "I do think there will be a consolidation in the business. I do think that one of the things that's going to differentiate agents is their ability to do things other than negotiate contracts, whether it's financial services, marketing, public relations, or entertainment."[6]

Some sports agent firms have tried to increase their income potential and retain their existing client base by offering top-level services in areas such as financial planning and endorsement representation. Problematically, some firms have attempted to provide services that they do not have the wherewithal to provide. Examples of this would be poor financial planning or inadequately developed athlete endorsement opportunities. Agents sometimes fail to retain clients because they lack the requisite expertise to compete in those areas. To avoid competency-related problems, firms that lack expertise in certain areas will sometimes outsource these services to other firms. This outsourcing frequently occurs with legal services, financial planning, investments, and marketing services. Over time, this strategy has hurt some sports agent firms as players have left their firm to sign with the firm used in the outsourcing. To dissuade clients from leaving, some firms have hired legal and business professionals to fill those corporate voids. This approach is only cost effective, however, if a firm represents a sufficient number of athletes for these professionals to service.

ProServ Inc. and IMG were the pioneers of the full-service sports agency firm, which makes available, under one roof, all the services players are likely to desire. Visits to the websites of corporations that have established divisions that provide athlete representation and related services are instructive with respect to the comprehensiveness of the services that such firms are capable of offering and the advantages afforded thereby over many of their smaller competitors. In describing its Sports and Entertainment Division, Assante's website emphasizes the "comprehensive and personalized one-stop resource, getting involved in all aspects of their lives." It goes on to provide the following listing of services that illustrate the multiple functions that large firms can serve on behalf of their athlete clients:

Our services include:

• Endorsement and marketing contracts, negotiations and sports agency services
• Business management, including budgeting, day-to-day cash management, bill payment and preparation of monthly financial statements
• Personal support services, including the recruitment, management and payment of contractors and domestic staff, home maintenance and relocation assistance
• Wealth management, retirement and estate planning
• The establishment of family and specialty foundations and trusts
• Accounting and tax services.[7]

SFX boasts a similar array of services on its website. SFX lists the following areas of expertise: "contract negotiation and all 'off-field' business and marketing endeavors, including endorsements, licensing, promotions, charitable endeavors, speaking engagements and personal appearances."[8]

Not to be outdone, Octagon's website touts the comprehensive nature of its athlete representation services, which include career guidance, contract negotiations, marketing and endorsements, team relations, public relations, charitable activities, and financial-planning services. In attempting to distinguish itself from its competitors and perhaps to ward off concerns regarding lack of individualized attention, Octagon emphasizes the notion of a business partnership. "The Octagon view is that you need someone capable of taking a long-term view of your career, seeing the bigger picture. We don't have a template for success; we'll create one for you. We won't advise you to grab the money, any money, while it's on the table; we'll use our marketing skills to help you build your image and capitalize on its value. And, most of all, we'll never make you feel like you are working for us; whatever you need to make the most of your career we'll be there, working for you, to make it happen."[9]

Factors other than the need to increase potential revenues from client representation have influenced the move toward consolidation. As the Internet and cable and satellite technology increase the amount of media, products, and services available to people around the world, opportunities for athletes have grown considerably. Having the potential to offer athletes high-level service and to position athletes for numerous endorsement opportunities, large companies without much prior experience in the sports agent industry have made major inroads into the industry and captured considerable market share.

To establish their presence as credible service providers in the athlete management industry, these large corporations needed to accumulate a well-known client list quickly. In the sports agent industry, firms receive new clients in large part based on their existing client list. Without any athlete clients to speak of, the principal and perhaps only way for these firms to quickly attain an all-star client list was to purchase the top sports agent firms.

The enticements offered to induce existing sports agent firms to merge with or to become divisions within larger corporations include significant amounts of cash. Leigh Steinberg is reported to have sold his business in 1999 to Assante Corporation in a $120-million deal.[10] Other inducements include equity in the purchasing company and incentives. An example of these types of inducements is Assante's purchase of Dan Fegan's basketball practice. In exchange for all of the assets of Fegan's practice, Assante was to pay "an undisclosed amount of cash and issue 171,200 Subordinate Voting Shares in Assante. The purchase agreement also provides an earn-out. The considerable earn-out will be earned to the extent that Fegan & Associates Inc. attains certain financial targets over the five years following closing. The earn-out will be paid in a combination of an undisclosed amount of cash and up to 1,428,835 Subordinate Voting Shares."[11]

This structure seems to be typical of the deals in the market today for companies being acquired. The initial down payment to the acquired company is made with cash, the acquiring company's stock, or some combination of the two. Subsequent payments to the acquired company are paid out at future dates and the amount earned is determined by a formula pegged against the acquired company's future performance. These "earn-outs" generally pay the acquired company some amount (again, in cash, stock, or some combination of the two) based on whether target revenue figures are met.

More importantly, consolidation offers existing sports agencies enhanced opportunity for longevity. Consolidation within a larger corporate structure allows the sports management division the opportunity to offer its athlete clients numerous new services, as well as the resources to invest in capital-intensive programs such as web applications, the production of their own sports events, and athlete training facilities.

Frank Craighill realized that his company's historical 20 percent growth would not be sustainable without capital due to the increasingly complex logistics of the athlete-agent industry.[12] Consequently he sold Virginia-based Advantage International to Octagon for $30 million. Other well-known sports agencies such as Steinberg, Moorad & Dunn, Tellem & Associates, and Falk Associates Management Enterprises (FAME) also elected to be bought by large conglomerates to remain competitive.

The Marquee Group began this trend of consolidation in the mid-1990s with its purchases of Washington, D.C.–based ProServ and Connecticut-based Sports Marketing and Television International.[13] Since Marquee's purchase, larger conglomerates with one piece of the puzzle have realized the enormous potential of the sports agent industry and have acted on their intuition. SFX Entertainment, an events promoter, Assante Corporation, a money management firm, and Octagon, a piece of the Interpublic Group's global marketing web, have each made considerable investments in the past few years to establish their presence as full-service athlete representation firms.

Along with purchasing sports agent firms, the conglomerates have added marketing agencies and other businesses to the mix. Including athlete and marketing agencies within their corporate structures gives firms the ability to sell entire packages to their large corporate customers. According to Ray Clark, whose Dallas-based sports services firm was purchased in 1999 for $12 million by New York–based Omnicom Group Inc., "Consolidation is running rampant because corporate clients want it. They don't want 15 sports marketing agencies. They want one that can solve all their needs."[14]

Besides their corporate clients, these conglomerates will also be able to offer special events and exhibitions to the public. SFX has sold sports fantasies on the Internet through its website, eSuperstars.com. There, sports fans may bid on events to play golf with their favorite PGA player or take batting practice with their hometown MLB team.[15]

It would be a bad investment for the purchasing company if it were unable to receive value from the synergy suggested by the difference in acquired price and market value. While it seems that some conglomerates are overspending to receive a well-known client list, the greatest value the conglomerates receive comes from the branding a company attains from the high-profile agents it purchased. The reputations of agents such as Steinberg and Falk will now be attached to the companies that acquired them. So long as their reputations are positive, that is positive for the acquiring company.

A few methods exist that try to keep these high-profile agents with the company. In the sports agent industry, key personnel are required to sign noncompete agreements, restricting their ability to work in the industry or take clients with them for a negotiated period of time after leaving the firm. Such a strategy might be effective in the short term, but defections have occurred. Probably the most publicized defection was agent David Dunn's departure from Assante with dozens of clients. Perhaps the most promising method for retaining agents is to give them an equity stake in the company with promises of future equity through stock and stock options. Generally, this is the logic behind the earn-outs discussed earlier. It works most effectively at publicly traded companies such as SFX, but might not be as valuable to owners of smaller agent firms purchased by private companies, including IMG. Holding equity in a public company, these executives need to worry about stock price changes and how possible skirmishes might affect the outsider's view of the company.

The Players

Consolidation of the sports agency business in the 1990s involved the merger of a number of smaller firms by four companies: SFX, Assante, IMG, and Octagon. These companies have molded their sports groups to compete in this revamped industry by combining sports agents firms, sports marketing firms, and sports branding firms. While each has found its way into the industry through different outlets, they have selected sports agent pioneers to lead them.

SFX

SFX Sports began as the result of the acquisition of regional musical venues around the United States.[16] Within a short time span, the company became the leading concert promoter in the U.S. market, owning 120 venues globally, including 16 amphitheaters in the top 10 U.S. markets, as well as owning or operating venues in 31 of the top 50 domestic markets.[17] Analysts expected SFX's revenues to increase by nine percent in 1999, resulting in a lower net loss of $39.2 million.[18]

In addition to concert promoting, SFX sells Broadway subscription series and individual productions in 55 markets.[19] SFX also owns production rights to Broadway shows such as *Ragtime* and *Phantom of the Opera*.

SFX entered the sports agent business in May 1998, purchasing FAME for a reported $82.9 million in cash and one million shares of stock, worth $38.75 million at the time, and $15 million over five years if FAME's cash flow hit certain earn-out levels.[20] In the deal, SFX received one of the most coveted sports agents, David Falk, and his most prominent client, Michael Jordan.

In July, shortly after the acquisition of FAME, SFX announced it would purchase the Marquee Group for approximately $100 million in stock.[21] The Marquee Group specialized in managing sports events, representing athletes and broadcasters, and producing television programs.[22] Originally a marketing company, the Marquee Group used $62 million it had raised in two public offerings to begin a consolidation boom by acquiring ProServ and Athletes & Artists, a firm representing hockey players and sports broadcasters, including Al Michaels and Chris Berman.[23] Prior to the merger, the Marquee Group also spent £5 million in an effort to become global by buying the two companies of English football's best-known agents, Jon Holmes and Tony Stephens.[24]

SFX's purchases in 1998 received attention from investors, competitors, and the United States government. Leigh Steinberg told a reporter in May 1998, "[SFX's acquisition of FAME] highlights the synergy between Big Entertainment and Big Sports, to the extent that sports have become content and programming in a much larger world."[25] On September 22, 1998, shares of SFX dropped 13 percent as the company's plans to consolidate the sports agent industry seemed to be in peril. At one point SFX even received a notice of a preliminary inquiry from the Department of Justice's antitrust division into its proposed purchase of the Marquee Group.[26]

Even under the watchful eye of the government, SFX continued its buying spree of sports agencies when it purchased Randy and Alan Hendricks' agent firm, Hendricks Management Company, in June 1999 for $15.7 million, plus $5 million in deferred payments with the chance to earn additional bonuses. This deal was followed by the purchase of Tellem & Associates in October for an undisclosed sum.[27]

By buying these firms, SFX added even more all-star talent to its long client list. Tellem's agency consisted of 35 basketball players and 20 baseball players, which included clients such as Albert Belle, Kobe Bryant, and Nomar Garciaparra. The success of the combined efforts of Falk and Tellem was exemplified during the 2001 NBA draft. SFX represented the overall number-one draft pick, Kwame Brown, and five other lottery picks, which constituted 46 percent of the NBA draft lottery. In addition, SFX represented 10 of the 28 players—36 percent— taken in the first round of the NBA draft.[28] In commenting on their "smashing success," Falk remarked that the "acquisition of Arn [Tellem's] agency has significantly strengthened our presence in professional basketball."[29] Tellem's remarks focused on the marketing clout of SFX as a reason for their success in the NBA draft: "We were about to make deals, especially in the card area, that were unprecedented in the history of sports."[30]

At the same time, SFX also increased its marketing abilities by acquiring the marketing firm Integrated Sports International of New Jersey (ISI) in the middle of 1999, and later Sean Michael Edwards Design, Inc. (SME). SME focuses on sports-related brand-identity building. Its list of clients in 1999 included the four major sports leagues, World Championship Wrestling, PGA Tour of America, and several top university programs.[31] In 2001, SFX purchased Signature Sports Group, which manages 30 professional golfers and golf events. This purchase followed SFX's acquisition in 2000 and 2001, respectively, of Greg Norman Production Co. and Tony Rosenberg Promotions.[32]

As a result of its various acquisitions and other efforts, as of mid-2001, SFX possessed an impressive client list. Its athlete clients include Michael Jordan, Dikembe Mutombo, Alonzo Mourning, Eddie Griffin, Eddy Curry, Kwame Brown, Roger Clemens, John Rocker, Kobe Bryant, Jason Giambi, Nomar Garciaparra, and Larry Walker. One report states that SFX represents one-sixth of the players in both the NBA and MLB (approximately 15% of players in each league).[33]

With its knowledge of the entertainment industry and well-known list of agents and clients, SFX has made a number of strategic moves. The company dubbed this compilation of companies SFX Sports and appointed David Falk as its CEO. The upshot of the loss of individual corporate identity is "branding."

As alluded to earlier and as discussed in Chapter 6 in greater detail, consolidation has not been without its problems. The August 2000 acquisition of SFX by the conglomerate Clear Channel Communications eventually led to a restructuring of SFX Sports and David Falk taking on the title of "Founder" in the restructured company.[34]

ASSANTE CORPORATION

Without any connection to the entertainment industry, Assante surprised the sports world with its $120 million purchase of Steinberg,
Moorad & Dunn in October of 1999.[35] Assante, a publicly traded company located in Winnipeg, Manitoba, at that time managed more than
$3.4 billion and had $22.9 billion under administration with its 2,500
employees operating in more than 150 offices in North America.[36] Unlike the other cases, insiders feel Assante's purchase of Steinberg's
group was not solely a strategic move into the potentially high-profit
sports agent industry. Some think the firm's motives were to increase
the amount of assets it manages and to attract high net-worth individuals using the high-profile image of the athletes.[37] Assante supposedly
contemplated being able to profit by signing the athletes to contracts
and from the investments their clients make with the company, while
receiving free advertising.

Assante realized few reputable large sports agent firms remained in
the industry, and if it wanted to try its strategy, it needed to move
quickly. Steinberg, whose client list at the time consisted of 150 active
and retired athletes (primarily NFL talent), managed players such as
Troy Aikman, Drew Bledsoe, and Jake Plummer.

As he observed his independent competitors being acquired by
large companies, Steinberg realized to remain competitive he needed
a large amount of cash, an amount only available in a conglomerate.
Steinberg told reporters that the merger would help his 24-year-old
firm expand as advertising, television, and other media deals have
become more important than the contracts he negotiates with the
players' teams.[38] To take advantage of the new wave of endorsement
opportunities available at Assante, Steinberg planned to get his players involved with anything sports related, including TV sports quiz
shows, TV biography shows, and even putting the diaries of his players on the World Wide Web.[39]

As for the development of Assante's sports group, Steinberg stated
in an interview that he would oversee expansion into television and
Internet sports-related programming, the acquisition of ten or twelve
more firms, and Assante's involvement in the management and marketing of athletes in all lines of professional sports.[40] In line with its
promise, in December Assante purchased Maximum Sports Management, a sports agent firm based in Roanoke, Indiana, and owned by
African American Eugene Parker. The third largest athlete representation firm in the NFL, Maximum managed 60 players in football and
basketball, including stars such as Deion Sanders, Emmitt Smith, and
Charlie Ward. Assante also purchased NKS Management, Inc. and

Philpott, Bills & Stoll, two Los Angeles–based companies specializing in managing the business affairs of entertainers. Assante strengthened its position in the representation of NBA players with the purchase of Dan Fegan's firm at the end of 2000.[41] NBA athletes under contract with Fegan in 2000 included Kenyon Martin, Austin Croshere, Dale Davis, Chris Dudley, Howard Eisley, Jerome Kersey, Joe Smith, and Shawn Marion.[42] Earlier in 2000, Assante purchased M.D. Gillis & Associates of Kinston, Ontario, a company that represents NHL players.[43]

Just as is true of SFX, Assante's sports group has not been trouble free. As discussed in Chapter 8, the ongoing legal dispute between Leigh Steinberg and David Dunn that began in 2001 reveals that consolidation is no cure-all for legal entanglements between agents and creates its own web of complex issues.

IMG

Mark McCormack's company IMG, based in Cleveland, Ohio, is the largest agency in the world with 2,000 employees working in 77 offices spanning 38 countries. Accounting for over $1 billion in revenue, IMG boasts a prestigious list of sports clients, including Tiger Woods, Pete Sampras, and Peyton Manning, as well as corporate clients, including US West, Texaco, and Nokia.[44]

Already an established full-service firm, IMG has mildly participated in the consolidation boom, acquiring an Atlanta-based Olympic consulting firm and a California TV production outfit that specializes in sports in early 1998.[45] Subsequently, IMG purchased Charlotte, North Carolina–based Muhleman Marketing Inc., known for marketing NASCAR racing and helping teams with set-licensing arrangements.[46] With a well-known reputation and a good sense of understanding of the trends in the industry, IMG should have little to worry about. This idea is supported by its impressive client list, which includes, beyond those already noted, Derek Jeter, Kenny Lofton, Brett Hull, David Duval, Jennifer Capriati, Lindsay Davenport, Venus Williams, Serena Williams, and a record-setting six first-round selections in the 2001 NFL draft.[47]

OCTAGON

A subsidiary of the New York–based Interpublic Group, Octagon is comprised of several sports-related companies purchased by Interpublic over the last few years. Interpublic, the parent of three of the world's largest ad agency giants McCann-Erickson World Group, Ammirati Puris Lintas, and the Lowe Group, covers almost every aspect of brand marketing, including promotional marketing, direct response, media buying, public relations, and sports marketing.[48] In 1998, the company tallied $10 billion in billings from its 2,500 employees working in 75 offices located in 35 countries.[49] Major customers have included General Motors Corporation (since 1916), Coca-Cola, Burger King, and Mercedes Benz.[50]

One of the first companies to acquire sports agent firms, Interpublic Group realized the trend in advertising and moved quickly to stay ahead. Interpublic purchased its first sports agent firm, Advantage International, in 1997. Advantage, representing the core of Octagon, manages clients in several sports, including tennis stars Anna Kournikova and Michael Chang and NBA all-star David Robinson.

Adding to its portfolio, Octagon initially purchased the following companies: CSI, a London company with 90 employees in five cities worldwide that specializes in selling and distribution and sports TV rights, in February 1998;[51] API Group in London, a sports marketing firm, on May 21, 1998; APA, a sports management group founded by former Olympic sprinter Alan Pascoe, in 1998; Pros Inc., an agency representing golf stars such as Tom Kite, Justin Leonard, and Davis Love III in March 1999; and Brands Hatch Leisure PLC, the largest single organizer and promoter of motorsport events in the United Kingdom in December 1999.[52] Octagon also signed partnerships with Koch Tavares, a leading sports marketing agency in Brazil, in early 1999 and the Italian-based Flammini Group, an agency specializing in motor sports. It also acquired the exclusive TV rights for home matches of English football clubs in the UEFA Cup in September 1999.

In the midst of its buying spree, Octagon publicly released its new organizational strategy in September 1999. Octagon announced it was going to rebrand its sports marketing and entertainment groups into Octagon Marketing, Octagon Athlete Representation, Octagon CSI, and Octagon Motorsports. The Octagon name was also added to each of the subsidiary's 34 sports firms, which at the time accounted for 800 employees and $700 million in estimated annual billings.[53] In this restructuring, Advantage became Octagon Athlete Management. Frank Lowe, CEO of Interpublic's Lowe Group, remained CEO of Octagon.

These moves by Octagon have positioned the company as one of the top sports agency and marketing firms worldwide. In his decision to brand the name of the company, Lowe felt it was a logical step: "Having spent the last two years building a group whose focus is on providing a marketing-led approach to sport, we all felt that the time is now right to launch what is essentially a new brand of sports marketing."[54] Along with sports marketing, Octagon offers a high level of service in athlete representation, consultancy, event management, property representation, TV rights, sales, and distribution, TV production and archive, rights ownership, and licensing and merchandising.[55] Octagon represents more than 250 athletes, including those previously mentioned along with star athletes such as Sergei Fedorov and Michael Vick.[56] Among its 100 blue-chip multinational companies, Octagon represents IBM, Guinness, and MasterCard.[57]

In 2000, Octagon made aggressive moves to establish its presence in the major American team sports. During 2000, it purchased Sullivan & Sperbeck to increase its representation of NFL players, and the baseball division of Bob Woolf Associates and baseball agent Gregg Clifton's business to increase its representation of MLB players.[58] These purchases added 90 players to Octagon's client roster—25 NFL players, 40 hockey players, and 25 MLB players. These acquisitions also added to Octagon's roster of high-profile athletes including baseball players Tom Glavine, David Wells, Benito Santiago, B. J. Surhoff, and Turk Wendell.[59]

In late 2001, Octagon demonstrated its willingness to expand beyond traditional areas of athlete representation when it purchased Carlisle Sports Management, one of two major independent companies that represent athletes who compete in extreme sports.[60] This acquisition represents Octagon's effort to establish a foothold in the potentially lucrative extreme sports marketplace.

Conclusion

Other manifestations abound of what Leigh Steinberg characterized as the synergy between sports and entertainment. For example, Wilhelmina Artist Management, a modeling agency, raised eyebrows when it signed NBA star Stephon Marbury.[61] Tennessee Titan running back Eddie George is another well-known athlete signed by modeling agency Wilhelmina. While sports agents Lamont Smith and Peter Schaffer will represent George in contract work, Wilhelmina will provide exclusive representation with respect to endorsements.[62] Wilhelmina's signing of top amateur golfer Matt Kuchar to an exclusive marketing contract was seen as a significant move by the company into the sports business. The move by Wilhemina also suggests, however, that notwithstanding the comprehensive nature of the "one-stop" service offered by major firms such as SFX, a market may exist for athletes interested in having multiple representatives. A representative for

Wilhemina remarked that "We are not wanting to be in the sports agent business, but we would love to work with sports agents to help them on the marketing and endorsement side of their talent."[63]

Other companies better known for business relationships in more traditional segments of the entertainment industry have also begun to make sports inroads. Unlike Wilhelmina, which stated that it has no interest in attempting to get athletes into television and movies,[64] other companies have made just such a pitch and are attempting to secure clients. Well-established talent agencies such as Michael Ovitz's Artists Management Group (which has added a sports management division), International Creative Management (ICM), and William Morris Agency seek to exploit connections in the television and movie industry to convince clients that these firms are better qualified to pursue their interests in these areas than traditional agencies.[65] Despite some problems, such as cultural differences between the sports and entertainment worlds, some predict increased representation by talent agencies of athletes. An ICM executive noted, "I think as the entertainment business and sports business come closer and closer together, through ownership, through fan support, through marketing, there will be more and more desire for athletes to be part of the world of entertainment. . . . In five years, we're going to have a lot more athletes coming to us as they learn what we're up to. And we're going to be a lot more selective in who we take on."[66]

Some companies, like the athletic apparel giant Nike, entered the fray briefly but are no longer involved in the athlete representation side of the sports business. Others will clearly come and go as well.

An example of the type of problems, many unanticipated, that might arise from the consolidation of the industry was brought to the forefront with complaints from at least two players' associations regarding potential conflicts of interest. Unions representing NFL and NHL players complained about such conflicts that arose as a result of SFX's representation of "players as well as owners of NHL venues."[67] At least in part as a result of such complaints, SFX reorganized. Whether the reorganization resolved questions of conflict of interest remains to be seen, given that Tom Hicks, owner of the NHL Dallas Stars and MLB's Texas Rangers is vice chairman of Clear Channel, a major shareholder of SFX.[68]

Consolidation—such as the purchase by SFX of Arn Tellem's firm, which combined the already significant numbers of NBA stars under one roof—is likely to renew concerns that such an agency will yield so much leverage in negotiations that it "could dictate the market."[69]

A future issue of concern is the anticompetitive impact on any market that once had many players and is reduced to a few. The potential antitrust issues, however, are not yet ripe in this arena. There are still many smaller players successfully battling for clients against the acquiring giants. As competition stiffens and smaller firms become unable to compete, antitrust actions could begin to be filed.

No matter how the structure of the industry evolves, the basic manner of doing business—one key point person recruiting a single athlete—does not appear to be evolving. The truth be told, recruitment of the athlete still occurs the old-fashioned way: person-to-person, one-on-one recruitment of clients. The complexities and problems associated with recruitment and representation are our next topics of discussion.

Part II
Problems

Chapter 4

The Basics
Competition for Clients

> *It's a huge problem. [ESPN's] David Aldridge wrote unabashedly that*
> *Master P was trying to take Antoine Walker during the [NBA] lockout. I*
> *was disturbed by that. We have a contract with players, and there's got to*
> *be some honor among thieves. But there is not. And I think that that goes*
> *on daily.*[1]
>
> *—Agent David Falk responding to a question regarding attempts by*
> *agents to steal other agents' clients*

The nature of "the business" continues to evolve, and a major influence on its evolution is the competition for clients. As the above quotation suggests, competition among agents is fierce and can lead to unethical behavior. In fact, because of the competition, many individuals with outstanding business or academic records are not able to sign a student athlete as a client. Johnny Rutledge's affidavit that appears in the Introduction reveals unsavory recruiting steps agents allegedly took.

As any athlete will attest, a prospective agent is not a difficult person to find. According to a former NFL defensive back, choosing a sports agent is "the perfect arena for a con man."[2] Consequently, the athlete's threshold question to the agent is often, "Who else do you represent?" This valid inquiry is sometimes the greatest barrier to entry for the prospective agent. One prospective agent described breaking into the business as being like the schoolyard basketball game "ice." In that game you are not allowed to begin to tally the baskets you score against your opponent until after you sink the first one. Sports agents face a similar dilemma: until you negotiate a contract for your first client you are frozen out while others with clients continue to score.

Dr. Michael Jackson, a professor of sports management who has advised Temple University students and others in the agent selection process, describes the difficulties prospective agents encounter: "Surgeons have cadavers to experiment on. Our players are not cadavers. The agents have to have experience."[3] Agent Bucky Woy writes about the importance of that first client in his book *Sign 'Em Up Bucky: The Adventures of a Sports Agent*: "As far as Consulting Services' [Woy's firm] success in the sports agenting field is concerned, I owe everything to Mr. Easy [professional golfing great Julius Boros]. When he agreed to let me represent him in many business dealings, people took a new look at Bucky Woy and this Consulting Services outfit he was pushing. . . . He opened all the doors for me with the players who had been viewing me with suspicion during my first year in business."[4] It is not surprising that Woy's entire book is dedicated to Boros. Similarly, sports agent attorney Bob Woolf closes his autobiographical work *Behind Closed Doors* by thanking his first client, baseball player Earl Wilson.[5]

Some agents, most notably Leigh Steinberg, boast that they do not solicit clients. These agents insist that athletes come to them because of their reputations. Baseball Hall of Famer Frank Robinson learned about his agent Ed Keating while appearing on the old television game show "Sports Challenge." Edward King once said that "typically, an athlete chooses Agent A over Agent B because Agent A has done more favors for the athlete or his family or has been friendlier."[6]

Because of the lucrative fees many agents receive,[7] the level of competition among sports agents to provide services and to obtain that first client has become extraordinary. As with any industry, as the field of competitors for a limited number of clients has increased, so have the cutthroat methods of competition.

Payments to Athletes

Letters do not work, agents say, because student athletes "don't write back and they receive dozens of pieces of mail." Even an eye-catching brochure featuring models, yachts, and sunny beaches in Miami, including an invitation to the athlete to come visit, does not always attract the student athlete's attention. Mike Rozier, a winner of the Heisman Trophy, estimated that he received 1,200 letters while at the University of Nebraska, "most of which came from people I had never heard of, and who did not even know me, or want to know me. All they wanted was to line their pockets with the money that I soon would earn in professional football."[8]

It is the face-to-face meetings that agents maintain are most successful. Norby Walters's vivid description of what many agree occurs in face-to-face meetings between a prospective agent and student athlete remains revealing: "The kid knows everybody's breaking all the rules so he's primed and ready for a businessman to come along. He's talking turkey as soon as you sit down. 'How much for my family? How much for me? How much interest? Do I have to pay it back?' "[9]

Hall of Fame NFL linebacker Lawrence Taylor described the nature of the interaction between an agent and a prospective client in his autobiography. His first encounter with his soon-to-be agent Ivery Black came between his junior and senior years in college. Taylor explained that Black made it clear that the rules of the NCAA do not allow the giving of money, so his policy was to *lend* athletes money until they were drafted, after which they would repay the loan. This is a standard explanation of what appears to be a common practice.[10]

It is this type of transaction, and variations of it, that many see as the prime barrier to entry into the field by ethical professionals. One former agent maintains, "The mentality on the part of the athlete is for 'right here and right now.' What can you do for me now?" He sees one of the agent's greatest contributions to the client is providing a perspective beyond the here and now. Any payment in the manner described by Walters and Taylor violates many of the rules of the NCAA and provisions of state athlete agent act statutes.

The stories of what agents provide to athletes for their signing range from anecdote to fact. A 1999 feature story in the *Wall Street Journal* highlights allegations of a new client recruitment method, promises of "romantic liaisons" with supermodels from New York's Wilhelmina Models Inc. modeling agency.[11] Agent Eric Fleisher made these allegations claiming that he was the victim of unfair competition. *Sports Illustrated* reported that Walters and Bloom paid more than $800,000 in varying sums to approximately fifty athletes, five of whom were first-round picks in the 1987 NFL draft.[12] Similarly, agent Jim Abernethy claims that he spent more than $500,000 over a one-year period in recruiting clients.[13] Other specific overzealous recruiting techniques reportedly include the offer of one-third of an agent's management corporation to George Rogers;[14] a series of incidents involving Florida State football players that culminated in one agent taking several players on a $6,000 shopping spree at Foot Locker in 1994;[15] agent Robert Caron's alleged cash payments totaling $3,900 to University of Southern California football player Shawn Walters;[16] the payment of a $2,500 promissory note to University of Alabama basketball star Derrick McKey;[17] Auburn basketball player Chris Porter's acceptance of $2,500 from an agent;[18] agent Jeffrey Nalley's purchase of $1,000 worth of clothing for Penn State star Curtis Enis;[19] the offer of $65,000 to former Louisiana State linebacker Michael Brooks;[20] allegations that a Florida player received wheel rims valued at $1,500 and another received weekly payments totaling up to $500 per month from an agent;[21] the promise to Wayne Waddy, a running back at Texas Christian University, of $75 for each touchdown he scored;[22] the promise to a Memphis State University basketball player of $500 per month with a $200 Thanksgiving bonus and a $1,000 Christmas bonus;[23] the alleged payment of $54,000 to University of Iowa running back Ron Harmon, his girlfriend, and family members;[24] and an additional $1,500 paid to Harmon for revealing a teammate's phone number to an agent.[25] Harmon was also reportedly offered $2,000 to aid the agent in recruiting linebacker Larry Station.[26]

In his autobiography *The Boz*, NFL and former college star Brian Bosworth explains that other athletes are sometimes involved in the student athlete recruiting process: "You get hit on constantly by agents in college, or by friends of agents. Even pro players call and try to sign you with their guy. Howie Long [then] of the Raiders called me to see if I wanted to hook up with his guy. I didn't even *know* Howie Long, much less his guy."[27]

Another client recruitment technique is the payment of a fee to the student athlete's coach or some other person with influence over the athlete. In 1988, *Newsday* exposed payments made by agent Lance Jay Luchnick to coaches. *Newsday*'s investigation revealed that Luchnick agreed to pay one coach, Ron Davis, a percentage of basketball player Cliff Livingston's contract if he could deliver him as a client. Livingston was "eager to help his old coach," and when he learned of this deal, he signed with Luchnick.[28] Davis reportedly received more than $14,000 for his role in bringing the two together.[29] Similar accusations were initially raised in 1998 against once prominent South Carolina–based agent Tank Black.[30]

A recruitment technique employed with increasing frequency is agents' use of street agents to help them to secure clients. NCAA rules do not prohibit an agent from having contact with an athlete. Increasingly, however, state athlete agent regulations require agents wishing to have contact with a student athlete, whose collegiate athletic eligibility has not expired, to register, pay a fee, and contact administrators at the student athlete's college. In order to circumvent such rules, or merely as a means of establishing a relationship with athletes, agents will use a "street agent" or "runner." The role of the runner is to funnel money and gifts from an agent to an athlete as a means of establishing an indirect relationship between the athlete and the agent, thereby placing the agent in a more advantageous position than his competitors. Runners can be high-school coaches, summer league coaches, friends, roommates, family members, girlfriends, or anyone who can "win over players with flattery, cash and other gifts."[31] Notes Washington, D.C.–based agent Bill Strickland, the improper use of runners places agents who do not use runners at a disadvantage.[32] A college sports official adds, "Sometimes the player is unaware of the source. . . . The benefit to the agent . . . would be at a later time, when he would make it clear to the player that he or she should show gratitude, or there could even be threats."[33]

The case of Myron Piggie is revealing in this regard. The name Myron Piggie is synonymous with some of the worst incidents that can occur in the athlete representation world, particularly when it comes to intermediaries that funnel star athletes. Piggie was a coach of a youth basketball team in Kansas City, but he also had a criminal record that caught up with him. Piggie was also the classic street agent who possessed enough control over young, future collegiate stars and professionals that he could play a major role in influencing which schools they ultimately attended and which agents they signed with for professional representation. The crimes to which he pled guilty and that caught the attention of basketball fans were defrauding the NCAA and four universities because he compromised the status of amateurs by providing them with cash and other gifts.

Piggie had been hired by a wealthy philanthropist, Tom Grant, to coach a youth basketball team. Piggie had no experience and a criminal record. Following his team's success, Nike signed Piggie to a five-year, $425,000 consulting agreement. Piggie was close to the talent who Nike wanted to wear its products and serve as endorsers if they reached superstar status. Ultimately Piggie was removed from the fray as he was incarcerated based on his fraudulent activities. In 2001, Piggie was sentenced to 37 months on a single count of conspiracy to commit mail and wire fraud and one year for failure to file income taxes. The terms will be served concurrently without the possibility of parole. He was also required to pay restitution in the amount of $320,000 to four universities, a prep school, and the IRS. The U.S. Attorney who went after Piggie stated, "We look at someone like Myron Piggie as a pimp and the players as prostitutes."[34]

For younger players, financial inducements such as cash and shoes are often enough. When they are not, these forms of payment sometimes have been accompanied by threats. Chicago Bears free safety Maurice Douglas testified at the Walters-Bloom trial that Lloyd Bloom told him, "if I didn't return the money and the cars, he'd have somebody break my legs."[35] The reference to money and cars related to a $2,500 initial payment and other periodic payments made by Walters and Bloom; the pair also leased a car for him.[36] The *Chicago Tribune* reports that Walters and Bloom made "veiled references to their friends [in Las Vegas] as well."[37]

Of course, not all agent/player relationships are the product of improper inducements. Many athletes and their parents evaluate the capabilities of potential agents as one would in the hiring of any professional. They sometimes use extensive, formalized interview programs to select their agents.[38] Nevertheless, these interview techniques appear to be the exception.

We close this section with an account that provides a textbook example of the tangled web created when agents employ improper techniques to secure clients and when athletes succumb to the temptations that accompany such techniques. Indeed the affairs surrounding the relationships between Marcus Camby and agents John Lounsbury and Wesley Spears (neither of whom was apparently aware of the other's efforts to sign Camby) epitomize the solicitation techniques described above, including agent gifts and payments to an athlete, the drawing in of an athlete's family and friends, the use of threats to secure representation, and alleged athlete complicity.

In a *Sports Illustrated* article,[39] Lounsbury and Spears characterized Marcus Camby as the "ultimate greedy athlete, constantly with his hand out." In describing his interaction with Camby, Lounsbury is quoted as saying, "Marcus was very good. . . . I would call him all the time, and he'd have a few sentences, a little time. But when he wanted money, he increased the amount of time he gave me. He knew how to play me. He'd ride around in my car, tell me what I wanted to hear, then take the money. 'I'm struggling, man.' Those were Marcus's famous words. That's what he said anytime he called and needed something. 'I'm struggling, man.' "[40]

In the same magazine account, Camby admits to having received favors from Lounsbury, including a stereo system, cash payments of between $300 and $500, and meeting a woman procured by Spears for sex at Spears's homes. Camby denies, however, that Lounsbury gave only when requested to do so by Camby. Said Camby, "I didn't have to ask for anything. I had so many people offering me things without asking. I got offers from big-time agents, names you would recognize. I got offered cars, houses for my mother, college tuition for my sisters. When you're getting all those offers, why would you need to ask for anything."[41] Camby also denies that he received $40,000 in cash and gifts that the agents assert they spent on him.

Camby's relatives and friends also became entangled in the web. Camby's mother, Janice Camby, reported that Lounsbury, despite her protests, insisted she take money from him. Lounsbury admits to purchasing gifts for and giving $1,500 in cash to Janice Camby.[42] Lounsbury allegedly offered money to one of Camby's childhood friends. Spears engaged in similar efforts to win favor with Camby's other friends. One of Camby's associates indicated that the athlete never intended to sign with Spears. He described the nature of the interactions with Spears as a "two-bit shakedown" of the agent.[43] Camby admitted to the essence of this characterization: "I wasn't asking for nothing. . . . He would give it. It was basically my friends who were milking him. . . . They have been my boys since I was growing up. It was an opportunity to do things for them. Taking the cash, cars, and jewelry . . . , 'was all part of the hustle' fun by Wray and Murray [Camby's friends]. Things just got out of control. So far out of control. No one knew it would twist this way."[44]

Finally, Camby's entanglement with Spears also involved allegations of extortion. Spears is reported to have exploded and made threats against Camby when he discovered that the athlete would not sign with him. According to one news account, Spears threatened Camby, saying

he had $75,000 invested in Camby and his friends, and Camby promised him face to face he would sign with him. . . . He also . . . [said] he had Camby on video taking money from him and witnesses from clothing stores. . . . Spears insisted that refusing to select him as Camby's agent will result in a lawsuit "that will tarnish Camby's image . . . and UMass will get in trouble."

Spears [told] Camby, "You told me you are going to sign with me, and you are going to sign with me. . . ."

"UMass would go down and you wouldn't be the number-one pick and no endorsements. The thing that bothers me most is that you lied to me."[45]

As is often the case, however, the techniques used to solicit an athlete and to win favor with his associates were to no avail. Despite favors and threats, rather than securing Camby as a client Spears was charged with extortion and promoting prostitution. As a result of a plea bargain, charges were dropped against Spears on the condition that he complete two years of probation and one hundred hours of community service.[46] Lounsbury did not fare much better. He was forced into bankruptcy, a consequence, he says, of giving gifts to Camby.[47] After Camby signed with ProServ, he gave $28,500 to Lounsbury, reportedly so that the agent could avoid being killed by loan sharks.[48] Consequently, Lounsbury surrendered his certification as an NBA agent. A separate unrelated incident, in which he was charged with providing airline tickets to two University of Connecticut basketball players, also resulted in Lounsbury settling charges filed by the Connecticut Department of Consumer Protection.[49]

The Racial Undertone

There is an omnipresent racial edge to this business that should be noted. We do not discuss it at length in the text but readers should remain aware of the white agent/black athlete dichotomy even where it is not highlighted. One-time agent Norby Walters fit the stereotype. Walters signed an astounding number of first-round draft picks as clients during his first year in the business. Through his firm, General Talent International, Walters represented such Black stars as Janet Jackson, Patti LaBelle, and Ben Vereen. Many pointed to the middle-aged Walters's success with African American entertainment acts as a "magnet" for young African American athletes, who reasoned, "if he can do it for them, he can put me in a Rolls Royce too." Walters entered into a partnership with Lloyd Bloom, a former Studio 54 discotheque bouncer. In a 1989 article, the *New York Times* stated, "the plan seemed so simple. Mr. Walters, a prominent music booking agent, would join forces with Mr. Bloom, an enthusiastic, young former football player. Together the two men, both white, would woo black college athletes with the promise that they could do for the athletes what the booking agent had done for such black entertainers as Luther Vandross and Kool and the Gang."[50]

Robert Ruxin, in his book *An Athlete's Guide to Agents*, tells the story of an agent who attempted to make student athletes believe he was Black. According to two student athletes who encountered the agent, "I thought he was black, having spoken to him on the phone. . . . His actions were black. . . . Like, he walked with a slight limp. You know, how a lot of blacks walk, kind of cool. A strut."[51] This is the omnipresent undercurrent in the business: white agents and African American clients. A key feature of this undercurrent is the relatively low percentage of African American athletes who patronize African American sports agents. The question that reverberates was prominently stated in the subtitle of a *Howard Law Journal* article, "A Search into Why Black Athletes Do Not Hire Black Agents."[52] At the heart of this question is a belief that there would be a natural affinity between this world of Black athletes who numerically predominate certain sports (for example, basketball and football) and well-qualified Black agents. The fostering of these relationships, however, has been impeded by stereotypes and the long-time dominance of white agents over Black agents.

In *In Black and White: Race and Sports in America*, the stereotype issue is explained as "the white man's ice is colder." Specifically,

A classic story, most often credited to Malcolm X, provides an insight into the black community's perception of the competence of our own professionals. The story has it that in a small southern town on some hot summer day, people stood in a long line wrapped around a corner to purchase ice. On the other side of town a black ice vendor sat with plenty of ice, doing very little business. When a black patron in the long line was asked why he would stand in the long line rather than purchase the ice in his own neighborhood, he responded, "Well everybody knows the white man's ice is colder."[53]

At the heart of the stereotypical belief that it is more advantageous for athletes to secure white representation is what some Black agents allege is being said by some white agents. According to African American athlete agent Fred Slaughter: "[White agents] just tell the kid, 'Only a white man can make that deal for you,' They have actually said that. And some kids, kids who are sitting in a well-furnished office with computers clicking and listening to a guy with gold teeth say that, they'll think, 'Wait a minute: if he's saying that, he must be right.' There are a lot of problems. It's been rough."[54]

Although the number of successful African American agents may have increased in recent years, these racial tensions persist in the sports agent business. Like other sectors of society, any examination that does not consider these racial issues is necessarily incomplete. This is particularly true when it comes to the business of sports. The reality is that it remains exceptional for African American athlete agents to represent top draft picks in the major sports.

In an interview conducted in early 2000, Eugene Parker stated "there were few if any black agents at the highest level, so the challenge has been twofold: first, to convince team officials of his competence, and second, to convince players of the same thing."[55] Black agent Roosevelt Barnes added, "you have to let [team management] know from the beginning that you know what you're doing. Once they understand that, they deal with you above board. . . ."[56] Barnes added that "convincing players and their parents of his abilities has been more difficult."[57]

A report in the SportsBusiness Journal is telling. In their 2002 "By the Numbers" sports industry analysis the only African American sports agents listed among the top ten in the NBA, NFL, Major League Baseball, and the NHL who represent the clients with the most money are Bill Strickland with clients in the NBA and Eugene Parker representing clients in the NFL. The NFL African American agent number increases slightly on the list of representatives of the 100 highest-paid athletes in that league. There, African Americans Roosevelt Barnes, Carl Poston, and Lamont Smith join Eugene Parker on the list. Neither baseball list includes an African American or an individual with a Spanish surname.[58]

Sports agent Bill Strickland sees it cutting both ways: "we still have black athletes who don't feel that black professionals can do the job. Some guys think the white man's ice is colder, when ice is ice. Some agents who are incompetent say let's get down because we are both black."[59]

The Gender Barrier

The gender of an agent plays a role in competition as well. Although female agents are beginning to emerge in the athlete representation industry, men continue to dominate. An October 1998 *SportsBusiness Journal* article reported that although women represent a few players, they lag far behind in representing players in the major money-making leagues, the NBA, NFL, MLB, and NHL. At the time of that article, only one of the 225 agents registered with the NHL Players' Association was a woman. The statistics were similar for the other major sports. In 1998, women represented only 2 percent of the agents registered with the NFLPA. Only five women represented players on forty-man rosters in the MLB.[60] It is the case on some occasions that the female representative is the wife, mother, or sister of the player.

Explanations vary for what amounts to a "glass ceiling when it comes to representing male athletes" in the major sports.[61] In the article, one female agent, Leslie Giordano, who at the time had negotiated contracts for eight NFL players over a four-year span, attributes the paucity to the fact that "no one has encouraged them [women] to do it." Rather than gender discrimination, Giordano noted the difficulty for anyone, male or female, to break into the business. "No one has said to my face that [discrimination] may be a factor why I haven't signed a particular player. . . . I feel like I'm just now starting to do something. It takes a while.' "[62]

Wendi Huntley, who represents a number of players in the WNBA, expressed a similar concern regarding the inequitable treatment of women in the competition for male "big league" clients. She noted that as she was attempting to recruit an NFL draft pick, the athlete told her that a competing agent had said, "You don't want to be represented by a girl, do you?" According to Huntley, "an assault based on the number of NFL players I represent would have been one thing but on this basis . . . that's comedy."[63]

Huntley also reflected on a key issue that many female agents must deal with: making sure the athlete understands that the relationship is to be all business. "I don't want any clients talking about, 'hey, baby.' Let's be clear, I am their agent, not their baby."[64]

The *SportsBusiness Journal* article indicated that another explanation ℉ered by male and female agents for the lack of female agents is ` greater comfort level male players have with men. "A player-agent relationship is an intensely personal one, and individual players un-like major corporations and organizations, are not under any public pressure to hire women."[65] Others reject comfort level as a legiti-mate basis for a male not to hire a woman agent. "For years people said they were uncomfortable with and didn't want to work with peo-ple of other races or women, and that's not good enough. . . . It will take strong women with a lot of determination to break through the barrier."[66]

Huntley perceives a "sisterhood" among WNBA players and female agents. "But time will tell. The women are not making enough money for the big-time male agents to really come in and compete. In the WNBA it is estimated that half of the players in the draft were not rep-resented by agents and those who were had agents primarily in order to explore international leagues beyond the WNBA. Since the demise of the rival American Basketball League (ABL) there is no leverage necessitating WNBA management to negotiate in the manner the in-dustry is accustomed to on the men's side."[67]

As with race, a degree of bias toward women remains in society. Like other sectors of society, however, as women become more successful and experienced in this field, their presence should increase. Unfor-tunately bias is a difficult barrier to overcome.

Agents' View of Their Business

One of the ironies of the sports agent business is that not only do out-siders look down on it but so do many agents, if not always seriously, often sarcastically. Agent Andy Miller, whose clients include NBA play-ers such as Kevin Garnett, Al Harrington, and Chauncey Billups, is reported as having said that 90 percent of agents are "scum of the earth."[68] Veteran agent Joe Linta stated in a 1998 interview that "I am very afraid of what the business has become. . . . It has gotten out of hand—the amounts of money involved, how crazy agents are."[69] One of the most successful agents, Leigh Steinberg, once expressed a simi-lar view when he called the sports agent business "the ultimate sleaz-oid profession."[70]

Agent Scott Boras has come to epitomize what some consider the worst and others consider the best attributes of agents. Boras repre-sented Alex Rodriguez in negotiations that led to the record-setting 10-year, $252-million contract for the shortstop to play for the Texas Rangers. The agent's fee will reportedly come to $12.6 million for his work on that single transaction.[71] Boras has also negotiated on be-half of players that have led to some of the other biggest contracts in professional baseball. For example, he negotiated the first $100-million deal in baseball on behalf of Dodgers' pitcher Kevin Brown in 1998.

Boras' successful negotiations on behalf of his clients have resulted in him being disliked by many and described as a "man who doesn't have a soul . . . so he sells his clients."[72] On the other hand, others recognize that he zealously represents his clients through his hard work, brilliant negotiation strategies, knowledge of the business of baseball, and preparation.[73]

Some agents have decided to opt out of the industry due to the harsh realities that now define it. In commenting on his decision to discontinue player representation, former basketball player and agent Len Elmore stated, "In all candor what chased me from the industry was the shrinking revenue caused by wage scaling and my unwillingness to pay a young kid to become my client. I simply did not desire, nor could I afford, to 'stoop to conquer.' Betrayal by client family members and significant others who, in my opinion, sought to control the wealth and attendant power amassed by 'their boy' also had negative impact. Thus, I was left with a harsh business reality. It was time to fold them and move on."[74]

David Ware told a group of agents at a NFLPA meeting that he resented accusations that agents are a "little higher than snakes and a little lower than scorpions." Ware continued, "If you don't like the business, you should get out." In noting how much he enjoyed what he did, Ware argued that the agent has an "obligation to be a zealous advocate of his client."[75]

Ware's statements came in response to the constant grumbling of many agents regarding the difficulty in signing clients "honestly," that is, without making payments that violate state agent regulations and cause athletes to violate NCAA regulations. In any case, Ware has been successful in recruiting clients. His representation of 1988 Heisman Trophy winner Barry Sanders in his negotiations with the NFL's Detroit Lions is just one of his achievements. Ware, along with agent C. Lamont Smith, were the first African Americans to represent a Heisman Trophy winner. In 1999, Ware also took over the representation of some clients who had been represented by Tank Black.

In reality, however, most agents are not successful and they have not found the business to be financially rewarding.[76] The position of sports agents entering the business illustrates why there is not a lot of success. Numbers are a key factor. There are, at varying times, more agents than there are athletes in a given league; thus competition for clients is intense.[77] Moreover, even if an agent does sign a client, there is no guarantee that the agent will make any money. If the athlete does not make the team after a contract has been negotiated, neither the athlete nor the agent gets paid absent an initial signing bonus; since the agent is generally paid a percentage of the athlete's earnings, the agent earns nothing if the athlete earns nothing. As was noted, in exceptional circumstances the agent may be paid on an hourly basis like most attorneys or accountants, and in such cases the agent may be compensated for the time expended. However, such arrangements are rare.

Ironically, it is possible for an agent to exert the most effort for the athlete that is going to bring the lowest fee—the rookie free agent who is *not* drafted out of college. Often such a rookie will enlist a sports agent to help find a team that is interested in giving the athlete a tryout. The agent must then contact more than two dozen teams in the appropriate leagues to try to find one or more that will give the player a tryout. If, after the tryout, the player does impress the team, then the agent can negotiate a contract for the player. But even then there is still the chance that the athlete will not make the team's final cut and the agent will not earn a fee for his or her efforts. Compare the work and the risk involved here to an early-round draft pick where there is no shopping for a team or a tryout and where the agent's responsibility is to negotiate a contract in the athlete's best interest. Although the contract negotiation itself may be difficult and time consuming, the compensation to the sports agent will inevitably be higher than in the rookie free-agent situation.

In the sport of baseball, some agents exhibit the patience of Job while their clients serve time in the minor leagues, often for years. During this time the agent takes little or no fee while waiting for the call from the major league team to come. During this waiting period the agent is probably, in addition to providing the player with gloves, bats, and other equipment, providing financial support. Most agents accept this toil with rookie free agents and minor leaguers as part of the price an agent must pay to become a success in the business. Among themselves, however, some complain about what a "pain" their athlete clients are. Ware notes that he for one "resent[s] guys who talk about the business and still take a fee for it."[78] Baseball agent Stanley O. King views the investment in his baseball clients as an "annuity," except, he notes, "the baseball type doesn't always pay off."[79]

Those individuals engaged in athlete representation take differing routes in pursuing the business, and they also possess mixed feelings about their profession. Many attorneys who enter the athlete representation profession will begin their careers at a traditional law firm that has carved out a niche for sports representation or one that will allow an individual attorney to pursue athlete representation while also working on the firm's other business matters. Often these attorneys will either leave to open up their own firm or become associated with a company that has more of a focus on athlete representation.

The above description tracks the experiences of Kevin Robinson, who has been what he describes as a "sports attorney" since 1999. He began his representation of athletes at a law firm in Denver. After he secured his first athlete client, the firm decided to terminate the sports representation aspect of its business. The firm's managers decided it was not worth the expense and time to continue in the business. Thereafter, Robinson began to pursue sports representation with A. J. Mills, Jr., P.C. of Boulder, Colorado.

Robinson considers himself fortunate to have become associated with a sports management firm because it allowed him a better opportunity to secure clients. This association helped him to overcome a significant obstacle to breaking into the business: the reluctance of experienced agents to bring on board and mentor aspiring agents for fear that the latter will "sign clients and then leave the firm."[80] He sees this reluctance to mentor as a manifestation of the competitive nature of an industry that he describes as "hostile." He also recognizes that competition by agents for clients and the desires of athlete clients (many of whom based their representation decisions on what they obtain from agents), causes many agents to provide improper inducements as a means of signing clients. "There are a lot of agencies and firms that have their grips on players, [by offering improper inducements], by the time they are sophomores in college."[81] Consequently, "it becomes difficult for other agents to compete."

While aware of the unflattering realities of the athlete representation business, Robinson is not jaded. He remains optimistic regarding the profession because of the positive role he believes he can play in the lives of his clients. "Our goal is that these young men become responsible, productive business men . . . and productive members of society."[82] Robinson also believes that some clients possess views that align with these goals: "You have . . . a set of athletes . . . who have an advisor and [look] at appropriate things like experience, what types of contracts [the adviser has] negotiated in the past . . . [and the adviser's] competency."[83]

Even some experienced agents retain a more positive view of the profession. Notes one, "[many] of the agents in the business are good guys who take good care of their clients."[84]

Conclusion

This chapter set forth the basics of the competition among agents in the business. Although the financial upside can be huge, only a few sports agents reap truly large financial rewards. The next chapter discusses the legal mechanisms employed to sanction agents.

Chapter 5

Unscrupulous and Criminal
The Problem Agents

Problems associated with unethical agents have clearly seeped into the public consciousness. Newspapers and television news programs, both sports and nonsports-oriented alike, report with regularity on problems that ultimately stem from agents' intense competition for clients. Widely reported incidents in recent times include the criminal case of agent Tank Black, athlete agents who misuse and misappropriate client funds, agent conflicts of interest, agents who are implicated in funding student athlete shopping sprees at sporting-goods stores, and agents who bestow cash and gifts upon student athletes and thereby precipitate the NCAA's imposition of sanctions against the colleges for which these athletes play. These incidents have alerted the public and those intimately involved in the sports industry to the challenges of ethics and credibility that confront the athlete agent industry.

As discussed in detail in Chapters 11 and 12, certain of these incidents led to a rush to quash sports agent problems by regulating the industry. Conspicuously absent from this flurry of legislative activity—focused on protecting the interest of academic institutions—are efforts to engage in a far-reaching reassessment of the multiple dimensions of the ethics and competency issues that confront the athlete agent industry. The narrow focus of such legislative efforts is exemplified in the state of Florida's agent legislation: "The Legislature finds that dishonest or unscrupulous practices by agents who solicit representation of student athletes can cause significant harm to student athletes and the academic institutions for which they play. It is the intent of the Legislature to protect the interests of student athletes and academic institutions by regulating the activities of athlete agents that involve student athletes at colleges or universities in the state."[1] At the end of the 1980s more than a dozen states had enacted statutes that attempted to regulate the activities of sports agents.[2] Entering the new millennium, this number had more than doubled.[3]

Despite the benefits to be derived from state-promulgated agent legislation, it often ignores other improprieties spawned by agents who are unscrupulous, unethical, unqualified, criminal, or some combination of the four. The payment of monies to student athletes by sports agents is the most publicized impropriety committed by sports agents. As alluded to above, however, additional wrongs occur frequently. These improprieties include athlete income mismanagement and excessive agent fees.

Income Mismanagement

The stories associated with the mismanagement of athletes' income are no more disturbing than stories associated with the mismanagement of the assets of other high-income individuals such as physicians, lawyers, and other business persons. Incidents of income mismanagement in sports, however, receive much more publicity because of the notoriety of the parties involved.

At the heart of many athletes' financial headaches is the fact that agents are subject to few educational or professional requirements, must adhere to vague ethical standards, and are subject to minimum regulation. A Beverly Hills entertainment attorney who also served as a sports agent commented, "I don't like to be lumped and called a sports agent. I was the Rams' general counsel for eight years. What I saw coming through the door representing the player was an embarrassment."[4] One attorney who represents athletes in agent abuse cases also criticizes deficiencies in the ranks of players' representatives: " 'There's no scientific study of the percentage of players that have been abused somehow in their investment, but it's in the high 90s,' he asserts. 'Virtually all of them are abused. The question is to what degree.' "[5]

As illustrated below in discussions of the Tank Black and Summit Management matters, problems relating to mismanagement of athlete finances are not restricted to athlete agents. Increasingly, athletes are seeking recourse for alleged mismanagement by the nebulous "financial adviser" who, according to agent Mark Bartlestein, preys on people "who are very inexperienced and very vulnerable. They get in there and recruit players harder than anyone."[6]

The following account given by NFL player Antoine Winfield describes the tactics allegedly used by financial advisers and agents to secure athletes as clients. "Winfield says [Dunyasha] Yetts gave him money by losing on purpose in card games. 'In college, we were broke, there's no money,' he explains, 'and if someone comes around and throws money in your face, you are going to take it.' Winfield says he and Yetts went on trips to Las Vegas and the Bahamas, courtesy of Yetts. 'He was giving me suits' valued at $1,500 and free Ohio State football tickets that, Winfield says, he sold. 'He was giving cash,' Winfield went on. 'If we needed the money, he would pay the rent.' Winfield says he realized his acceptance of the gifts violated NCAA rules. 'We knew it was illegal,' he says, adding: 'If you got caught, you would be in trouble.' "[7]

The problems associated with financial advisers raise particular cause for concern since they may fall through the regulatory cracks. These advisers often are not agents and therefore are not subject to player association certification or state regulatory requirements. Notes Charles Banks, a traditional financial planner, "It's the new bad fad. As the fees on the agent side come down and salaries go up, everyone is getting in on the financial side and no one is really looking out for the player who doesn't understand the difference between a stockbroker, an investment manager and a life insurance salesman."[8]

As will be discussed in Chapter 10, the NFLPA in 2001 undertook a major new initiative aimed at addressing problems associated with financial advisers. As discussed below, complaints filed by the Securities and Exchange Commission (SEC) also suggest that the activities of financial advisers will be more thoroughly scrutinized in the future.

A February 2002 issue of *U.S. News and World Report* contained an investigative report concerning NFL players who have been or allegedly have been victimized by financial managers.[9] The report revealed that cases involving acknowledged and alleged mismanagement of players' investments follow similar patterns. The alleged surefire deal fails; investment funds are used to cover personal expenditures, which allows financial advisers to maintain a certain (often lavish) standard of living; and investment funds are used to cover other failed transactions.

One of the more notorious cases of alleged irregularities identified in the *U.S. News* article that seems to fit this pattern, if the facts as alleged are proven to be true, involves financial adviser Donald Lukens. An SEC complaint filed against Lukens alleges that athletes were among the individuals whom he "duped" to make high-risk investments.[10] The complaint more specifically claims that Lukens "violated federal securities laws by systematically defrauding at least 100 (and perhaps more than 200) clients and brokerage customers collectively of tens of millions of dollars in a series of investment schemes during at least the mid-to-late 1990s."[11] According to the SEC complaint, "in soliciting these funds, Lukens routinely and falsely described the investments as 'safe' and 'secure,' promising high returns, provided baseless personal guarantees, made other materially false or misleading statements, and failed to disclose material information, including significant risks."[12]

Lukens allegedly misappropriated or diverted for personal and business use the money given to him for investment purposes. In his answer to the SEC complaint, Lukens denies having engaged in any wrongdoing.

Lukens is also alleged to have formed Global Sports & Entertainment, a financial and investment advisory firm in the mid-1990s. Global is thought to have represented at least 40 professional athletes at various times. Global's athlete clients reportedly included Kurt Thomas and Byron Russell of the NBA.[13] Lukens is accused of having defrauded NFL player Simeon Rice of $2.4 million.[14] Additionally, Lukens, who filed for bankruptcy, listed among his creditors the following former or current professional athletes: Eric Dickerson ($1.835 million), NFL player Sean Gilbert ($350,000), NFL player Steve Atwater ($1.2 million), and NFL tight end, Shannon Sharpe ($300,000).[15]

Another illustration of the aggressive posture taken by the SEC involves Dunyasha Yetts (discussed previously), who allegedly "violated the federal securities laws by operating [as] an unregistered broker-dealer in Dublin, Ohio, and defrauding at least 14 customers of approximately $1.8 million in an investment scheme that continued from 1998 through to early 2001."[16] Yetts allegedly formed and operated Worldwide Financial Group and World Wide Sports Group.[17] The SEC claims that Yetts fraudulently induced customers to invest with him and Worldwide Financial.[18] The complaint further asserts, "Yetts did not invest those funds for his customers' accounts. Instead, Yetts misappropriated or diverted their funds for personal and business expenses."[19] NFL player Antoine Winfield, who is identified as Worldwide Financial's largest client, was allegedly defrauded of $1.35 million.[20] Yetts denies that he defrauded Winfield.[21]

The NFLPA has decertified Yetts. Conduct on which the NFLPA focused in revoking his certification reportedly included Yetts's mismanagement of Winfield's funds and money given to Winfield to induce him to sign a representation agreement with Yetts.[22]

In August 2001 former NFL running back Terry Orr was sentenced to 14 months in a federal prison camp after pleading guilty to one count of wire fraud. He was also ordered to attempt to make restitution to three of his former teammates on the Washington Redskins and to another investor. Three former football players—Raleigh McKenzie, Art Monk, and Brian Mitchell—each invested $50,000 in a deal involving a shoe company. Their investments were lost when the shoe company failed. In addition, Orr used some of the money invested by the former players and another investor for personal expenditures and to satisfy debts arising from another failed investment. For example, Orr used $22,000 of the $50,000 obtained from Monk to make mortgage payments; $15,000 was used as a down payment on a Suburban SUV.[23]

The U.S. News & World Report article also identifies the following as instances of alleged or proven improprieties by financial advisers:

- An SEC investigation regarding whether Von Cummings mishandled $1 million of former NFL running back Robert Smith;[24]
- The case of Linda Frykholm, who defrauded several investors, including Brian Simmons of the Cincinnati Bengals, of a total of $15 million that was used "to finance a lavish lifestyle.";[25]
- The SEC arbitration in which Sean Jones, a financial adviser and former NFL player, was ordered to pay $500,000 to former NFL cornerback Cris Dishman. Dishman alleged that Jones failed to disclose the high level of risk associated with certain investments. Jones, who denies the allegations, has requested that a court overturn the three-person arbitration panel's ruling;[26]
- Money lost by NFL players who entered into investment deals with Luigi DiFonzo, who committed suicide in August 2000.[27]

Often issues of competence and ethics merge to create disastrous results for athlete clients. The most notorious recent mismanagement story involves South Carolina–based agent William "Tank" Black.[28] Like Norby Walters and Lloyd Bloom, Black began to have success at a rapid rate. The principal business entity through which Black operated was Professional Management, Inc. (PMI). Like many other firms that depend on one, if any, marquee clients for most of the firm's existence, initially Sterling Sharpe was PMI's lone recognizable client. Yet prior to his downfall, Black's firm was on track to represent an unprecedented five NFL first-round draft picks. Black had also acquired first rate clients that included NBA's Vince Carter and NFL stars Fred Taylor, Duce Staley, Ike Hilliard, and Terry Allen.

The unraveling of Tank Black's emergence as a super-agent began simply enough when NFLPA lawyer Richard Berthelsen stated at a meeting of football agents that he could not take action against agents who made under-the-table payments because the agents present at the meeting never named names. At that point Ray Anderson, then of AR Sports in Atlanta, stood up and said, "I'll give you a name, Tank Black."

Anderson's statement led to an NFLPA investigation of Black and PMI. Thereafter, investigations were launched by the Securities Exchange Commission (SEC), the Internal Revenue Service (IRS), the FBI, the United States Attorney's Office, and authorities in the states of

Florida and Louisiana. The allegations asserted against Black went beyond claims of under-the-table payments. Black was accused of fraudulently leading clients to believe they were investing in a publicly traded security, leading clients into a pyramid scheme, and, perhaps most damaging from a prosecutorial standpoint, laundering drug monies.

Michael Fuchs, an SEC lawyer involved in the Black case, told *Sports Illustrated*, "Professional athletes are prime candidates for financial fraud. Many are unsophisticated in financial matters and suddenly find themselves with a six- or seven-figure salary. They're young, they're trusting, and they've been taken care of most of their lives."[29] Cumulatively, Black's clients allegedly lost millions of dollars as a result of having placed the ultimate degree of trust in a single individual who seized the opportunity to take advantage of their trust in an extraordinarily grievous manner.

The various investigations of Black prompted Reverend Jesse Jackson, the Florida branch of the NAACP, and others to raise the question of racial motivation. Some felt that the investigation of Black constituted another illustration of the "system" trying to pull down an African American who was achieving unprecedented levels of success. One of Black's attorneys succinctly expressed this view: "Tank is setting records and beating these white [agents] at their own game."[30] In fact, it appears highly unlikely that race played any role in the initial attention directed toward Black. Ray Anderson, an African American, was motivated by a desire to protect his own business interest when he reported a competitor he believed was involved in wrongdoing. This is not to say that race is not a factor in the athlete agent business. Race impacts many aspects of the industry including access to opportunities for agents of color, who agents pursue as clients, and who clients will select as agents. Yet allegations of racism based on the vigorousness of the prosecution of Black appear unfounded. As Berthelsen told *Sports Illustrated*, "this case with one individual has more violations of our regulations than all of our previous cases combined."[31]

As this book goes to press, civil and criminal prosecutions of Black and those associated with him have either been resolved or are pending. Black and James Franklin, general counsel of Black's PMI, pled guilty and admitted that they assisted convicted drug traffickers and others in moving cash from drug proceeds.[32] Black admitted to playing a part in laundering more than $1 million. In June 2001, Black received a six-year, 10-month sentence, to be followed by three years of supervised probation after he pled guilty to money laundering charges asserted in the case before U.S. Federal District Chief Judge Lawrence Zatkoff.[33] He was also fined $15,000. In January 2002, a Florida jury convicted Black of "conspiring to commit mail and wire fraud and of conspiring to defraud the U.S. and obstruct a Securities and Exchange Commission investigation."[34] Black, who was to be sentenced in May 2002, faces up to 25 years in prison. The conviction grew out of allegations that Black stole upwards of $13.5 million from football players whom he represented as a financial adviser.

Still pending are state and federal civil and criminal actions that accuse Black of misappropriating millions from his pro athlete clients.[35] A Louisiana action accuses Black of conspiracy to bribe persons connected to LSU's football program. James Franklin was sentenced to 32 months in prison, two years of postprison probation, and a fine of $10,000. In a separate Florida action, a federal judge sentenced Alfred "Tweet" Twitty, Black's assistant, to six months of house arrest for helping pay former University of Florida football players while they were still students, and for defrauding NFL players of millions of dollars.

Another recent matter raises issues of competency and ethics. A federal indictment was issued in January 2001 against another South Carolina–based sports management firm, Summit Management Group. In a 56-count indictment, federal prosecutors allege that several high-profile players, including baseball player Mookie Wilson and football players Charles Woodson and Stephen Davis, were collectively defrauded of between $3 and $5 million by the management firm.[36] The firm also is alleged to have persuaded high-profile college and high-school athletes to hire them as financial managers. Prosecutors apparently began the investigation in 1999 following Stephen Davis' complaint that Summit had misappropriated his money. According to the indictment, certain athletes granted powers of attorney to Summit. For example, Corey Jenkins, a first-round draft pick of the Boston Red Sox, allegedly handed over for Summit's management the $575,000 signing bonus he received from the club. The indictment alleges that Summit failed to use portions of the money to pay the athlete's bills, including house and car payments, as it had agreed.[37] The indictment also charges Marion Jones and James Brown of Summit with violating fiduciary duties owed to their clients.

One of the most widely reported cases of income mismanagement was that of retired Los Angeles Lakers basketball star Kareem Abdul-Jabbar, who sued agent Tom Collins. Abdul-Jabbar alleged that Collins mismanaged his basketball earnings by placing them in questionable investments, including a rib restaurant in Texas, a hotel in Alabama, two hotels and a restaurant in California, an exercise rope, a sports club, a limousine service, a commodities brokerage firm, and a cattle-feed business. Abdul-Jabbar also claimed he had been defrauded. He sought damages of a reported $59 million in his 1986 lawsuit.[38] The case was settled in early 1990, but the settlement terms were not publicly disclosed.[39]

Another well-publicized case of financial mismanagement involves Technical Equities Corporation, a growth-oriented holding company run by sports agent Harry Stern,[40] which declared bankruptcy in 1986. Technical Equities allowed individuals to invest in high-tech, manufacturing, and real estate deals. Many of the firm's athlete clients invested their life savings in the company. The firm's financial collapse involved not only seventy sports figures but also nearly seven hundred others, including doctors and lawyers.[41]

In another incident, agent Jack Rodri was sued by two of his clients, then NFL running back Eric Dickerson and former professional boxer Ken Norton. In separate suits both athletes alleged that Rodri mismanaged their earnings.[42] The Norton-Rodri suit was particularly shocking because Rodri had represented Norton throughout most of his professional boxing career as well as during his retirement.

In still another instance, NFL quarterback Jim Kelly sued his former agents for alleged gross negligence in the handling of his business affairs. Kelly sought to recover $130 million in damages, $28 million in punitive damages, and $200,000 in attorneys' fees.[43]

The author of a recent article identifies the following instances of financial improprieties:

in August 1996, four National Football League (NFL) players filed a joint civil suit against their former agent, Joe Courrege. The lawsuit alleged that Courrege solicited the athletes by preaching Christian principles and then defrauded them by using fictitious names and corporations to complete fourteen questionable real estate deals. They claimed total damages of $200,000. Norman Young mishandled his athlete clients' funds through his agency Probus Management, Inc. Clients complained that their bills were not paid, promises of off-season employment and endorsement deals were not kept, and their phone calls were not returned. The National Football League Player's Association (NFLPA) sued Probus on behalf of some of his clients. Unfortunately, because Probus had court judgments totaling hundreds of thousands of dollars and no discernable assets, the athletes did not recover any of their mishandled money.[44]

In the Walters-Bloom trial Joel Levy, an accountant for both Lloyd Bloom and his client, then Kansas City Chiefs running back Paul Palmer, testified about the misuse of client funds. Levy maintained that Palmer gave Bloom $125,000 to start a credit restoration business. With these funds, Bloom allegedly made a $82,242 down payment on the lease of a $160,000 1987 Rolls Royce Corniche, commonly referred to then as the most expensive vehicle in the world. He also used the funds to pay other personal expenses, including "credit-card debts, clothing and karate lessons."[45] Levy testified further that Bloom "had a sickness with money and trouble handling his own money."[46]

LEGAL MECHANISMS

Criminal Prosecution

In several alleged cases of financial mismanagement, the legal system has been deployed as a means of holding agents and financial managers accountable for their misconduct. Sometimes the legal process is invoked in the form of criminal prosecution. In this regard, the federal indictments issued against Summit Management and its principals are illustrative. Federal prosecutors have alleged that "as a part of a scheme and artifice to defraud and obtain money from professional athletes," Marion D. Jones and James E. Brown fraudulently represented that Summit "had assembled a highly qualified team of trained professionals, including certified public accountants, attorneys, investment portfolio managers, pension fund experts, asset managers and consultants for real estate investments, tax and estate planners, insurance managers and career counselors, to insure the financial growth and success of its clients."[47] More specifically, the indictment charges that Summit engaged in mail fraud, wire fraud, bank fraud, and money laundering.[48]

If proven, the charges asserted by federal prosecutors carry the potential of imprisonment and fines. For example, the indictment identifies the maximum penalty for each count of mail fraud as imprisonment for five years and a fine of $250,000. In addition, prosecutors have sought forfeiture of a minimum of $445,947.27 from Marion Jones and James Brown, which represents proceeds traceable to their alleged money-laundering offenses. A minimum of approximately $1,218,825.64 is sought in forfeiture from Jones, Brown, and another defendant, Andre Lewis.[49] This amount represents "proceeds the Defendants obtained, 'directly or indirectly, as a result of [bank fraud offenses].' "[50] In January 2001, the four defendants named in the indictment pled not guilty to the federal charges.[51]

A criminal prosecution ended in the conviction of Atlanta-based agent Fairron Newton. A federal grand jury issued an indictment that charged Newton with fraud, tax fraud, money laundering, and filing false tax returns. Newton arranged for the salaries of NFL football players (including Charlie Garner, Tim Bowens, Fred Baxter, and Shaun King) to be paid directly to his company, Options Plus Financial Services. Newton promised to pay the players' bills, debts, and expenses. In 1995, without the knowledge of the players (who were in no way involved in criminal misconduct), Newton began filing fraudulent tax returns in order to generate tax refunds that were received by Options Plus.[52] In June 2001, Newton was sentenced to serve two years in prison, ordered to pay restitution of more than $240,000, and ordered to serve 200 hours of community service.[53]

Criminal prosecution against Howard J. Golub, who at one time served as a financial manager for approximately seventy athletes, resulted in his being sentenced in January 1989 to ten to twelve years in prison and ordered to pay restitution in the amount of $163,600 to clients following a guilty plea.[54] Golub had been indicted by a grand jury on five counts of fraud and nineteen counts of theft. His clients included baseball players George Foster and Lance Parrish, basketball players Louis Orr and Cedric Maxwell, and football player Rich Karlis.[55]

One of the earliest agent-related criminal prosecutions took place against agent Richard Sorkin.[56] While acting as a sports agent, Sorkin gambled and lost in the stock market more than $1 million in earnings of more than fifty hockey and basketball players. Investigations revealed that Sorkin bet as much as $100,000 per week on horses, baseball, and football.[57] The district attorney found that Sorkin lost $626,000 gambling and $271,000 in the stock market. Other missing funds could not be traced or otherwise accounted for.[58]

Civil Suits

Players also invoke the civil process in their attempts to hold agents legally accountable and to recover money lost as a result of financial mismanagement. For example, Mookie Wilson won a judgment against James Brown and Marion Jones, the principals of Summit Management Group.[59] Wilson alleged that Summit and its principals "failed to make mortgage, car and credit card payments" for him. He also alleged that Summit "used his credit card and power of attorney for personal gain."[60] A judge awarded Wilson damages of $450,000 that consisted of "$360,000 for money lost, $50,000 for punitive damages and $40,000 for lawyer's fees."[61] Wilson's attorney doubts that his client will recover much, if any, of the money the court awarded him.[62]

In a much-celebrated case in the early 1990s, former baseball player Bill Madlock filed a malpractice and fraud action against his former agent and attorney Steve Greenberg, stemming from unsuccessful investments made on Madlock's behalf.[63] The arbitrator who heard the case "cleared Greenberg and his law firm of all charges with the exception of two counts of negligence."[64] Because the statute of limitations had expired, Greenberg, who characterized these findings of negligence as technical glitches, was not required to pay any damages.[65]

A common form of mismanagement involves players' allegations that agents or financial advisers persuaded them to enter into investments with promises that the players would reap tax-related benefits. When the IRS informs the players that they have a tax deficiency, players may seek recourse against their agents or financial advisers. Such was the case when former baseball star Keith Hernandez filed a suit in which he asserted numerous claims, including breach of contract, fraud, and breach of fiduciary duty. The gist of Hernandez's lawsuit was that his sports agent, who at one time handled virtually all of his financial affairs, improperly established an investment that failed as a tax shelter.[66]

In pursuing civil actions, athletes are most likely to assert claims of fraud, negligence, breach of fiduciary duty, and breach of contract. A lawsuit filed in 2000 by football players Ike Hilliard and Fred Taylor against Tank Black and several other individuals and entities is representative. The plaintiffs asserted that they were " 'unsophisticated with respect to business and financial matters' and that they 'relied completely on the advice and expertise of Defendants Black, Franklin, and PMI' who 'exercised substantial if not complete control and authority over the financial decisions of Plaintiffs and others.' "[67] The plaintiffs generally alleged that the defendants, among other things, improperly lured them to invest several millions of dollars into investment schemes, and that defendants engaged in conduct in violation of securities laws. Finally, the athletes asserted causes of action sounding in breach of fiduciary duty, breach of contract, conversion, negligence, and civil conspiracy relating to the investment schemes.[68]

In *Williams v. CWI, Inc.*, NBA player Reginald Williams and his wife sought to recover $50,000 that they had entrusted with Waymon Hunt, a financial adviser.[69] Rather than invest the money, Hunt diverted it for his own purposes.[70] The federal district court judge who heard the matter ruled that Hunt was liable to the plaintiffs under either a breach of contract or fraud theory. A noteworthy aspect of this case is the court's perspective as to why players appear particularly susceptible to financial abuse by agents and other financial advisers.

Like many young professional athletes, Mr. Williams was earning a considerable salary but had no experience in making investments or managing money. He needed reliable expert advice and did not find any readily available.

Because Mr. Williams' predicament appears to be a recurring problem for basketball players and other athletes who suddenly receive large disposable incomes, it seems that it would be appropriate for either the NBA, or the

player's team, or the players' association to develop a three-pronged program
to assist these young people. First, they could offer at least rudimentary education in business and finance. Second, they could assemble a package of low
risk blue-chip investments for young players that will provide for their futures
as well as a system for referring them to wise and ethical professionals who
can advise them on managing money. Third, they might offer a financial incentive for players to place a portion of their funds in a deferred investment
program. Perhaps the League and the players' association could even establish their own high-grade, low-risk investment fund. In this way, young athletes would be protected from highly speculative ventures like the one involved
in this case.[71]

Other notable cases in which athletes have filed lawsuits relating to
alleged mismanagement of their financial affairs by agents and financial managers include an action alleging fraud, breach of contract,
negligence, and breach of fiduciary duty in which a court awarded
damages in the amount of $868,047.84 to former NBA player Bill
Willoughby against his agent, Jerry A. Davis;[72] an arbitration case in
which an athlete alleged his agent made unsuitable investment recommendations and misrepresentations relating to the sale of securities;[73]
Kendricks v. Grant Thornton International,[74] in which 127 investors, many
of whom were professional athletes, filed a lawsuit against an accounting firm alleging, among other claims, fraud, aiding and abetting
fraud, breach of contract, breach of fiduciary duty, negligence, negli-
gent misrepresentation, and securities law violations; baseball player
Charles ("Walt") Terrell's lawsuit against an agency firm that allegedly
mismanaged his funds and defrauded him;[75] and an arbitrator's
award of $204,886 to football player John Farley for damages arising
out of investment advice.[76]

In responding to such a panoply of allegations, agents and financial
managers not only deny that they acted incompetently, but also assert
that it was the athlete who squandered his or her resources. A lawsuit filed by former football player Vincent Clark against his financial
manager is illustrative. Clark asserted that his financial adviser performed services including "paying Clark's bills, providing Clark with
spending money, investing the balance, managing the investments,
and procuring and maintaining appropriate insurance."[77] After suf-
fering a career-ending football injury and the realization that his financial resources were not what he believed they should have been,
Clark sued Weisberg alleging various forms of improper financial
management. According to the court, Weisberg responded as follows:
"Weisberg claims that like many professional athletes, Clark spent almost all of the money he earned. Weisberg believes that Clark failed
to acknowledge that 'he now has insufficient funds because he wasted
his assets by making exorbitant purchases, transferring large sums

of money to his family members and friends, and refusing to save for the future or consider the consequences if he were injured or unable to continue playing football, and not because of any action taken by Weisberg.' "[78] In another lawsuit involving Vincent Clark, *Clark v. Robert W. Baird Co., Inc.*, the defendants successfully obtained the dismissal of certain claims, including allegations of RICO violations and fraud.[79]

The stories of abuse described above should not make us forget that there are legitimate financial success stories. *Sports Illustrated* reported that former major league outfielder Gary Maddox paid IMG $12,000 a year to manage his investments and has been very successful. Similarly, major league pitcher Orel Hershiser, a former business major, worked with his agent to invest $1 million per year for an annual expected yield of $300,000 during his retirement.[80] The number of success stories probably rivals the disasters, but it is the latter that receive the most extensive press coverage.

Excessive Fees

In 1983, agent Bob Woolf negotiated a five-year, $800,000 contract for hockey player Andrew Brown.[81] Woolf contracted with Brown to receive a fee of $40,000, or 5 percent of Brown's projected $800,000 salary. The team for which Brown played—the Indianapolis Racers of the fledgling World Hockey Association—suffered financial difficulties. Consequently, Brown received only $185,000 of the anticipated $800,000 when the Racers went bankrupt.[82] Nevertheless, the Racers agreed to pay Woolf his $40,000 fee calculated on the basis of the full $800,000 player/team contract. The fee received by Woolf approximated 20 percent of the total compensation actually paid by the team to Brown rather than the 5 percent that was contemplated. Brown sued Woolf alleging misrepresentation and breach of fiduciary duty.[83] The Woolf case illustrates one problem associated with agent fees: the receipt of the entire fee "up front" from the athlete's signing bonus or first few paychecks.

Issues relating to the timing of fee payments to agents and excessive fees charged by agents have become less problematic due to actions taken primarily by players' associations. These actions include limits on the amount of fees that an agent is permitted to charge for negotiating a contract on a player's behalf and restrictions on when agent fees are payable.

The current *NFLPA Regulations Governing Contract Advisors* address both of these issues. Section 4(B)(1) of those regulations imposes a 3 percent maximum on fees for contract negotiation–related services.

"The maximum fee which may be charged or collected by a Contract Advisor shall be three percent of the 'compensation' . . . received by the player in each playing season covered by the contract negotiated by the Contract Advisor."[84] Another section of the regulations defines 'compensation' so as to "include only salaries, signing bonuses, reporting bonuses, roster bonuses, and any performance incentives earned by the player during the term of the contract (including option year) negotiated by the Contact Advisor."[85] The 3 percent represents a decrease from earlier NFLPA regulations. Prior to 1988, the NFLPA allowed agents to charge for contract negotiation services up to 5 percent of "a player's compensation in excess of the minimum salary for the first three years of the contract."[86] This decrease is not particularly significant given that in all of the major professional leagues the average fee for contract negotiations alone is around 3 percent of the value of the contract negotiated.

The NFLPA's regulations also address when agent fees are payable. As a general proposition, the regulations mandate that an agent or "Contract Advisor," as stated in the regulations, is "prohibited from receiving any fee for his/her services until and unless the player receives the compensation upon which the fee is based."[87] So the player's receipt of compensation for athletic services is a condition to the payment of fees to an agent. The regulations allow an exception in cases of deferred compensation to be received by a player. They recognize that a player may desire to pay an agent in advance with respect to deferred compensation. Under such circumstances, the advance payment of fees is collectable by the agent only after the player has performed the services "necessary under his contract [with his team] to entitle him to deferred compensation."[88]

Regulations promulgated by the NBPA contain limitations similar to those imposed by the NFLPA. NBPA regulations impose a 4 percent maximum on the fees agents can charge for contract negotiations. Moreover, a ceiling of 2 percent is imposed on the fees that an agent can charge NBA players who sign for the league minimum with their teams.

Interestingly, the Major League Baseball Players Association (MLBPA) imposes no universal maximum limit on the fees that an agent can charge as a percentage of player compensation. MLBPA Counsel Gene Orza maintains that the market will regulate itself. He argues that because of the athletes' knowledge of the market, agents charging too much will soon be out of business. This being said, *MLBPA Regulations Governing Player Agents* (MLBPA regulations) include provisions intended to protect players signed to minimum salary contracts. The MLPBA regulations state, "No Player Agent shall charge a Player any fee for negotiating that Player's individual salary unless the salary

negotiated exceeds the minimum salary for that year established by
the Basic Agreement."[89]

Conclusion

Broadly these are the most frequent legal issues being grappled with
in the sports agent business. As you will note, they are largely focused
on athlete earnings in terms of wealth management. The next chapter
will focus on broader ethical and qualification issues that go beyond
monetary concerns.

Chapter 6

Conflicts of Interest

Factual scenarios involving financial mismanagement potentially implicate several of the obligations identified in Chapter 1 that agents owe to their principals. These obligations include the duty of an agent to comply with all applicable laws and the agent's duty to notify the principal of all matters that may affect the principal's interests.[1] Allegations of financial mismanagement also implicate agent obligations related to conflicts of interest—the subject explored in this chapter.

Agents have been under the microscope for engaging in practices where conflicts of interest may be present. As discussed in Chapter 1, critical features of the agent/athlete relationship are the agent's obligation of undivided loyalty and the duty to act in good faith at all times.[2] These duties preclude an agent from acting on behalf of parties adverse to his or her principal.[3] A conflict of interest occurs when a duty owed to one party is compromised by a separate interest or agreement with a third party. As revealed below, agents are likely to confront numerous situations in which they must act with care to avoid violating the basic duties of undivided loyalty and good faith that they owe to their athlete clients.

Agent Self-Interest: Undisclosed Financial Interests

Historically, the conflict of interest scenario involving the athlete/agent relationship that has been most problematic is one involving nondisclosure by an agent of a financial interest that conflicts with that of the athlete client. One such notable instance involved former Philadelphia Eagles football player Reggie White and his former agent Patrick Forte. White alleged that while Forte was negotiating with the Eagles regarding White's player contract, Forte was also negotiating a contract for himself to be an assistant to the president of that NFL franchise. In a suit filed in U.S. District Court in Philadelphia, White maintained that this constituted a conflict of interest and affected Forte's performance in his player-contract negotiation.[4] The suit was eventually settled and both parties were prohibited from commenting on the settlement terms.[5]

Similar issues were present in *Detroit Lions, Inc. v. Argovitz*,[6] which pitted agent Jerry Argovitz against former Detroit Lions running back Billy Sims. Argovitz was negotiating on behalf of Sims with both the NFL's Detroit Lions and the then-competing USFL's Houston Gamblers. During the course of his negotiations with the Lions on behalf of Sims, Argovitz informed the athlete that he had applied for the Houston franchise. Sims, however, was unaware of the extent of his agent's interest in the USFL franchise. After Argovitz's ownership application for the Gamblers' franchise was assured, Argovitz reduced his offer on behalf of Sims to the Lions and dropped prior demands for so-called skills guarantees that had the potential to provide Sims with even greater income. While these negotiations continued, Argovitz also decided to seek an offer from the Gamblers and provided one of his partners with information regarding the offer Sims had received from the Lions. Based on the information about the progress of Argovitz's negotiations with the Lions, Sims believed that the Lions were not negotiating in good faith and were not interested in his services. Therefore, he did not urge Argovitz to seek a final offer from them even though the Lions were willing to provide him with the guarantees that Sims had sought from the team.

Sims agreed to join the Gamblers on the terms of the team's offer and signed a contract with the team on July 1, 1983. Argovitz did not contact the Lions and request a final offer so that both offers could be presented to Sims. After the true nature of the Lions' interest in him was revealed, Sims signed a contract with the Lions on December 16, 1983. Subsequently, he and the Lions went to court requesting that the contract with the Gamblers be invalidated because it was a product of fraud and because of the conflict of interest by Sims' agent, Argovitz.

The court ruled in favor of Sims. In so ruling, it concluded that Argovitz had breached his duty to contact the Lions and receive and present its final offer alongside that of the Gamblers to Sims. It also concluded that to deny rescission of Sims' contract with the Gamblers would be unconscionable in view of Argovitz's egregious and pronounced breach of his fiduciary duty to Sims during negotiations on behalf of Sims with the Lions.

Finally, the court found that Sims' knowledge of Argovitz's application for the franchise or approval of the franchise did not absolve the agent of his duties to Sims. The court found that Argovitz could not have expected Sims to understand the extent to which his agent's interest and position as president of the team undermined Argovitz's efforts as an unbiased third-party negotiator. The court pointed out,

"Argovitz's conflict of interest and self-dealing put him in the position where he would not even use the wedge he now had to negotiate with the Lions, a wedge that is the dream of every agent."[7] This "wedge" was the offer from a franchise in a rival league. Argovitz knew that if he called the Lions, the Lions would offer Sims a contract and Sims would not be available to the Gamblers, of which Argovitz was an owner. Moreover, Argovitz improperly had Sims sign a waiver of any claims Sims might have against him without telling Sims to obtain advice independently, arranged a $500,000 loan from the Gamblers to Sims at 1 percent above prime, out of which he knew his $100,000 fee would be paid, and did not demand benefits for Sims, a proven NFL talent, comparable to those that Jim Kelly, another player, obtained from the Gamblers.[8]

Argovitz violated the agent's basic duties of undivided loyalty, good faith, and honest and fair dealing in several ways. Without obtaining appropriate consent, Argovitz represented a third party in a transaction in which his client was involved, possessed direct interest in the transaction that was antagonistic to his client's interest, and failed to disclose all information relevant to the principal's interests.[9] This conduct amounted to an extreme failure to adhere to the fiduciary relationship that existed between him and Sims.

Conflict of interest concerns have also arisen where leaders of players' unions represent individual union members in their contract negotiations with their respective teams. The argument against such representation is that the union leader's primary responsibility is to safeguard the rights of all union members, and circumstances may exist where an act may be advantageous to the union leader's client but not to the union as a whole or where an act could be advantageous to the union but not to the individual athlete.

The late Larry Fleischer, former head of the NBPA, represented individual athletes while he was the union's leader. Similarly, former National Hockey League Players Association (NHLPA) chief Alan Eagleson represented individual athletes in that league. Eagleson's conflicts in representation and other areas became so extreme that the members of the union initiated an independent investigation of his interests in 1989.[10]

MULTIPLE REPRESENTATION AND OTHER POTENTIAL CONFLICTS

Agent representation of athletes presents conflicts in addition to those described above. In examining the following scenarios, consider whether a conflict exists and, if so, what steps an agent might take to avoid the conflict. Also consider what, if any, additional variables become relevant if the agent is also an attorney. These additional "complications" will be examined in the following chapter.

1. An agent represents players from different teams in the same sport. Does either a potential or real conflict of interest exist? Is it inevitable that the agent will consciously or unconsciously favor the interests of one client over another?

2. Is the potential for a conflict of interest enhanced when the athletes play at the same position? Does the following situation present a conflict of interest? Former professional quarterback Warren Moon left the Canadian Football League and sought a position in the NFL. Moon's agent Leigh Steinberg shopped Moon to numerous teams including the New York Giants, the team for which another one of Steinberg's clients, Scott Brunner, played quarterback.[11]

3. Suppose an agent represents multiple players on the same team. Should this be permissible? Does it create a potential or an actual conflict of interest? Consider the following factual scenario: The same agent represented two Kansas City Royals baseball players, Hal McRae and Frank White. Allegedly, the agent refused to finalize a contract on behalf of White until the team had extended McRae's contract.

   In such a scenario is the conflict real or potential? What, if anything, can the agent do to avoid a conflict?[12] Is the players' consent to dual representation necessary to avoid a conflict of interest?

4. In the NBA and the NFL, each team has a salary cap that limits the amount of money a team may allocate for player salaries. Suppose an agent represents multiple players on one team and the players are seeking remuneration from a limited fund. Does this situation present a potential or a real conflict of interest? If so, what is the nature of the conflict? Does it lie in the fact that the athletes expect their agent to seek the greatest amount of compensation possible from this limited fund for each of them?[13] Is a conflict unavoidable since a negotiation leading to increased compensation for one player will lead to decreased compensation for the other player?[14]

5. Does the gravity of the scenario described above intensify if the athletes play the same position, or is this irrelevant?

6. Agents are compensated based upon a percentage of the compensation received by athletes. Compensation includes the salary to be earned under the contract as well as certain bonuses such as a signing bonus. Standard athlete/agent contracts provided

by the major professional players associations restrict agents from collecting fees until the player has received compensation, or in cases of deferred compensation, until the athlete has performed the services on which the compensation is based.

Suppose an agent encourages a young player to sign a long-term contract that includes a large signing bonus, "modest annual salaries and substantial deferred compensation" rather than a "short term contract with a modest signing bonus, substantial annual salaries and little or no deferred compensation."[15] Given that agents are typically compensated based upon a percentage of an athlete's compensation, does this advice represent a conflict of interest? What steps, if any, can an agent engage in to avoid a conflict of interest?

7. Suppose an agent represents numerous clients. Does multiple representation undermine the agent's obligation to zealously represent his or her client given the substantial time demands placed on agents engaged in contract negotiations and the short period of time in which negotiations must occur? Is it relevant whether the agent is a member of one of the larger athlete representation agencies such as SFX , IMG, Octagon, or Assante? Is a member of a small athlete agent firm? Is solely responsible for representing his or her clients?

8. Suppose an agent encourages an athlete to endorse a product that may not be in the athlete's best interest. Does a conflict exist given that the agent will receive a percentage of the endorsement contract that the player signs? How can a conflict be avoided?

9. Does a conflict exist when an agent represents multiple players who may be suitable for an endorsement contract? Is the conflict resolved if an agent recommends both players for the contract? As noted by one commentator, "is there the possibility that, had the clients retained independent counsel, their interests could have been more vigorously represented?"[16]

10. Changes in the sports industry have caused coaches to increasingly seek representation by agents or attorneys in their contract negotiations with teams. Does a conflict exist when an agent represents a player and a coach on the same team? If so, what is the basis for the conflict? Does it reside in the fact that the dual representation may result in the agent advocating a position that favors the team/coach to the disadvantage of the athlete client? Assume that a goal of a coach is to have players arrive at training camp and begin preparations for the start of the playing season as early as possible. Might an agent who represents both a

player and a coach on the same team unconsciously encourage a player to sign early and facilitate an early arrival? Would doing so constitute a conflict of interest? What level of coach involvement in contract negotiations on behalf of a team creates a conflict when the agent represents the coach and the athlete?

11. Is there a conflict of interest if a player represents fellow players on the same team? This situation arose for a short period of time when Percy Miller, popularly known as Master P, represented NBA players during a period when he failed two NBA tryout attempts.

The foregoing scenarios demonstrate the complexity of the conflicting issues that may arise in the sports agency industry. The discussions that immediately follow and that appear in Chapter 7 are not intended to provide definitive answers to the previous questions. They may, however, provide information that proves helpful in attempts to resolve conflicting issues that arise out of the agent/athlete relationship.

Standards Governing Conflicts

As was noted at the beginning of this chapter, the agent's fiduciary obligation to his or her athlete client imposes upon the former a duty to act in his or her client's best interest. As stated in the Restatement (Second) of Agency, "Unless otherwise agreed, an agent is subject to a duty to his principal to act solely for the benefit of the principal in all matters connected with his agency."[17] Under agency law principles, the fiduciary nature of the relationship along with duties of loyalty, good faith, and honest and fair dealings, impose an obligation on agents to avoid conflicts of interest.

Player Union Regulations

Regulations promulgated by players associations that govern agents recognize the agent's duty not to engage in conduct amounting to conflicts of interest. For example, the *National Basketball Players Association Regulations Governing Player Agents* include general provisions exhorting agents to avoid conflicts of interest, as well as specific provisions that prohibit agents from representing management and from holding financial interest in certain business ventures. These provisions provide:

To further effectuate the objectives of these Regulations players are prohibited from:

(e) Holding or seeking to hold, either directly or indirectly, a financial interest in any professional basketball team or in any other business venture that would create an actual conflict of interest or the appearance of a conflict of interest between the individual player and his agent;

(f) Representing the General Manager or coach of any NBA team (or any other management representative who participates in the team's deliberations or decisions concerning what compensation is to be offered individual players) in matters pertaining to his employment or any other matters in which he has any financial stake by or association with any NBA team;

(g) Engaging in any other activity which creates actual or potential conflicts of interest with the effective representation of NBA players; provided that the representation of two or more players on any one club shall not itself be deemed to be prohibited by this provision;

(h) Soliciting or accepting money or anything of value from any NBA club in circumstances where to do so would create a conflict or an apparent conflict with the interests of any player he represents . . . ;

(k) Concealing material facts from any player whom the agent is representing which relate to the subject of the individual's contract negotiation.[18]

Sanctions for violating these regulations may include suspension or revocation of the agent's certification to be involved in individual contract negotiations on behalf of NBA players. Similarly, *MLBPA Regulations Governing Player Agents* threaten the suspension or revocation of a player agent's certification if he or she engages in enumerated conduct that creates an actual or potential conflict of interest. According to such regulations, holding a financial stake in any baseball club or other financial venture creates an actual or potential conflict of interest, or more generally creates an actual or potential conflict of interest in the agent's effective representation of a player.[19] Agent regulations of the NFLPA and the NHLPA also contain such prohibitions.

Players' unions have relied upon these regulations in several prominent recent situations involving possible conflicts of interest on the part of agents. In 2001, IMG terminated a sponsorship sales agreement with the NHL after the NHLPA complained that the arrangement constituted a violation by IMG of rules that prohibit agents from representing both players and management.[20] The complaint lodged against IMG by the NHLPA is illustrative of an emerging approach by players' unions to prevent potential conflicts. A year prior to this complaint, IMG Hockey President Mike Barnett was forced by the union to terminate a 20-year business relationship with Wayne Gretzky after the former player joined a group of investors seeking to purchase the NHL's Phoenix Coyotes.

Pressure by the NHLPA and MLBPA resulted in a restructuring of SFX. These players' unions raised concerns of potential conflicts of interest by SFX following its acquisition by the conglomerate Clear Channel Communications. A major shareholder of Clear Channel is Tom Hicks, who owns MLB's Texas Rangers and the NHL's Dallas Stars. On January 1, 2001, "attempting to shield itself from conflict issues and appease the NHLPA and MLB Players Association . . . SFX Entertainment Inc. separated its athlete representation division into a semi-autonomous business unit."[21] Later in the year, SFX divided the division into individual agencies that are devoted to particular sports.[22] The following discussion of the baseball group aptly describes the nature of the restructuring:

> Under the new structure, SFX Baseball Group is owned by Clear Channel, but Clear Channel has no ability to interfere in the business of the group. Even David Falk, head of SFX Sports, has no authority over the baseball agents in the group. . . . The group is run by the baseball agents whose businesses were acquired by SFX over the past few years. . . . [Randall Hendricks, a longtime baseball agent who is CEO of the new company] compare[s] the structure of the new company to a blind trust. "They own the stock, but we have an agreement with Clear Channel and our new company. . . . They cannot remove any officers or directors. They don't have the powers of normal shareholders. . . . We can take a position in the interest of our clients even if it's adverse to [Clear Channel]."[23]

Apparently, the new structure came too late to satisfy agents Jim Bronner and Robert Gilhooley, who filed suit against SFX arguing that the conflict presented by Clear Channel's ownership indirectly resulted in their losing baseball player Juan Gonzalez as a client.[24] Bronner and Gilhooley, who were fired by SFX after they filed suit, also allege that SFX fraudulently withheld information regarding the takeover by Clear Channel when they sold their company to SFX in February 2000.[25]

Another interesting potential conflict arose during Michael Jordan's tenure in a management and ownership role with the NBA's Washington Wizards. Jordan's long-time agent and business adviser David Falk currently represents players on that team as well as players who may join that team. The issue was raised regarding Jordan's ability to avoid preferential dealings with his own business manager.[26] Jordan, Falk, and the league all asserted that there was no conflict. Some critics argue, however, that on the surface the relationship appeared to run afoul of NBPA regulations that prohibit agents from representing management representatives who participate "in the team's deliberations or decisions concerning what compensation is to be offered individual players in matters pertaining to his employment or any other matters in which he has any financial stake by or association with any NBA team."[27]

Unrelated to the Jordan conflict, agent David Falk notes that it is not the existence of a conflict alone that is a problem; "The question is whether you have a debilitating conflict." Falk and others maintain that because of the limited number of agents with actual expertise in sports business issues, most successful agents are bound to have conflicts: "Invariably you're going to have conflicts even if you only have two clients." Falk makes a valid point. If an endorsement deal is offered to an agent to give to either of his two clients, only one can be given the deal and necessarily the other is shortchanged.

Conclusion

In summary, all agents are subject to the duty to avoid conflicts of interest that grows generally out of the law of agency. In addition, all agents are governed by regulations promulgated by the players associations. Whether agents are subject to additional proscriptions will often depend on the existence of state-enacted agent regulations or whether the agent is also an attorney. Discussion of state-enacted agent regulations is reserved for Chapter 11. We turn in the next chapter to a discussion of conflicts of interest and other complex issues that are present when an agent is also an attorney.

Chapter 7

Ethics
Attorney Versus Nonattorney Agents

The sports agent industry has evolved such that licensed attorneys comprise a significant number of the agents who represent athletes. The intersection of the legal profession and the agent profession is often an uneasy fit. Rules governing the practice of law do not seem particularly well equipped to handle the unique nature of the sports agent profession. Law professor Walter Champion notes that "[the] ethical code of a well-established profession . . . may not perfectly fit to the emerging, evolving and dynamic relationships that are inherent in the sports arena."[1] This uneasy fit creates a myriad of issues, including the following:

1. What standards govern the determination and management of conflicts of interest when an agent is also an attorney?
2. Is the attorney who represents an athlete as an agent bound solely by generally applicable principles of agency law such as the duty of loyalty that proscribes conflicts of interest and regulations of players' unions?
3. In order to avoid standards and regulations attendant to their professional status, under what circumstances may a licensed attorney disclaim his or her status as an attorney when representing athletes? and,
4. Under what circumstances do nonattorney agents, and attorney agents negotiating contracts and engaging in other activities on behalf of clients in jurisdictions in which they are not licensed, violate prohibitions against the unauthorized practice of law?

Standards Governing Attorney Agents: Conflicts of Interest

As it relates to most matters, there is not much difference between the standards to which the lawyer and nonlawyer agent will be bound. General agency law principles, as well as those that govern the practice of law, impose duties on both attorney agents and nonattorney agents. Examples of such duties include requirements that services be rendered competently, and that clients be represented with the utmost loyalty and good faith.[2]

While a nonlawyer agent is subject to general agency law principles and league and players' union regulations, the attorney agent will also be held accountable to the code of ethics for lawyers. Failure to adhere to this code may result in disciplinary action, including a fine, reprimand, suspension, or even disbarment. Such sanctions are in addition to any that might be imposed for the agent's failure to adhere to general agency law principles or union regulations.[3] Various state supreme courts impose the professional ethics requirements on attorneys. These ethical standards are set forth in the Model Rules of Professional Conduct, formulated by the American Bar Association. Many states have adopted these standards. The disciplinary rules of the ABA apply when a breach of these rules occurs in the lawyer-client relationship.[4]

The code of ethics that governs attorneys with respect to conflicts of interest illustrates the additional standards that apply to the attorney agent. Rule 1.7 of the Model Rules of Professional Conduct generally addresses conflicts of interest. It also provides guidance with respect to the circumstances under which conflicting representations can be undertaken,[5] and provides "a general standard for lawyers analyzing the propriety of representing multiple clients with adverse interests."[6] Model Rule 2.2 is specifically focused on multiple representations— "the common representation of two or more clients in a single transaction or several related transactions."[7] As the hypotheticals in Chapter 6 suggest, the sports attorney may "frequently encounter representations where the conflicts associated with multiple-client representations are subtle and appear insignificant when representation is first considered. In reality, sports transactions are often complex and involve clients occupying disparate positions."[8]

Chapter 6 described various situations in which agents or attorney agents represent multiple players, such as where an agent represents players who seek compensation from a limited fund. Ethics rules governing attorneys deliver some guidance in regard to a potential conflict resulting from multiple representation. These rules provide that the fact of a potential conflict does not automatically preclude multiple representation.[9] According to Rule 1.7, "an attorney may proceed with conflicting representations only after obtaining the client's consent and only if she 'reasonably believes' that none of the clients' interests is likely to be compromised by the representations."[10] Model Rule 2.2 instructs attorneys in situations involving multiple representation to take the same precautions: consultation and consent. The model rules define consultation as the "communication of information reasonably sufficient to permit the client to appreciate the significance of the matter in question."[11] Allowing for multiple representation where proper precautions are taken is premised on notions of freedom of contract. It is also based on the belief that a person should be allowed to select the lawyer that he or she wants to represent his or her interests.[12]

Leagues and players' unions recognize the reality of multiple representations of players by agents and perhaps the premise on which the above-described ethical rule is based. For example, NBPA agent regulations expressly state that an agent who represents one or more players on the same team has not automatically violated its proscriptions against conflicts of interest.[13]

In summary, if the lawyer makes a good faith determination, from the perspective of a "disinterested lawyer," that he or she can adequately represent the interests of multiple clients, the lawyer can do so, but only if the consent of all clients is obtained.[14] The question of whether appropriate consent has been given carries its own risk for the agent. Notes one author discussing general conflict of interest concerns that arise from multiple representation:

> Although the athlete-clients may have given their consent to the potential conflicts of interest, there should be concern as to whether the consent was informed consent. This involves the question of whether the athletes understand the amount of time and effort which is necessary to negotiate their contract and undertake other areas of their representation, in order to adequately discern a possible lack of attention from their attorney due to other clients' demands on the attorney's time. Furthermore, it is difficult to draw a line between the point when the conflict of interest is merely potential and the point where the time and resource demands upon the individual attorney make the conflict an actual conflict.[15]

Similarly, Professor John Walton states that

> According to Rules 1.7 and 2.2, an attorney may proceed with conflicting representations or intermediations only after obtaining the clients' consent and only if she "reasonably believes" that none of the clients' interests is likely to be compromised by the representation. However, the admonition in the Rules is misleading simply because it essentially ignores the possibility that the attorney's judgment may be clouded when evaluating the clients' conflicting interests. Moreover, it provides no hint of how complex the consent to conflict process can be. [16]

As also discussed in Chapter 6, the court in *Detroit Lions v. Argovitz*,[17] which involved a dentist acting as an agent, provided a very strict standard in determining when adequate consent has been given. In that case the court held that an agent must fully inform the client of all relevant facts and obtain the principal's consent: "the agent must show that his principal had full knowledge, not only of the fact that the agent was interested, but also of every material fact known to the agent which might affect the principal and that having such knowledge the principal freely consented to the transaction."[18] On the question of consent, the court stated consent will be deemed to be freely given under circumstances where the agent "inform[s] the principal of all facts that come to his knowledge that are or may be material or which might affect his principal's rights or interests or influence the action he takes."[19] The rule enunciated in *Argovitz* suggests that consent will be deemed proper only when the disclosure made by the agent "include[s] not only a specification of the extent of the agent's financial interest, but a disclosure of significant risks that the player confronts in the conflicting relations and important alternative courses of action that are available."[20] Note two commentators, the "impression is left that the court requires a level of disclosure so exacting that it is difficult to imagine a reasonable person continuing to be represented by the agent with the conflict."[21] Yet, *Argovitz* can also be interpreted as giving agents the flexibility to engage in multiple representations so long as proper disclosures are made to the clients.

Attorney, Agent, or Both?

Given that attorneys must comply with state-imposed professional codes of conduct, the violation of which may result in disciplinary action, it is not surprising that some attorney agents have claimed that the representation of athlete clients does not involve legal work. Thus, they argue that they should not be subject to professional codes with respect to such services. Attorney agents, attempting to disavow their attorney status in this context, find justification in the fact that nonattorney agents who provide competent services on behalf of their athlete clients are not subject to the same requirements. Most fundamentally, these attorney agents argue that it is unfair to impose standards on them to which nonattorney agents are not bound. As captured by one analyst: "some sports lawyers argue that based on the nature of the representation industry, that if they enter the industry and hold out themselves as a sports agent, they avoid application of the ethical rules of the legal profession."[22]

One problem with this argument lies in the nature of the services provided by agents. A principal service provided by the athlete agent is the negotiation of the athlete's contract with his or her team. As pointed out by one commentator, "There can be little doubt that the general service of negotiation is an area of traditional legal representation."[23] On the other hand, athlete agents provide services that do not fall within the scope of what is typically considered legal representation. Many of these services relate to the athlete's business affairs for which legal training is not required, such as advice on personal and financial matters. Indeed, it has been suggested that changes in the industry make agent expertise in accounting and business planning as relevant, if not more so, as legal training.

Only a few courts and administrative bodies have addressed the issue of whether an attorney agent is subject to the ethical rules that govern attorneys. Therefore, it would be unwise to draw any definitive conclusions regarding how a particular court or administrative body might resolve the issue. Nevertheless, these rulings provide some indication of judicial thinking in this regard.

An advisory opinion of the Illinois State Bar Association directly addressed whether attorney agents are governed by the Illinois Code of Professional Responsibility that regulates attorney conduct.[24] The panel considered whether "the representation of athletes is actually the practice of law in that it may include a wide range of business counseling, as well as contract negotiations. This doubt could be prompted by the fact that nonlawyers frequently engage in these activities." The panel concluded that "when an attorney engaged in the private practice of law represents a client in contract negotiations and general business counseling, these activities constitute the practice of law."

In another matter, *Cuyahoga County Bar Association v. Glenn*,[25] an attorney agent represented Richard Dent in contract negotiations with the Chicago Bears. The attorney's mishandling of Dent's funds amounted to violations of state disciplinary rules governing the conduct of attorneys. The Ohio Supreme Court assumed, without discussion, that the attorney was subject to such rules in upholding sanctions imposed by a state bar disciplinary panel.

The Georgia Supreme Court also upheld a state bar's discipline of an attorney agent who violated professional standards governing attorneys. As in *Cuyahoga*, the court in *In the Matter of Fredrick J. Henley, Jr.* assumed without discussion that the attorney who represented a professional football player was governed by standards regulating attorneys.[26]

One commentator endorses the view suggested by these cases:

The fact that a person is believed to be a member of a profession is certainly a reason for the selection of the agent by the client. The client's interests are thus best protected by continuing the obligation of the profession beyond the scope of the practice. It may also be argued that the activities of a sports agent or an attorney may be indistinguishable, for which reason it is appropriate to adopt a policy which supports the application of the ethical code regardless of form. From the forgoing, it appears the better rule is that the ethical codes of any regulated profession should apply to the activities of that professional while acting in the capacity of a sports agent.[27]

The perspective expressed above may be premised, in part, on protecting the public's reliance interest. Attorney status carries with it assumptions made by the public as to the training, competence, ethics, and accountability of attorneys. In the case of the attorney agent, he or she also may profit from such assumptions in that they may result in a recruiting advantage.

Cases outside of the agent context seem to support the position taken above. *In re Dwight* is illustrative.[28] There an attorney provided accounting and investment services, in addition to legal services. In the transaction at issue, the attorney provided financial advice to a client. In responding to a complaint filed by the client with the Arizona Bar, the attorney contended that when he provided the financial advice he was not acting in his capacity as an attorney, but rather as a financial adviser. The court rejected his defense: "As long as a lawyer is engaged in the practice of law, he is bound by ethical requirements of that profession, and he may not defend his actions by contending that he was engaged in some other kind of professional activity."[29] In articulating a rationale for its ruling, the Arizona Supreme Court stated, "only in this way can full protection be afforded to the public."[30]

The California Supreme Court reached the same result in *Kelly v. State Bar of California*.[31] In that case, an attorney who had represented a client in various legal matters participated in a business transaction—the sale of an airplane—that did not involve practicing law. Nevertheless, the court concluded this action would not insulate him from attorney discipline. Making reference to previous cases, the court stated, "We have held that when an attorney serves a single client both as an attorney and as one who renders nonlegal services, he or she must conform to the Rules of Professional Conduct in the provision of all services."[32] Similarly, in a case decided prior to *Kelly*, the California Supreme Court concluded as follows: "where an attorney occupies a dual capacity, performing, for a single client or in a single matter, along with legal services, services that might otherwise be performed by laymen, the services that he renders in the dual capacity all involve the practice of law, and he must conform to the Rules of Professional conduct in the provision of all of them."[33]

An Arizona court pointed to the difficulty in differentiating between legal and nonlegal work as a rationale for holding attorneys, who perform both legal and nonlegal work for clients, to the code of professional ethics. It stated:

> The duties of a lawyer who also holds other professional licenses cannot be circumscribed by the fine distinctions that we might draw between the nature of the services performed under a particular license. How is one to tell whether, in advising the Petersons about the tax consequence of the condemnation settlement, respondent acted as an accountant or a lawyer? Respondent could have given the same advice as a lawyer without having been licensed as an accountant. He might have given the same advice under his accountant's license, even though he had never been admitted to the bar. More importantly, how is any client to know when a lawyer *cum* accountant *cum* investment adviser removes one hat and puts on another? Respondent admitted the distinctions between attorney, accountant, and tax adviser are far from clear.[34]

The court concluded that an attorney will be viewed as an attorney whenever he enters into a relationship to provide services that the client might reasonably believe are law related.

Disavowing Attorney Status, Unauthorized Practice, and Other Issues

The cases discussed in the preceding section strongly suggest that an attorney agent who engages in dual representation—providing legal and nonlegal advice to a client—will be subject to the appropriate state professional standard. But this conclusion does not end our inquiry. Other questions arise both within and outside of the dual representation context. These questions include:

1) Is an agent who is a licensed attorney, but who makes no representations or otherwise holds him- or herself out as an attorney, subject to professional rules governing attorneys? Stated somewhat differently, is an attorney agent who effectively withholds information of his or her attorney status from clients subject to professional standards of responsibility?
2) Is client knowledge or lack of knowledge of an agent's status as an attorney irrelevant so long as the attorney agent is licensed and performs legal and nonlegal work on behalf of the client? In other words, in cases of dual representation, is the attorney agent bound by professional standards of conduct regardless of whether the client is aware that the agent is an attorney?
3) Should an attorney who acts as an agent on a full-time basis and

does not otherwise practice law be subject to the professional code of conduct that governs attorneys? Some commentators have suggested that an attorney agent who relinquishes his or her law practice may not be subject to attorney codes of professional conduct.[35] This view seems premised on the notion that the attorney agent who does not hold himself out as an attorney does not implicate the reliance interest of clients.

4) What other steps, aside from not having a legal practice, might an attorney agent take so as to effectively disavow attorney status and thus be subject to general fiduciary principles of agency law rather than ethical mandates of state bar associations?

5) What of the agent who graduated from a law school program but never became licensed and does not hold him- or herself out as practicing law? Does this constitute an effective means of "disavowing ties to the legal profession" so as to effectively avoid application of its code of conduct?[36]

6) Has the nonattorney agent who provides services that include those traditionally considered to involve the practice of law (for example, contract review and negotiation) engaged in the unauthorized practice of law? Does the fact that services typically provided by agents are performed competently by nonattorneys bring such services outside of the parameters of what constitutes practicing law?

7) Has the attorney agent who provides services for clients in states other than those in which the attorney is licensed to practice law run afoul of rules prohibiting the unauthorized practice of law? Will an attorney agent who provides such services be precluded from recovering his or her fee if the athlete refuses to pay?

The above issues defy easy resolution. The answer to several of these issues, however, may hinge on determining whether the attorney agent who renders services, such as contract negotiation on behalf of athletes, is engaged in the "practice of law." There are no appellate court rulings that address this question as it relates to the services provided by sports agents. Guidance may, nevertheless, be found in appellate court decisions in which courts attempt to define what constitutes the practice of law. For example, the New Jersey Supreme Court in addressing whether a lawyer, unlicensed in New Jersey, had engaged in the unauthorized practice of law recognized that the issue is often difficult to determine. "Often issues related to the unauthorized practice of law involve exercises in line drawing between the proper realm of another profession or business activity and the practice of law."[37] The court went on to articulate the general standard that "one is engaged in the practice of law whenever legal knowledge, training, skill, and ability are required."[38] In examining the facts of the case before it, the court determined that unauthorized practice of law had occurred.

The California Supreme Court addressed the "unauthorized to practice issue" in what has come to be viewed as a leading case on the subject, *Birbrower, Montalbano, Condon & Frank, P.C. v. ESQ Business Services, Inc.*[39] Birbrower, a New York law firm, represented ESQ, a California corporation, and its affiliated entity. Attorneys for Birbrower performed substantial work for ESQ. This work included the negotiation of an agreement between ESQ and another company, giving advice in a dispute regarding the agreement, making recommendations regarding settlement of the dispute, and initiating and interviewing arbitrators for an arbitration proceeding. However, neither the attorneys who performed these services nor any other attorney of Birbrower was licensed to practice in California. ESQ brought a malpractice claim against Birbrower. The law firm counterclaimed to recover its attorneys' fees. ESQ claimed that the fee agreement was unenforceable because Birbrower had engaged in the unauthorized practice of law in California.

The relevant California statute provided that "No person shall practice law in California unless the person is an active member of the State Bar." The statute did not define "practice of law" or "in California." Since the statute failed to define "practice of law," the court looked to case law for guidance. It approvingly cited a case in which practice was defined broadly to include "the doing or performing of services in a court of justice, in any matter depending therein, throughout its various stages, and in conformity to the adopted rules of procedure. . . . Included in [this] definition [is] legal advice and legal instrument and contract preparation, whether or not these subjects were rendered in the course of litigation." The court added that a lawyer need not be physically present within the state in order to be practicing law in California. The court concluded that a lawyer could violate the unauthorized practice statute "by advising a California client on California law in connection with a California legal dispute by telephone, fax, computer, or other modern technological means. Conversely, . . . we . . . reject the notion that a person automatically practices law 'in California' whenever that person practices California law anywhere, or 'virtually' enters the state by telephone, fax, e-mail or satellite. . . . We must decide each case on its individual facts."[40] The court concluded that the facts clearly established that Birbrower had practiced law in California. Consequently, Birbrower was unable to recover compensation for services performed since it ran afoul of a statute that prohibits compensation for work rendered when the attorney was not a member of the State Bar.

Readers are also reminded of the advisory opinion of the Illinois State Bar Association discussed above. In that matter, the attorney represented athletes and coaches in contract negotiations and practiced law. Although this fact pattern appears to involve dual representation, the Bar Association's definition of practicing law is relevant. The Bar Association concluded that "when an attorney engaged in the private practice of law represents a client in contract negotiations and general business counseling, these activities constitute the practice of law."[41]

A final area worthy of noting is the topic of solicitation. The heart of this issue is the same as the ethical concerns discussed above—the business advantage potentially gained by the nonattorney agent by virtue of being subject to fewer operational constraints. Attorney ethical rules against client solicitation highlight the relative difficulty attorney agents face in recruiting athlete clients as compared to the nonattorney agent. There exist longstanding rules against solicitation of business by attorneys. The primary basis for antisolicitation rules is to prevent overreaching by attorneys against the public.

As discussed in Chapter 4, recruitment of athlete clients is inherently difficult. But the rules against attorney solicitation generally provide that: "A lawyer shall not by in-person or live telephone contact solicit professional employment from a prospective client with whom the lawyer has no family or prior professional relationship when a significant motive for the lawyer's doing so is the lawyer's pecuniary gain."[42] Such is certainly the case where the agent seeks to contact the college or even high-school athlete with whom he or she has had no previous contact. In the end, the possibility of legal action by appropriate governing bodies or by clients exists to avoid the contracts or to withhold fees against the attorney agent, whereas no such consequence is present for the nonattorney.

Conclusion

As the last section highlights, the dichotomy that has been created in seeking to hold attorneys to high ethical standards is one that arguably provides a business advantage to nonattorney agents over attorneys. This dilemma adds to the complicated nature of the sports agent business. The argument is not that attorneys necessarily make "better" agents than nonattorney agents, but that they should not be disadvantaged by rules that hold them to higher ethical standards. Many of the ethical rules discussed herein, some would argue, should be applied to all agents. In fact, agency law principles impose standards on all agents that narrow the differences in the ethical obligations imposed on attorney and nonattorney agents.

Chapter 8

Agent Wars

Agents Against Athletes

Sometimes wrongdoing by agents is not against athletes, but other agents. Similarly, in many instances, athletes will engage in conduct that runs contrary to the obligations that agency law imposes upon them. Although an athlete, unlike an agent, is not a fiduciary with respect to his or her agent, the athlete possesses certain obligations vis-à-vis his or her agent. Athletes are required to reimburse agents for reasonable expenses incurred on their behalf, to indemnify agents for any loss that agents incur in properly carrying out duties on behalf of their athlete clients, and to afford the agent a reasonable opportunity to perform his or her duties.[1]

Another fundamental obligation that agency law imposes upon an athlete is the duty to reasonably compensate agents for the services that they properly performed.[2] Not surprisingly, most claims by agents that an athlete has breached the relationship revolve around pay disputes. A 1998 *New York Times* article reported that the arbitrator who (at the time) handled agent/player disputes stated he "has handled 88 cases in the last two years. . . . Most of the disputes . . . involve disagreements over fees."[3] Illustrative is the federal lawsuit filed in the mid-1990s by agent Mark Gandler who alleged that hockey player Andrei Nazarov failed to pay for services that the agent had performed pursuant to a representation agreement between the two.[4]

Agency principles provide that if a "principal wrongfully terminates the agency contract, he is liable to his agent for damages for breach of contract in addition to reasonable compensation for services rendered up to the date of termination."[5] This principle was applied in *Total Economic Athletic Management of America, Inc. v. Pickens.*[6] Football player Bruce Pickens contracted for Total Economic d/b/a Team America to advise him in negotiating his NFL player contract. Before Team America began negotiations, Pickens retained agent Tom Condon who negotiated Pickens' contract with the Atlanta Falcons. Pickens and

Howard Misle of Team America gave different accounts of the circumstances leading up to the player signing an undated representation agreement with the agency. The five one-year contracts negotiated by Condon resulted in total compensation to the athlete, including various bonuses, of $4,100,000.

A jury awarded Team America $20,000 in damages. On appeal, a Missouri court rejected Pickens' defense that the contract was unenforceable due to illegality. Pickens asserted that Team America engaged in illegal conduct when it gave a car to him as an inducement to sign a representation agreement. NFLPA rules preclude agents from giving items of value to athletes to induce them to sign representation agreements. The court concluded the resulting contract was not illegal under Missouri or Nebraska law simply because the alleged inducements would violate NCAA and NFLPA rules.

As for Team America's contention that the jury award of $20,000 was too low, the court sided with Pickens. It enunciated the following standard for determining the amount to which a terminated agent is entitled: "the player's breach of an agency agreement does not necessarily entitle the agent to commission. . . . the agent is entitled to his commission only if he can show that, had he been permitted to continue performance, he would have been able to consummate the contracts upon which he claims commission. Contrary to Team America's assertions, it was not entitled to commissions based solely on the contract negotiated by others."[7] The court concluded that the evidence supported the jury's damage award.

Often, an athlete who has been sued by an agent based on the athlete's failure to pay will defend his position by asserting that the agent engaged in improper conduct. This conduct includes providing substandard services, breaching other basic obligations that agents owe to principals, or engaging in illegal conduct (such as Pickens alleged). For instance, an agent assumes a duty that he or she "possesses a degree of skill commensurate with the job to be done and that he will use such skill with diligence."[8] An agent commits a breach when he or she fails to act with the care and skill employed by a reasonable person under the same circumstances.[9] If such a failure is established, an athlete possesses a defense that, at a minimum, may entitle him or her to offset losses against any fees owed when the losses resulted from the agent's failure to exercise due care.

The paradigmatic illustration of this scenario remains the dispute in the early 1980s between agent Leo Zinn and football player Lemar Parrish.[10] Zinn sued Parrish to recover agent fees due to him under a representation agreement under which the agent was obligated to "use 'reasonable efforts' to procure pro-football employment for Parrish, and at Parrish's request to 'act' in furtherance of Parrish's interest by: a) negotiating job contracts; b) furnishing advice on business investments; c) securing professional tax advice at no added costs; and d) obtaining endorsement contracts. . . . Zinn's services would include . . . efforts to secure for [Parrish] off-season employment."[11]

Between 1971 and 1974, Zinn negotiated contracts on Parrish's behalf with the Cincinnati Bengals. In 1974, Zinn negotiated a series of contracts with the Bengals that included substantially better terms than previous contracts. After Parrish signed this series of contracts, he informed Zinn that he "no longer needed his services."[12] Parrish also informed Zinn of his intention not to pay Zinn a 10 percent commission on these contracts, which Zinn claimed totaled at least $304,500, including bonus and performance clauses. Zinn sued to recover the commission owed to him.

In addition to negotiating Parrish's contracts with the Bengals, Zinn performed other services including negotiating an endorsement deal (for which he received a commission), assisting Parrish in the purchase of an apartment building, forwarding to Parrish the stock purchase recommendations of other individuals (after having screened them), and arranging for the preparation of Parrish's taxes. Zinn was unsuccessful in securing other endorsements for Parrish, or securing off-season employment for Parrish.

Parrish defended his case by arguing that the representation agreement with Zinn was void because the agent had not been registered as an investment adviser as required by a federal statute. The court concluded that the nature of the investment services Zinn provided did not subject him to the registration requirements of the statute: "isolated transactions with a client as an incident to the main purpose of his management contract to negotiate football contracts do not constitute engaging in the business of advising others on investment securities."[13]

Parrish also argued that he was relieved of his obligation to pay Zinn because the agent inadequately performed services relating to procuring employment, endorsements, and off-season employment, and providing substantial tax and investment advice to Parrish. Applying a reasonable efforts standard, the court rejected Parrish's defense. With respect to the other services that Zinn agreed to provide, the court found that Zinn "was subject to an implied promise to make 'good faith' efforts to obtain what he sought."[14] Providing a word of caution that success with good faith efforts should not be confused with undertaking good faith efforts (the latter being the appropriate standard), the court found that Zinn had fulfilled his obligations to Parrish.

A 1999 opinion outlines the suit against former football player Matt Millen by Athletes and Artists (A&A), a sports management firm. They had agreed contractually that A&A would "represent Millen in his negotiations as a professional football broadcaster and that they would undertake the management of Millen's broadcasting career."[15] A&A sought to recover eight percent of $255,000 and $155,000 contracts that Millen had entered into with CBS Television and CBS Radio, respectively. Millen sent A&A a check in the amount of $10,000 which he claimed represented payment for all past and future services A&A provided or might provide. Thereafter, it appears that A&A represented Millen in exploring broadcast opportunities with NBC and Fox television networks. Ultimately Millen terminated A&A's services and obtained another person to assist in finalizing his deal with Fox, the company for which he agreed to work.

A&A sued to recover compensation for services it had rendered in connection with its representation of Millen. In addition to asserting technical legal defenses, Millen contended that A&A was not entitled to compensation because it played no role in the negotiations with Fox, and that A&A engaged in "unauthorized actions and made misrepresentations concerning negotiations with NBC."[16] The court ruled that A&A's breach of contract claims were barred by the statute of frauds since there was no writing that contained all of the essential terms of the agreement. The court, however, allowed A&A to take its *quantum meruit* claim to trial. It noted that A&A was entitled to compensation for services rendered to Millen. The value of such services had to be determined at trial since it might be no more than the $10,000 Millen had already paid or a much greater sum.[17]

Agent Versus Agent: The Quest for Clients

The term or duration of the agency relationship is determined by the terms of the contract. For example, the NFLPA's Standard Representation Agreement allows either the athlete or the agent to terminate the relationship with five days' written notice.[18] This contract further provides that in the event that the termination occurs subsequent to when the player has signed an NFL contract that was negotiated by the agent, the latter is entitled to the fee the parties agreed upon. If termination occurs prior, the agent is entitled to reasonable compensation for the services he or she provided.[19] The ease with which athletes can terminate their relationship with agents, the fierce competition by agents for clients, and the significant amounts in fees that are often at stake erupt into considerable conflict when one agent accuses another agent of stealing clients.

An illustrative case involves football player Patrick Worley. Worley ended up being sued by agent Gary Wichard and his firm, with whom he had entered into a representation agreement. Worley initially signed with an agent on January 3, 1989. Thereafter, on January 18, 1989, he signed an exclusive representation agreement with Wichard's firm. A few months later on April 17, 1989, Worley signed an exclusive representation agreement with another firm to negotiate a rookie contract that eventually would come to $3,050,000. In the reported case, a default judgment for agent fees that was originally entered in Wichard's favor was overturned.[20]

A recent case involving baseball star Ivan Rodriguez further demonstrates how these factors converge to create conflict.[21] Rodriguez signed a series of terminable at-will one-year agency contracts with Speakers of Sport. In an effort to expand its representation of baseball players, ProServ approached Rodriguez. It promised that it "would get him between $2 and $4 million in endorsements if he signed with ProServ—which he did."[22] As a consequence of his agreement with ProServ, Rodriguez terminated his contract with Speakers. A year after he contracted to have ProServ act as his agent, Rodriguez signed with another agent when ProServ failed to secure the endorsements. Subsequently, Speakers filed suit alleging that ProServ improperly interfered with its contractual relationship with Rodriguez.[23]

A federal appellate court upheld the trial court's grant of summary judgment dismissing Speakers' lawsuit. In reaching this conclusion, the court recognized that the competitive nature of the athlete agent business is reflective of our business system. Proceeding from this premise, the court adopted an approach that affords a broad range of acceptable activity when it comes to attempts by one agent to recruit another agent's client. "There is in general nothing wrong with one sports agent trying to take a client from another if this can be done without precipitating a breach of contract. That is the process known as competition, which though painful, fierce, frequently ruthless, sometimes Darwinian in its pitilessness, is the cornerstone of our highly successful economic system. Competition is not a tort . . . , but on the contrary provides a defense (the 'competitor's privilege') to the tort of improper interference."[24]

Despite its recognition of the competitive nature of the business, the court noted an important limitation: the competitor's privilege does not validate inducing clients by way of fraud.

A similar standard was adopted by a court in a case involving baseball superstar Barry Bonds.[25] The court found that to establish interference with prospective economic advantage, Bonds' former agent would have to show that his new agent, BHSC, engaged in some wrongful conduct beyond "mere interference." The court noted that evidence—showing that BHSC hid the fact that it contacted Bonds and that BHSC had a history of contacting athletes under contract with other agents—would not establish an interference claim. One commentator observes that while these cases "appear legally accurate, they provide a broad spectrum of competition that borders on interference thereby tolerating unfair and corrupt dealing."[26]

Agents on occasion have sued teams alleging that they interfered with the former's relationship with an athlete. Such an instance that resulted in litigation involved a lawsuit by agent John Manton against the Los Angeles Lakers. Manton claimed that in 1979 he entered into a contract pursuant to which he agreed to represent Earvin "Magic" Johnson. According to Manton, the Lakers improperly induced Johnson to breach the representation agreement so that the team could negotiate directly with Johnson and get him to sign for a lesser sum than Manton could have procured.[27]

A dispute that falls within none of the typical categories of conflicts between agents and athletes is nevertheless worth noting. Former NFL quarterback Jim Kelly authored an autobiography in which he expressed his contempt for certain of his former mentors, including his former agent A. J. Faigin. In the book, Kelly stated in part:

> I learned my lesson the hard way about whom to trust and whom not to trust in business. I had had complete faith in my first agents, Greg Lustig and A.J. Faigin. . . .
> Then Danny and the Trevino brothers started taking a closer look at my business affairs. And the more they looked, the more they didn't like what they found.
> Finally, I saw the light. In 1988, I fired Lustig and Faigin and put my brother [Danny] and the Trevinos in charge of all my business dealings. Then I filed a major lawsuit against my former agents, as well as the former owners of the Gamblers for defaulting on the payment of my signing bonus.[28]

As adroitly stated by the court, Faigin "took umbrage [with these comments] and sued both Kelly and Vic Carucci, the journalist who assisted Kelly in writing the book."[29] In his libel action, Faigin argued that the relevant statements "Falsely implied that he was dismissed for unlawful conduct, thus damaging his reputation and jeopardizing his career."[30] A jury found the language at issue to be defamatory in that it tended to harm Faigin's reputation, but also concluded that Faigin failed to prove the falsity of the language. Consequently, the jury rendered a decision favorable to the defendants. The jury's verdict was upheld on appeal.

Acrimony Among Agents

Disputes may also erupt when agents who worked together decide to end their relationship. Intervention by an arbitrator or a court is often necessary when former associates cannot decide on their own how to divide fees and clients. For example, a dispute resulting in litigation arose between agents Steve Weinberg and Howard Silber over how to divide up clients and fees after a joint venture agreement, including one involving professional football players, turned acrimonious.[31] After they filed lawsuits against each other, Weinberg and Silber agreed to arbitration. Following the arbitration hearing, but before the arbitrator rendered a decision, Weinberg negotiated a nine-year, multi-million-dollar contract for Washington Redskins running back Stephen Davis. The arbitrator ordered that Weinberg pay $2,079,495 to Silber for fees earned from representation of Davis. The arbitrator also ruled that each party should take nothing with respect to their dispute regarding other athlete clients.

In court, Weinberg requested that the arbitrator's ruling be vacated. Silber requested that the decision be confirmed. Relying on the considerable deference given by courts to arbitration decisions and the extremely narrow scope of review of such awards, the court rejected Weinberg's request to set aside the judgment. In so doing, the court rejected Weinberg's arguments that the arbitration agreement between him and Silber was void and unenforceable, that the evidence failed to support the arbitrator's decision, and that the arbitrator was biased.

Often former business associates, after a relationship has soured, must turn to courts to determine who is entitled to fees earned from representing athletes. The relationship between sports agents Lawrence Jacobs, Robert Bond, and Dan St. John, who formed ProSports Management, ended up in court when they could not decide upon a division of fees and clients. The relationship between the three agents, which began in late 1992, began to unravel in 1996. Bond and St. John accused Jacobs of breach of fiduciary duty to ProSports, conversion, larceny, and embezzlement with respect to conduct by Jacobs revolving around commission fees he received from football player Kevin Carter. Jacobs argued in defense that the funds were rightfully payable only to him and not to ProSports. Finding that the evidence supported the contention that he had committed embezzlement, conversion, and larceny, the court concluded that ProSports was "the owner of the commissions and Jacobs was required to turn over all funds to the corporation."[32]

As this book goes to press, a dispute involving allegations of client stealing between Leigh Steinberg and David Dunn has received significant attention. Dunn, a partner in the long-time successful firm of Steinberg, Moorad & Dunn (a division of Assante), left the partnership to begin his own firm, Athletes First. He reportedly started Athletes First with as many as eighteen clients who had previously been represented by Steinberg, Moorad & Dunn. Athletes including Kerry Collins, Rob Johnson, Drew Bledsoe, Ryan Leaf, Amani Toomer, and John Lynch terminated their relationships with Steinberg, Moorad as a prelude to signing representation agreements with Athletes First.[33]

The dispute reached new levels of intensity and acrimony when Steinberg and Moorad filed a lawsuit against Dunn in the California Superior Court in Los Angeles in May 2001. In August 2001, the state court action was withdrawn and a lawsuit was initiated in federal district court. Allegations of improperly taking clients and the legal ramifications thereof were set forth in the complaint. The key goal of Leigh Steinberg and remaining partner Jeff Moorad was to gain an injunction against Dunn, which would stop him from representing the players. In addition to allegations that Dunn improperly signed up clients of Steinberg & Moorad, plaintiffs asserted that Dunn had breached a five-year employment contract and violated the provisions of a covenant not to compete.[34] In arguing his client's position, Dunn's attorney stated that "Dunn left because he didn't feel that athletes were being taken care of properly and because promises made to him were not honored."[35]

This case raises several interesting questions, including whether athletes have the right to be represented by the sports agent of their choice, even if that representative has "stolen" them from their previous firm and even where there exists a noncompete agreement. The importance of the dispute was signaled when the NFLPA spoke in support of this athlete right.[36] The NFLPA filed a brief seeking to intervene in the lawsuit between the agents. According to NFLPA general counsel Richard Berthelsen, "By doing this, we are not taking the side of either Leigh Steinberg or David Dunn, we are instead taking the side of the player who wishes to have an agent of their choice to represent them." Acknowledging the possible ramifications of the NFLPA's position on future acquisitions, Berthelsen stated, "[It] certainly would impact covenants not to compete . . . , which I guess would be important for companies considering [acquisitions]."[37]

In August 2001, a federal district court judge issued a temporary restraining order against David Dunn and Athletes First. The order prohibited the defendants from "soliciting former or current clients of Steinberg, Moorad and Dunn." It also prohibited Athletes First "from arranging, facilitating or promoting any further terminations by former SMD clients."[38] In a show of support for Dunn and Athletes First, twenty-one players signed a declaration indicating that they wanted Dunn and Athletes First to represent them.[39]

Conclusion

The final case is illustrative of the continuing battles and the role the law may play in resolving agent disputes. None of the parties involved in athlete agent relationships or in competition for those relationships is beyond suing or being sued. Starting with an examination of amateurism, the final chapters examine the rules and laws that attempt to control the wide-ranging issues in this business.

Chapter 9

The Last Amateurs on Earth
Amateurism and Opportunity

"Ancient Amateurism is a myth."[1]
—David C. Young

Chapters 10 and 11 will explore private and public efforts to address the problems associated with the athlete agent industry. The major impetus behind such efforts, particularly state-enacted agent legislation, is to protect the interests of institutions of higher education that may be jeopardized by student athlete and agent interactions that violate NCAA rules and regulations. The NCAA has established a complex set of rules and regulations that govern all aspects of intercollegiate sports. Included within this regulatory structure are rules that circumscribe the student athlete/agent relationship. These and other rules within the NCAA's regulatory regime are premised on several notions, including the amateurism ideal. Consequently, a predicate to understanding the NCAA regulatory scheme and state agent statutes that are sensitive to this regime is exploring the controversial notion of amateurism. If not for the dominant desire to preserve amateurism, the web of NCAA regulations would be much less complex.

Much of the controversy surrounding the amateurism issue revolves around how the term "amateur" should be defined. In simplest terms, an amateur is whatever the organization regulating the particular athletic event or organization says it is.[2] This definition generally appears in the organization's constitution or bylaws. For example, the NCAA describes the amateur principle as follows: "Student-athletes shall be amateurs in an intercollegiate sport, and their participation should be motivated primarily by education and by the physical, mental and social benefits to be derived. Student participation in intercollegiate athletics is an avocation, and student-athletes should be protected from exploitation by professionals and commercial enterprises."[3] Other NCAA provisions specifically delineate how amateur status can be lost.[4]

Consistent with the NCAA amateurism principle, an amateur has been popularly defined as someone who participates, and always has participated, in sports solely for pleasure and for physical, mental, or social benefits. The amateur receives no financial gain of any kind, direct or indirect, for his or her athletic prowess.

The payment of any money to amateur athletes has traditionally been viewed as contradicting the true meaning of amateurism.[5] Questions of amateurism most often arise when compensation of some sort is given to student athletes. Current NCAA rules prohibit such payments. Pursuant to NCAA rules, amateur status is lost when a student athlete: "(a) Uses his or her athletics skills (directly or indirectly) for pay in any form in" the particular sport in which the individual competes, or "(b) Accepts a promise of pay."[6] Often "boosters," alumni, and educational institutions "cheat," however, by making payments to student athletes when it is advantageous for them to do so. Cheating sometimes appears in the form of a monetary payment or sometimes in the transfer of goods or services. Athlete agents, seeking an advantage, also cheat by engaging in conduct that ranges from directly paying student athletes to bestowing gifts upon an athlete's friends and relatives.

Payments by agents to student athletes are particularly successful in recruiting student athletes from economically disadvantaged families. Ironically, if these student athletes cannot find time to earn money from working within the framework of NCAA rules, they are forced to ask their families for extra money in order to pay for things that range from clothes, to expenses for a date, to a stereo system like the one possessed by the student in the dorm room next door. If an athlete's family cannot afford the expenditure, the athlete may be tempted to look elsewhere. Often a willing donor is the athlete agent, booster, or alumnus. Such payments violate NCAA rules, some state athlete agent statutes, and players' union regulations.

Coupled with the issue of money is a generally held view that unlike their professional counterparts, amateur athletes participate in sports for the glory of the sport alone. Both the pay and the motive issues are commonly viewed as having originated in ancient Greek athletics. However, we shall see that this interpretation is questionable at best: as David Young has remarked, "Ancient amateurism is a myth." The next sections examine the origin of rules against giving compensation to amateur athletes.

Origin of Rules Against Compensation

THE ANCIENT GREEKS

The amateurism ideal in sports is commonly posited on the Olympic model, which in turn is assumed to be derived from ancient Greek athletics. The "myth" of ancient amateurism is that a society existed, presumably the Greeks, in which athletes participated in sport solely for the glory thereof and received no compensation for their participation or winning. This view is reflected in one of the most extensive studies of the relationship of college athletics to the colleges and universities, which was conducted by the Carnegie Foundation in 1929 and published in *American College Athletics* by Howard J. Savage.[7] Adopting this view, Savage writes, "The essential differences between the amateur and the professional in athletics were clearly understood among the ancient Greeks."[8] Classicist David C. Young, however, in his book *The Olympic Myth of Greek Amateur Athletics*, writes that he "can find no mention of amateurism in Greek sources, no reference to amateur athletes—no evidence that the concept 'amateurism' was even known in antiquity. The truth is that 'amateur' is one thing for which the ancient Greeks never even had a word."[9] In fact, Young examines various levels of compensation that were received in ancient times and uncovers a prize in one event that was equal to ten years' wages.[10]

The absence of compensation was not an essential element of Greek athletics.[11] As another classicist notes, the ancient Greeks "had no known restrictions on granting awards to athletes."[12] Many athletes were generously rewarded; according to Young, the only real disagreement among classical scholars is when these payments or awards to athletes began.[13]

The myth regarding ancient Greek athletics was apparently developed and perpetuated by individuals who profited in various ways from the development of such a system.[14] Young examines the work of scholars who are most often cited for espousing this view of Greek amateurism. He cites an article written by classical scholar Paul Shorey in *The Forum* as one of the first misstatements of the actual history:

And here lies the chief, if somewhat obvious, lesson that our modern athletes have to learn from Olympia, if they would not remain barbarians in spirit. . . . They must *strive*, like the young heroes of Pindar, *only* for the complete development of their manhood, and their sole prizes must be the conscious delight in the exercise . . . and some simple symbol of honor. They must not prostitute the vigor of their youth for gold, directly or indirectly.

[T]he commercial spirit . . . is fatal, as the Greeks learned in their *degenerate* days. . . . Where money is the stake men will inevitably tend to rate the end above the means, or rather to misconceive the true end . . . the professional will *usurp the place of the amateur.* [Emphasis Young's][15]

This passage was written prior to 1896, when the first modern Olympiad was held in Athens, and was directed at potential Olympians. Young points out that Shorey writes about "the Greek record for the high jump" although there was no high jump at the time,[16] that the statements attributed to Pindar throughout the text do not exist,[17] that dates are off by five hundred years,[18] and that Shorey actually knew very little about Greek athletics.[19] Young goes on to identify other scholars who made the same erroneous statements and shows how the myth was perpetuated because these scholars inevitably cited each other for authority.[20] One scholar, Harold Harris, in his *Greek Athletes and Athletics*, actually created an account of an ancient Greek athlete with detailed dates that Young concludes is a "sham" and "outright historical fiction"[21] and was probably designed to serve as "a moral lesson to modern man."[22]

The "modern man" for whom the lesson was apparently designed seems to have been the gentleman amateur athlete of Victorian England:

Harris' bogus Greek athlete and Shorey's false history of ancient athletics are not isolated cases nor mere instances of sloppy scholarship. They are representative examples of a far-flung and amazingly successful deception, a kind of historical hoax, in which scholar joined hands with sportsman and administrator so as to mislead the public and influence modern sporting life. We shall never know whether these men performed their deception consciously or unconsciously, nor does it much matter now. But the deception itself is still with us, and we need to inquire into its results and its causes.[23]

In simplest terms, Harris, Shorey, and other early scholars of Greek "amateurism" were part of a process that sought to justify an elite British athletic system that was to find its way into American collegiate athletics. The fact that scholars were promulgating these definitions of amateurism meant that nonscholars would inevitably do so. Probably the leading voice in the United States in favor of segregating pay and amateurism was Avery Brundage, former president of the United States Olympic Committee and the International Olympic Committee. Brundage was one of the main opponents to Jim Thorpe's efforts to recover his Olympic medals, which were taken away because Thorpe had played semiprofessional baseball. One of the ironies of Thorpe's losing his medals was his statement that "I did not play for the money there was in it, but because I liked to play ball."[24] Other athletes assumed false names while playing semiprofessional baseball; Thorpe did not even realize he was jeopardizing his eligibility.[25] Similarly, during Brundage's reign, Olympic hurdler Lee Calhoun lost his amateur status because he received wedding gifts as part of his appearance on the television show "Bride and Groom."[26]

Brundage's view of Olympic amateurism was published in an article entitled "Why the Olympic Games?":

> The ancient Olympic Games . . . were strictly amateur . . . and for many centuries, as long as they continued amateur, they grew in importance and significance. . . . Gradually, however, abuses and excesses developed. . . . Cities tried to demonstrate their superiority . . . by establishing special training camps . . . , by recruiting athletes from other communities, and by subsidizing competitors. Special prizes and awards and all sorts of inducements were offered and winners were even given pensions for life. What was originally fun, recreation, a diversion, and a pastime became a business. . . . The Games degenerated, lost their purity and high idealism, and were finally abolished. . . . sport must be for sport's sake.[27]

Brundage firmly opposed amateurs receiving any compensation whatsoever related to participation in sports and used the Greek amateur athletic story to justify his position.

ENGLAND

Young and other scholars contend that it was not the Greeks who developed the current collegiate ethic of amateurism. Rather it was scholars like Savage and Harris as well as the Avery Brundages of the day and the practices that developed in Victorian England. In fact, the first published definition of the term "amateur" by a sports organization was made by the Amateur Athletic Club of England in 1866.[28] That definition described an amateur as "Any gentleman who has never competed in an open competition, or for public money, or for admission money, or with professionals for a prize, public money or admission money, and who has never at any period of his life taught or assisted in the pursuit of athletic exercises as a means of livelihood; nor is a mechanic, artisan, or labourer."[29]

The purpose of the Amateur Athletic Club was to provide English gentlemen with the opportunity to compete against each other without having to compete against professionals.[30] The development of concepts of amateurism in Britain was largely based on class distinctions. The distinctions were forced by the use of so-called "mechanics clauses" in amateur definitions, like the one quoted above, which maintained that mechanics, artisans, and laborers could not participate in sports as amateurs.[31] According to Ronald A. Smith in his book *Sports and Freedom*, the British Amateur Rowing Association included such a clause in its eligibility rules in 1870.[32] It was from these rules that the modern eligibility rules of the NCAA evolved. In fact, any negative connotations that remain today regarding professionalism probably evolved from this distinction. Interestingly, part of the reason for the "mechanics clause" was that those who used their muscles as part of their employment in fact had a competitive advantage.[33]

UNITED STATES

Smith describes the profound amateur/professional dilemma that confronts American universities in this way: "If a college has truly amateur sport, it will lose prestige as it loses contests; if a college acknowledges outright professional sport, the college will lose respectability as a middle-class or upper-class institution. The unsatisfactory solution to the dilemma has been to claim amateurism to the world, while in fact accepting a professional mode of operation."[34]

The first two sports to face these questions of professionalism versus amateurism in the United States were baseball and rowing. Initially, the norm in sports in this country was professionalism. Baseball was played at the semiprofessional level as early as 1860, and the first professional team, the Cincinnati Red Stockings, was formed in 1868,[35] the same year in which the New York Athletic Club, the first amateur organization in the United States, was formed.[36]

"Professionalism" in college sports abounded. For example, in the 1850s Harvard University students rowed in a meet that had a $100 first prize purse, and in the 1860s they raced for as much as $500.[37] Smith maintains that amateurism, as historically conceived, was largely absent from college sports at the beginning of the twentieth century: "By the early twentieth century, there was probably no college in America which was able to preserve amateurism in men's sport, as competition for money and non-money prizes, contests against professionals, collection of gate receipts, support for training tables, provision for athletic tutors, recruitment and payment of athletes, and the hiring of professional coaches pervaded the intercollegiate athletic scene. Professionalism had invaded college sports and had defeated amateurism as it was understood in the nineteenth century."[38]

One of the more graphic illustrations of the benefits students received, even in the early 1900s, involved 1904 Yale football team captain James Hogan. After the final game in his career Yale rewarded Hogan by sending him to Havana on vacation.[39]

One reason that college sports developed beyond amateurism in the

United States, as opposed to its British counterpart, was the sheer number of competing institutions.[40] In England, upper-level education meant Oxford or Cambridge. With only two institutions, the odds of stepping outside the established bounds of amateurism were not that high. In the United States, on the other hand, the Ivy League and other private and public colleges and universities vigorously competed against each other in sports. Even if Harvard and Yale wanted to be the athletic and intellectual elite of the United States, as Oxford and Cambridge were in England, they could not do so. As Smith notes, with the Wesleyans and Cornells developing athletically, refusing to compete against them would cause Harvard and Yale to lose their athletic "esteem and prestige."[41] According to scholars like Smith and Daniel L. Boorstin, the English system of amateurism, loosely derived from the Greeks, simply did not have a chance of surviving in the United States.

Competition among a larger community of institutions was a major element in the weakening of Victorian notions of amateurism. Another factor is what Smith refers to as a difference in egalitarian beliefs: "The English amateur system, based upon participation by the social and economic elite and rejection of those beneath them from participating, would never gain a foothold in American college athletics. There was too much competition, too strong a belief in merit over heredity, too abundant an ideology of freedom of opportunity for the amateur ideal to succeed. . . . It may be that amateur athletics at a high level of expertise can only exist in a society dominated by upper-class elitists."[42] Even with this sort of ideological conflict, the NCAA's early years were heavily burdened by attempts to enforce various amateur standards.

In spite of this tradition, or perhaps because of it, in 1909 the NCAA, through its committee on amateur law, recommended and later adopted the following amateur/professional distinction:

1. An amateur in athletics is one who enters and takes part in athletic contests purely in obedience to the play impulses or for the satisfaction of purely play motives and for the exercise, training, and social pleasure derived. The natural or primary attitude of mind in play determines amateurism.
2. A professional in athletics is one who enters or takes part in any athletic contest from any other motive than the satisfaction of pure play impulses, or for the exercise, training or social pleasures derived, or one who desires and secures from his skill or who accepts of spectators, partisans or other interests, any material or economic advantage or reward.[43]

With this, Victorian England's amateur/professional distinction was incorporated into American collegiate athletics.

The first NCAA eligibility code sought to ensure that the athletes who participated in collegiate sports were in fact full-time registered students who had not been and were not being paid for their participation in athletics. The 1906 NCAA Eligibility Code provided:

The following rules . . . are suggested as a minimum:

1. No student shall represent a college or university in any intercollegiate game or contest, who is not taking a full schedule of work as prescribed in the catalogue of the institution.
2. No student shall represent a college or university . . . who has at any time received, either directly or indirectly, money, or any other consideration, to play on any team, or . . . who has competed for a money prize or portion of gate money in any contest, or who has competed for any prize against a professional.
3. No student shall represent a college or university . . . who is paid or received, directly or indirectly, any money, or financial concession, or emolument as past or present compensation for, or as prior consideration or inducement to play in, or enter any athletic contest, whether the said remuneration be received from, or paid by, or at the instance of any organization, committee or faculty of such college or university, or any individual whatever.
4. No student shall represent a college or university . . . who has participated in intercollegiate games or contests during four previous years.
5. No student who has been registered as a member of any other college or university shall participate in any intercollegiate game or contest until he shall have been a student of the institution which he represents at least one college year.
6. Candidates for positions on athletic teams shall be required to fill out cards, which shall be placed on file, giving a full statement of their previous athletic records.[44]

During the years subsequent to the establishment of this code, the NCAA has sought further to define its views on amateurism. One notable effort involved the formal incorporation of the Amateur Code into the NCAA constitution.[45] This step, said Palmer E. Pierce, former president of the NCAA, was intended "to enunciate more clearly [the NCAA's] purposes; to incorporate the amateur definition and principles of amateur spirit; [and] to widen the scope of government."[46]

The amateurism ideal undergirds several current NCAA rules. These rules reflect the extent to which the amateurism and the anticompensation principles have historically permeated the NCAA regulatory structure and influenced views held of intercollegiate athletics. One illustration of the impact of perceptions of college athletics is the pervasiveness of the influence of the amateurism ideal in judicial decision making. Many courts have adopted the NCAA's amateurism ideal. Illustrative of judicial recognition of the amateurism myth are the court's comments in *Walters and Bloom v. Fullwood and Kickliter*.[47] Although *Fullwood* involved a question regarding which entity possessed jurisdiction or the power to decide the dispute between the parties, Chief Judge Charles L. Brieant found it appropriate to state his views on amateurism. In his conclusion, referring to what must appropriately be called a stereotypical view of amateurism, Brieant wrote, "All parties to this action should recognize that they are the beneficiaries of a system built on the trust of millions of people who, with stubborn innocence, adhere to the Olympic ideal, viewing amateur sports as a commitment to competition for its own sake."[48] In his opinion, Brieant cited scholars who disagreed with Young's view and maintained that Greek tradition excluded compensation.[49]

The United States Supreme Court recognized the amateur ideal in *NCAA v. Board of Regents*.[50] Therein the Court stated that the "NCAA plays a critical role in the maintenance of the *revered tradition of amateurism* in college sports."[51] Similarly in *Gaines v. NCAA*, the court's decision was influenced by the revered amateurism ideal.[52] The court noted that the "overriding purpose of [NCAA] eligibility Rules, thus, is not to provide the NCAA with commercial advantage, but rather the opposite extreme—to prevent commercializing influences from destroying the unique 'product' of NCAA college football. Even in the increasingly commercial modern world, this Court believes there is still validity to the *Athenian concept* of a complete education derived from fostering full growth of both mind and body."[53] Finally, in *Banks v. NCAA*, a student athlete challenged the legality of the NCAA's no-draft and no-agent rules.[54] In upholding the validity of the restrictions, the court concluded that the "no-agent and no-draft rules are vital and must work in conjunction with other eligibility requirements to preserve the *amateur status* of college athletics, and prevent the sports agents from further intruding into the collegiate educational system."[55] The court relied in part on the amateurism principle in rejecting a student athlete's challenge of no-draft and no-agent rules. The court stated that "the NCAA's second primary goal is preserving amateurism as an integral part of the educational process."[56]

The ultimate decisions reached in *Fullwood*, *Gaines*, *Banks*, and other cases may have been sound notwithstanding judicial reliance on the amateurism ideal. What is problematic, however, is the extent to which an inaccurate belief in the amateurism ideal has influenced judicial resolution of legal disputes in intercollegiate athletics. In fact, Young would probably maintain that certain of these decisions are doctrinally incorrect and unfair. Young said that he wrote his book on amateurism because he "couldn't stand to see all these problems associated with amateurism blamed on all those poor dead Greeks."

NCAA Pay Restrictions

As briefly mentioned above, an individual loses amateur status and will be rendered ineligible to compete in intercollegiate competition in a particular sport through the receipt of "pay" related to his or her athletic skills.[57] "Pay" includes "any direct or indirect salary, gratuity or comparable compensation."[58] Amateur status will also be lost if an athlete or his or her relatives or friends accept benefits from a prospective agent.[59] Moreover, amateur status will be lost if a student athlete enters into "an agreement with an agent."[60]

NCAA restrictions on payments to student athletes related to their athletic abilities also extend to outside employment.[61] Until recently, NCAA rules limited the time an athlete on full athletic scholarship could work during the school year or at any time that class was in session or, in the case of football, after practice had begun.[62] The NCAA imposed this limitation through bylaw 15.02.4, which limited the amount of financial aid a student could receive to "tuition and fees, room and board, and required course-related books."[63] The by-laws specifically included as a source of funds that must be considered in this amount "employment during semester or term time."[64] The NCAA's employment rule presents a perfect "opportunity" for boosters, alumni, agents, or prospective agents to fill a gap for student athletes.

In 1997 the NCAA rules were revised, effective 1998, to allow student athletes to earn up to $2,000 per year from employment during the school term. These earnings will not be included when calculating financial aid. The irony of this rule modification is that few student athletes seem to be taking advantage of this opportunity. One possible reason for the lack of utilization of this rule change is the tremendous demand that is already placed on their time. The limited amounts that a student athlete might earn from employment might not seem to be worth the time expended given other demands on their time.[65]

The student athlete on full athletic scholarship may not be paid for athletic prowess nor does he or she apparently have time to work for additional spending money. The throwback to the aristocratic idea of the amateur is clear here. If the student athlete has adequate funds for the activities of student life, the ideal situation is not to work. This scenario clearly provides more time to concentrate on studies. However, if the athlete does not have the funds (from family or elsewhere) and may only work to a limited extent under the rules, what happens when the limited earnings are gone, or, if the athlete desires to make a larger purchase, such as an automobile? This window of opportunity is often seized by boosters, alumni, or sports agents. Indeed, some view payments in violation of NCAA rules as synonymous with other "victimless crimes." The athlete needs the money and no one is hurt in the transaction; the payment just happens to violate NCAA rules. Moreover, such payments are likely to run afoul of athlete agent legislation enacted by state legislatures and may be prosecuted under federal racketeering laws.

Conclusion

The societal desire to retain the oldest forms of amateurism is one of the strongest impediments to cleaning up the sports agent business. Improvement should come, particularly on the recruiting side of the business, as meaningful amateurism reforms take place. The chapter that follows begins the discussion of private and public efforts to regulate the athlete agent.

Part III
Solutions

Chapter 10

Knights of Columbus Rules?
Private Sports Agent Regulations

With the growth of problems in the sports agent industry, many concerned parties have sought regulatory solutions. Historically, the key entities involved in attempting to formulate legislation as the panacea for the problems that afflict the agent industry have been the NCAA, NCAA member institutions, players' unions, state and federal law enforcement and legislative entities, and, of course, professional athletes, student athletes, and sports agents themselves. This chapter examines the legislative efforts of private entities, and Chapters 11 and 12 explore public entities' efforts to regulate agents. The discussion below describes the private entities that have attempted to regulate sports agents, and evaluates the relative effectiveness of their efforts to control the activities of sports agents.

National Collegiate Athletic Association

INDIRECT REGULATORY EFFORTS

The NCAA is the oldest and most powerful governing body in college sports. The NCAA developed as the result of a meeting in 1905 (of thirteen colleges) to discuss safety reforms in intercollegiate athletics. The meeting was convened at the urging of President Theodore Roosevelt following deaths and other serious injuries that resulted from the violent brand of football that was played at the time.[1] Currently, the association has more than 1,000 members, commonly referred to as member institutions.

Although the NCAA sometimes appears to be a monolith, its actions represent the joint decision making of its member institutions. A former executive director defines the organization's basic premise as "institutional control of intercollegiate athletics."[2] In other words, each institution is ultimately responsible for the governance of its intercollegiate athletics program. Notwithstanding the notion of institutional control, the NCAA, through its promulgation of rules and regulations, sets national standards for the governance of intercollegiate athletics. These bylaw provisions, rules and regulations, as revised from time to time, are published annually in the *NCAA Manual* that is produced for each of the divisions—I, II, and III—of the organization.

Among the provisions contained in the *NCAA Manual* are those that establish specific guidelines for governing the relationship between a student athlete and a sports agent. A student athlete who fails to comply with these provisions may lose his or her eligibility. Section 12.3.1 articulates the NCAA's general rule concerning agents: "An individual shall be ineligible for participation in an intercollegiate sport if he or she ever has agreed (orally or in writing) to be represented by an agent for the purpose of marketing his or her athletics ability or reputation in that sport. Further, an agency contract not specifically limited in writing to a sport or particular sports shall be deemed applicable to all sports and the individual shall be ineligible to participate in any sport."[3] This provision precludes student athletes from engaging in a contractual relationship with agents. A student athlete who violates this provision will be deemed ineligible to compete in intercollegiate athletics for his or her college or university.

A student athlete may also lose his or her eligibility by accepting benefits from agents. Sections 12.3.1.2 (a) and (b) render an athlete ineligible if he or she (or relatives or friends) accepts benefits from "[a]ny person who represents any individual in the marketing of his or her athletics ability" or agent even if the agent has no "interest in representing the student athlete."[4] For example, payment by an agent of expenses related to sending a prospective student athlete to a summer camp would constitute an extra benefit, in addition to gifts of money, cars, and other items from agents to student athletes. Acceptance of such benefits runs afoul of NCAA rules that prohibit athletes from accepting "extra benefits" that are "not available to the student body in general." Such conduct by agents and athletes is also likely to violate state statutes regulating agents that are discussed in Chapters 11 and 12.

NCAA rules do not prohibit a student athlete from obtaining advice from lawyers regarding a proposed professional contract. The lawyer may not, however, represent the "student-athlete in negotiations for such a contract."

Despite the huge domain the NCAA is chartered to regulate, the association lacks authority to directly impose sanctions against all of the actors that may be involved in a violation of its rules and regulations. The NCAA has the power to impose sanctions against a member institution for violations of association rules by student athletes and athletic personnel of a college or university. Consistent with the NCAA's notion of institutional control, member institutions—not the NCAA—take action against student athletes and other athletics personnel who violate NCAA rules. The failure by an institution to take action may result in the imposition of sanctions by the NCAA. Sanctions take various forms, but they can include barring a member institution from television appearances and postseason play, which generally guarantee considerable profits for a college sports program or university budget. This authority provides the NCAA with the strength to govern, since schools hesitate to jeopardize such revenue-laden opportunities as participation in the NCAA basketball national championship tournament, which can yield a school millions of dollars. Ultimately, the authority that the NCAA wields is primarily economic.

One of the most stunning examples of the NCAA's power is the so-called "death penalty." Use of this penalty bars a member institution not only from championship competition but from playing altogether. The first and only school to receive this sanction, due to extensive recruiting and other violations, was Southern Methodist University (SMU). In 1987, SMU received a one-year version of the penalty for paying thirteen players a total of $61,000 from a slush fund. The payments were approved by the SMU athletic department. When the sanction was imposed, SMU's football players were allowed to transfer to other schools. The experts' projections at the time held that it would take at least five to six years to rebuild SMU's football program following the death penalty.[5]

Lesser penalties such as probation can be devastating as well. In 1989 the University of Kentucky's basketball program was placed on a three-year probation for recruiting and other violations. The *Sports Industry News* estimated that the school would lose $1.8 million over the three years. Kentucky's initial losses due to the NCAA sanction were $350,000 from the 1988 NCAA basketball tournament, $250,000 from their share of their conference's television syndication package, and $1,100,000 from their conference tournament.[6]

Thus NCAA rules and regulations indirectly impact agents by discouraging student athletes from entering into relationships with agents that run afoul of NCAA rules and regulations. These rules may also encourage institutions to take preventive action to avoid improper conduct between student athletes and agents. Moreover, as discussed in Chapter 11, an agent who violates an NCAA rule also risks having run afoul of state laws that govern the student athlete/agent relationship.

DIRECT REGULATORY EFFORTS

In contrast to the considerable economic power that the NCAA possesses in relation to its member institutions, its power over sports agents is severely limited. According to former NCAA Executive Director Richard Schultz, sports agent improprieties are "really one of the knottiest problems we have because there is not a lot we can do about it. All we can do is penalize the institution or the athlete."[7] This lack of regulatory authority combines with other factors to create opportunities for sports agent improprieties.

One failed NCAA attempt at direct regulation was a voluntary sports agent registration system.[8] Under the system, sports agents were required to complete a form, return it to the NCAA, and agree that they would not contact a student athlete or coach without first contacting the athletic director at that member institution. An NCAA memorandum that accompanied the registration form explained that the NCAA made available to the student athlete and others a list of the individuals who had registered under this program.

The NCAA's agent registration system was *voluntary*. In the memorandum that accompanied the registration form, the NCAA acknowledged that the system operated without the force of law behind it. Former sports agent Mike Trope succinctly described the ineffectiveness of the NCAA rules and regulations in his book *Necessary Roughness* when he wrote, "The NCAA rules are not the laws of the United States. They're simply a bunch of hypocritical and unworkable rules set up by the NCAA. I would no sooner abide by the rules and regulations of the NCAA than I would the Ku Klux Klan."[9] Similarly, athlete agent Norby Walters told a *Sports Illustrated* reporter, in reference to an NCAA rule forbidding student athletes to contract with sports agents before their eligibility was exhausted, "I'll sign anyone I want. The NCAA can't enforce [its rules]. I'll sign a sophomore if I want."[10] Much like Trope, he told *USA Today* that breaking NCAA rules is "like saying we bent the Knights of Columbus rules."[11] In a recent article, two commentators accurately describe the inherent limitations on the NCAA's authority to directly regulate athlete agents as follows:

only the federal government and the individual states possess the power to regulate agents; the NCAA simply lacks jurisdiction to regulate athlete agents. The NCAA is merely a voluntary organization with jurisdiction only over its member constituents (i.e., the colleges and universities that elect to join the NCAA). It does not even have jurisdiction over its athletes, and it must instead enforce its rules against its member institutions. In other words, if an athlete violates an NCAA rule or regulation, the NCAA will mandate that the member university not allow the athlete to participate further in intercollegiate sports.[12]

In 1989, some NCAA members began to acknowledge that it was possible that the voluntary agent registration system might have been doing more harm than good. Agents who registered could then tell prospective student athlete clients that they had a registration "validation" from the NCAA. In fact, all the registration validated was that the agent had taken the time to complete a form. NCAA Executive Director Richard Schultz himself referred to the system as "meaningless," and at the end of 1989 it was abolished.[13]

Players' Associations

Players' associations, which constitute trade unions for the athletes in the major professional sports, also regulate athlete/agent relationships. These unions operate under the guidelines of the National Labor Relations Act (NLRA).[14] The first players' union agent regulation program was instituted in 1983 by the NFLPA. The creation of the NFLPA program was followed by the NBPA and later by major league baseball's counterpart, the MLBPA, and hockey's counterpart, the NHLPA. In varying forms, these unions require sports agents to register with them and to receive "certification" before representing members of their unions.[15] The NBPA process basically requires the completion of a form, attendance at a seminar, and the payment of a fee. The NFLPA requires a prospective agent also to pass an exam related to this representation. The MLBPA does not allow a sports agent to register until he or she actually agrees to represent a client.[16] The sanctions for noncompliance with the rules set forth by unions include "decertification."[17]

The sports unions' power to regulate and certify agents represents a departure from the ways in which employees' unions typically operate. In most industries, unions (pursuant to collective bargaining agreements with employers) negotiate terms and conditions of employment as well as all union member salaries. In contrast, professional sports leagues, also pursuant to collective bargaining agreements, possess the exclusive authority to negotiate individual player salaries and other terms and conditions of employment such as minimum salaries, pension benefits, health insurance, playing conditions, travel accommodations, the ability of a player to move from one team to another, medical treatment, and grievance and arbitration procedures.[18] However, unlike other unions, sports unions have delegated their exclusive authority to negotiate individual player salaries. Thus, players are free to select representatives to negotiate the individual terms of their contract compensation packages within the framework established by the collective bargaining agreements.[19]

In 1983, the NFLPA asserted that it possessed the inherent authority to regulate agents who represented football players in contract negotiations with teams. Pursuant to its asserted authority, the NFLPA mandated that those agents who desired to represent its members be certified by the union. Similarly, in 1986, in response to complaints by players of abuse by agents, the NBPA established a comprehensive system of agent certification. One court described the abuses that prompted union regulation of agents:

> players complained that the agents imposed high and non-uniform fees for negotiation services, insisted on execution of open-ended powers of attorney giving the agents broad powers over players' professional and financial decisions, failed to keep players apprised of the status of negotiations with NBA teams, failed to submit itemized bills for fees and services, and, in some cases had conflicts of interest arising out of representing coaches and/or general managers of NBA teams as well as players. Many players believed that they were bound by contract not to dismiss their agents regardless of dissatisfaction with their services and fees, because the agents had insisted on the execution of long-term agreements. Some agents offered money and other inducements to players, their families, and coaches to obtain player clients.[20]

The NBPA established a comprehensive system of regulation and certification that addresses most, if not all, of the abuses cited above.

Like the NFLPA's agent regulations, only agents certified by the NBPA are authorized to represent its members.[21] The MLBPA asserts its authority in the MLBPA regulations by citing the NLRA and emphasizing that it is "the exclusive representative for all the employees in such unit."[22] It then cites its collective bargaining agreement with management, noting that players may negotiate contracts with teams "in accordance with the provisions set forth in this Agreement."[23] The certification requirement is solidified by a further requirement in the Major League Baseball Collective Bargaining Agreement (effective June 17, 1988) that a player may use an agent for negotiations "provided such agent has been certified to the Clubs by the Association [MLBPA] as authorized to act as a Player's Agent for such purposes."[24]

Courts have upheld the authority of players' associations to regulate agents. In *Collins v. National Basketball Players Association*, an appellate court upheld a federal district court ruling that recognized the authority of players' associations to establish agent regulations and to certify agents.[25] "The integrity of a prospective negotiating agent is well within the NBPA's legitimate interest in maintaining the wage scale and working conditions of its members."[26]

The authority of players' unions to impose sanctions against agents was recently recognized in *Black v. National Football League Players Asso-*

ciation.[27] Former agent Tank Black sought dismissal of disciplinary proceedings initiated against him by the NFLPA. Black asserted that the NFLPA's proceeding and a proposed ruling that revoked his contract adviser certification were the products of an antitrust conspiracy, the product of an arbitration system established pursuant to NFLPA regulations that violates the Federal Arbitration Act, and interfered with his business relations. The court rejected his claims. In *White v. National Football League*, agents Leigh Steinberg, Jeffrey Moorad, and Gary Wichard argued that they were not subject to discovery in a proceeding in which the National Football League Management Council alleged that the agents and the San Francisco 49ers entered into undisclosed agreements concerning player compensation.[28] The agents argued that they were not subject to discovery in the proceeding because they were not signatories to certain agreements, including the NFL Collective Bargaining Agreement, and because they were not subject to the penalty scheme provided for in these agreements. In rejecting the agents' arguments, the court cited approvingly to *Collins v. NBPA* and the notion that players' unions can regulate sports agents.

Unions have on occasion used their authority to discipline agents. For example, in 1996, the NFLPA suspended its first agent; Robert Caron was fined $5,000 and suspended for a year for conduct involving the University of Southern California (see discussion in Chapter 11).[29] Between then and 1999, the NFLPA is reported to have suspended seven agents for violation of its rules.[30] The NFLPA suspended agent Jimmy Gould for two years and fined him $15,000. Other agents suspended by the NFLPA include Jeffrey S. Nalley and Joel Segal.[31] Also, as discussed in Chapter 5, the NFLPA revoked the license of Dunyasha Yetts,[32] and Tank Black was decertified by the NFLPA in 1999.[33] Players' associations will also use their authority and the threat of suspension to influence an agent to voluntarily relinquish certification. This situation occurred recently when long-time agent Sal DeFazio resigned as a certified player representative. His resignation came in the aftermath of charges by the NBPA accusing him of improperly withdrawing more than a million dollars from players' accounts.[34]

Initially, a key flaw in the NFLPA system was that the union did not represent student athletes until they signed a professional contract.[35] Thus the relationship where the greatest problems were occurring—with the recent graduate—was not covered by the regulation. The NFLPA now asserts its authority over the interests of the rookie athlete as well.[36] This circumstance contrasts with the NBPA, where student athletes drafted by the league have been considered to be members of the union since the creation of its agent regulatory rules.[37]

Interestingly, the MLBPA's primary goal is education as opposed to punishing the shady agents. According to Gene Orza, assistant general counsel of the association, "we do not think that agents are bad. We believe players should have more information at their disposal when they go about choosing an agent."[38] The MLBPA system strives to make this information available.

Players' association certification obviously carries more force than the NCAA program did. The strength in the union certification programs lies in the ability of the players' associations to decertify or even to deny initial certification of an agent. The NCAA had no similar power. However, union regulations run the same risk as the NCAA system of "validating" an agent without a thorough evaluation. Some agents do not want to register. Orza notes that one attorney maintained, "I am not an agent, I am an attorney," and has been fighting the registration requirement on that basis.

NFLPA Financial Advisor Regulations

In early 2002, the NFLPA became the first sports union to adopt regulations governing the financial advisers of its members, The *NFLPA Regulations and Code of Conduct Governing Registered Player Financial Advisors* represent the union's response to an increasing number of incidents in which football players have been victimized by financial advisers. The stated goal of the regulations is to promote "the integrity of those who represent NFL players in financial matters."[39] Financial advisers are requested to voluntarily participate in the program. According to the regulations, participants in the program will be afforded "unique access and information on NFL players, their benefits, and compensation structure."[40] Perhaps more important, participating financial advisers will be viewed as having received the union's blessing as "qualified" and "pre-selected financial advisers."[41] The regulations include disclaimer language that states that the NFLPA does not endorse any Registered Player Financial Advisor. Nevertheless, registered status will obviously provide a competitive advantage to participants over financial advisers who elect not to participate or whose application for registration is denied.

The regulations contain definitions of key terms such as "financial advisor," which is defined as "any person who, for compensation in any form, gives any financial advice with respect to a Player's funds, property and/or investments of any kind."[42] The regulations contain definitions of numerous other terms, including "alternative investment," "broker," "control," "financial planner," and "investment advisor."

In addition to the definitions section, the regulations include provisions that delineate the criteria for determining an individual's and a firm's eligibility for certification as a Registered Player Financial Advisor. Other provisions delineate minimum education, training, and experience requirements. Applicants must have graduated from an accredited four-year college or university.[43] An applicant must also have had a minimum of three years relevant work experience and graduate training in his or her area of financial expertise (e.g., a master's degree in business administration) or a professional designation (e.g., certified financial planner). Establishing an area or areas of financial expertise is critical for the applicant given that the regulations prohibit registered financial advisers from providing financial advice to NFL players outside of the area(s) of financial expertise for which the union has granted registration.[44]

Several bases exist pursuant to which an applicant can be deemed ineligible for union registration as a Player Financial Advisor. For example, if an area of financial expertise requires registration or licensure with governmental entities such as the SEC, the applicant who has not duly complied is ineligible for registration as a Player Financial Advisor.[45] Other grounds for ineligibility include conviction, guilty pleas, or indictments for a felony or misdemeanor offense under state or federal law relating to matters involving finances and breach of trust, such as investments, fraud, breach of fiduciary duty, bribery, and theft.[46] Relatedly, an applicant must not have had a final civil judgment rendered against him, her, or it (in the case of firms) for matters such as fraud, conversion, misappropriation of funds, professional malpractice, or breach of fiduciary duty.[47] An applicant is ineligible if he or she has been disciplined by a regulatory agency such as the Securities and Exchange Commission, a self-regulatory organization (SRO) such as the National Association of Securities Dealers, Inc. (NASD), or a professional association for matters that generally call into question an applicant's trust and competence. Finally, an applicant will be deemed ineligible for failure or inability to pay debts and for seeking protection of bankruptcy laws within seven years prior to the time of application.

Affirmative obligations are imposed upon applicants who become registered financial advisers. Illustrations of such duties include periodically informing players of the investments made on the players' behalf and the economic status of such investments, periodically providing players with itemized statements of fees charged, and notifying of any change in the adviser's professional status.[48] Advisers must also retain for at least three years "promotional, solicitation, and advertising materials provided to any Player."[49]

The regulations create a fiduciary relationship between advisers and player clients. They provide that "[a] Registered Player Financial Advisor shall have the duty to act in the best interests of his/her Player-clients."[50] Consistent with this fiduciary obligation, advisers are required to assess the suitability of particular investments for their player clients by taking into consideration factors such as the player's assets and liquidity, risk tolerance, and short- and long-term liabilities.

Certain conduct is expressly prohibited by the regulations. Not surprisingly, "any device, scheme, or artifice to defraud a Player" is included in the prohibited conduct, as is "soliciting or obtaining any general power of attorney from a Player over his assets or investments."[51] Other prohibited conduct includes commingling the player's funds or property with the adviser's and, more generally, engaging in unlawful conduct or conduct involving breach of trust such as fraud, deceit, and dishonesty. Advisers are prohibited from engaging in any activity that "creates an actual or potential conflict of interest with the effective representation of a Player."[52]

The regulations provide arbitration and disciplinary procedures that constitute the exclusive methods for resolving disputes arising from denial of registration and violation of the regulations. The NFLPA's president or executive director is authorized to appoint a three-person panel to hear complaints regarding the denial of registration and to prosecute violations of the regulations. Appeals of adverse action proposed or taken by the panel can be made to an outside arbitrator to be selected by the NFLPA.

Financial advisers who wish to participate in the program must complete an application and pay a $1,500 fee. (The fee for NFLPA certified contract advisers—agents—is only $1,250). The application requests information that presumably will allow the union to assess the qualifications and integrity of applicants. In addition the applicant must be covered by a fidelity bonding and/or professional liability insurance.[53]

Association of Representatives of Professional Athletes

The agents themselves at one time had a set of self-regulating rules established through the Association of Representatives of Professional Athletes (ARPA).[54] This organization, composed of approximately 120 members at its peak, was a self-regulatory agency formed by agents to reform their industry. Membership in the organization was voluntary, as was compliance with the organization's rules. Although ARPA had its own code of ethics, there was no entity that mandated their enforcement. It received high praise from some circles; however, ARPA had virtually no power to implement its enforcement. The authors made several calls and it appears that ARPA is no longer in existence.

Conclusion

This chapter has provided an overview of private sector attempts to regulate agent conduct. An equally important and more widely discussed area is government regulation. The next chapter examines state and federal law attempts at legislation affecting the sports agent.

Chapter 11

The Laws

In a recruiting pitch to an athlete, Norby Walters said, "The normal sports agent . . . he's not gonna shake white America. I have been shaking those people for years in that music side of entertainment. Now it's time to shake 'em hard in the sports side of entertainment."[1] The "shaking" needs to come from the regulators of the sports agent industry. This chapter examines public attempts to regulate sports agents. In examining the problems that may restrict the effectiveness of existing public regulatory schemes, it looks at changes, such as the Uniform Athlete Agents Act, that may ameliorate certain of the impediments to effectively using existing laws to hold sports agents accountable to their clients and other persons and entities (the following chapter fully explores that act). It also considers the need for more rigorous enforcement of existing regulations and looks at the need for a uniform sports agent law.

With varying degrees of success, individual states have attempted to arrest the athlete/agent problems for two decades. This chapter briefly describes past and existing state legislation and addresses the issues that arise out of such legislation. As this work is being completed, a uniform law that regulates athlete agents has been promulgated and most, if not all states, are likely to adopt it.[2] As discussed in Chapter 12, uniform legislation addresses some of the problems that imbue existing state agent acts.

Federal Regulation

Although sports topics tend to generate a great deal of public and political interest, federal legislative intervention into the sports realm is rare. Examples of such legislation include the Amateur Sports Act and the Curt Flood Act. At present, no federal legislation specifically applies to regulating the activities of sports agents. As will be discussed in regard to state regulatory efforts, however, improper agent conduct may fall within the parameters of nonagent-specific federal law.

For example, federal charges of mismanagement of funds, fraud, and racketeering were made in the Walters-Bloom trial. The prosecuting tool used in that trial was the Racketeer Influenced and Corrupt Organizations Act, commonly referred to as RICO,[3] which is especially noted for the broad range of factual contexts in which it has been asserted by prosecutors.

RICO was initially designed to attack organized crime and to stymie political corruption. Since its enactment in 1970, RICO's scope has expanded significantly beyond these factual contexts. Indeed, RICO's applicability to agent/athlete contracts surprised commentators and agents. Lonn Trost, then head of the sports department at the national law firm of Shea & Gould, testified at the Walters-Bloom trial that he had informed agents that signing student athletes to contracts before their eligibility expired did not violate any criminal statutes.[4] Walters, Bloom, Trope, and Trost all turned out to be incorrect.

RICO created three criminal offenses. If a party violates two or more of a list of approximately thirty criminal statutes over a period of ten years, he or she may be found guilty of acquiring, controlling, or operating an "enterprise" through "a pattern of racketeering activity." If the party is convicted, the penalty for the RICO violation alone is seizure and forfeiture of the assets from the illegal enterprise and a fine of up to $25,000. In addition, under RICO, not only can the government bring an action but the civil provisions also allow private citizens to bring actions and gives them the right to recover three times their actual damages and reasonable attorneys' fees.

The most notorious case involving the application of the federal RICO statutes to sanction agents was the Norby Walters matter. In *U.S. v. Walters-Bloom*, criminal application of the RICO Act was deemed appropriate by the jury. In that case, the "pattern of racketeering" was the mail fraud perpetrated against the NCAA when the student athletes, paid by Walters and Bloom, had letters sent to the NCAA by their schools proclaiming that they were eligible to compete under NCAA rules when, in fact, they were not. *U.S. v. Walters-Bloom* also involved a reputed organized crime figure, Michael Franzese, who allegedly helped finance Walters's and Bloom's venture into the sports agent business in exchange for a 25 percent share.[5] It does not seem, however, that Franzese's involvement was an essential element in the jury's determination. Thus, as is the case with many RICO actions to date, the organized-crime component need not be present; all that apparently needs to occur is for an agent to induce two athletes to violate an NCAA regulation and for those athletes to proclaim to their institutions and the NCAA that they are eligible.

The Summit Management case also provides an excellent illustration of the use of nonsports-specific federal laws to prosecute alleged wrongful conduct by those who represent athletes. The violations alleged in the federal grand jury's indictment against the principals of Summit Management Group arose from alleged schemes to perpetrate fraud on several of the company's athlete clients. Central to the government's case are allegations of mail fraud stemming from the alleged improper transfer of funds from athlete's banking accounts to Summit's account that ultimately wrongfully deprived the athletes of their property. The indictment also alleges that the principals of Summit violated federal statutes that criminalize money laundering and bank fraud.

Successful legal actions may also be asserted against student athletes who participate in the fraud as well. Minnesota Vikings wide receiver Cris Carter was fined $15,000 and ordered to perform 600 hours of community service for failing to cooperate with federal authorities when they were investigating Walters and Bloom. Carter failed to reveal that he had received a $5,000 signing incentive from agent David Lueddeke.[6]

Recently, federal and state civil RICO actions have been asserted by private parties seeking compensation for alleged improper conduct by persons involved in sports. Football player Vincent Clark recently sued his brokerage company, Robert W. Baird Co., Inc., and agent, Kenneth Fox. In addition to asserting fraud, breach of contract, and fiduciary duty claims, Clark asserted civil violations of RICO. As in Walters-Bloom, the alleged RICO violation revolved around allegations of mail fraud. Although the court in *Clark* acknowledged the applicability of civil RICO actions to this context, it concluded that the plaintiff had failed to plead facts sufficient to support a civil RICO action and granted the defendants' motion to dismiss the claim.[7] In a state civil RICO action, *Jones v. Childers,* the plaintiffs met with more success.[8] Looking to the United States Supreme Court's standards for guidance in determining whether defendants had engaged in conduct that amounted to a violation of Florida's state RICO statute, the Eleventh Circuit Court of Appeals held that "The number of occasions on which Childers and TSI fraudulently induced the professional athletes to invest in a number of Israeli securities, the relationship between the fraud with respect to *Jones* and the fraud perpetrated against the other investors, the similarity of all victims—all professional athletes—and the similarity of the acts, taken collectively, demonstrates a pattern of racketeering activity which constitutes proof of a RICO violation."[9]

Another source of federal regulatory activity is the federal Securities and Exchange Commission (SEC). The SEC has reportedly exerted regulatory authority in the sports agent industry. This agency has "reprimanded" some of the larger sports management firms for violating existing investment advisory laws.[10] As discussed in Chapter 5, the agency is presently investigating agent Tank Black and has initiated legal proceedings against other agents.

Many commentators have maintained that aggressive federal legislation providing appropriate sanctions would be the best way to deter agent misconduct. Commentators in search of a more direct federal vehicle to regulate agents have set forth various types of sports agent–specific legislation ranging from a federal version of state legislation to a model based on federal securities law. Federal legislation would certainly provide the uniformity that heretofore has been absent and go a long way toward resolving problems associated with a lack of uniformity—conflict-of-law and commerce-clause problems. So far, no such legislation has been promulgated. Lloyd Shefsky, former president of the Sports Lawyers Association and a veteran of a three-year lobbying effort for sports agent legislation, cited three reasons for the lack of success in passing such legislation: "The first was it was not as important as current events like the arms race; second, the former jocks like [New Jersey Senator Bill] Bradley and [New York Representative Jack] Kemp did not want to be associated with sports; and third, and this is the best of all, they said, 'You want us to protect millionaires?' "[11]

Moreover, the enactment of federal legislation to regulate agents would not serve as a panacea. There is clear evidence that in other professions where legislation exists to control the professional ethics (for example, securities brokers), fraud and unethical activities persist within the industry. Ivan Boesky and Michael Milken were both aware of the rules against insider trading, but because of the potential for huge profits, they took the risk of breaking the laws and getting caught.[12]

State Regulation

Two tiers of state regulation are potentially applicable to athlete agents. The first level consists of generally applicable civil and criminal laws that might apply to improprieties committed by agents in negotiating and drafting of contracts, and improprieties that constitute violations of agents' fiduciary responsibilities to their athlete clients. The prosecution of Richard Sorkin under New York State criminal laws in 1977 is one of the earliest examples of the prosecution of a sports agent under existing state laws. Later, in 1989, prosecutors in Florida filed fraud and conspiracy charges against a Florida sports management firm. Former Atlanta agent Jim Abernethy was found guilty under a state statute covering tampering with a sporting event as well as commercial bribery and violation of deceptive trade law. The trial of the sports agent who represented Kevin Porter, a former Auburn University football star, led to a successful prosecution under state law in an Alabama county circuit court.[13] That conviction, however, was later reversed on appeal. As this book goes to press, South Carolina, Florida, and federal authorities have pursued or are pursuing agent Tank Black.[14]

The second level consists of sports agent–specific statutes. Subsequent to the adoption of the Uniform Athlete Agents Act, some states already introduced athlete agent legislation. As of January 1, 2001, twenty-eight states had enacted agent-specific legislation.[15] Interestingly, the state of Washington had enacted agent legislation, but repealed it in 1999.[16] Until the Uniform Athlete Agents Act is adopted in states with existing agent statutes, however, these statutes remain the governing law. For example, Mississippi's agent statute was repealed in order to be replaced by the Uniform Athlete Agents Act, which the state adopted effective July 1, 2001.[17] The Uniform Athlete Agents Act has also been introduced in Washington. Due, however, to the likelihood that most of the states with existing agent statutes and those without agent statutes will adopt the Uniform Athlete Agents Act, the discussion that follows provides only an overview of agent statutes that preceded the Uniform Athlete Agents Act.

Athlete Agent Statutes

As discussed in Chapter 10, NCAA rules and regulations that seek to protect the amateurism ideal have provided the major impetus for agent-specific regulation. Premised on the authority of state governments to protect the public interest, athlete agent legislation seeks to protect the financial interests of universities and colleges that may be undermined when the relationships between agents and student athletes violate NCAA amateurism and agent-related provisions. For example, a successful football program at a public or private Division I college could potentially lose millions that might be derived from television and postseason competition if it is sanctioned by the NCAA due to improper conduct between an agent and student athlete. A clear example of the financial harm caused by a student athlete's dealings with a sports agent involved the University of Alabama. The NCAA required the school to forfeit $253,477 for using two ineligible players in the 1987 NCAA basketball tournament.[18] The players were declared ineligible because of their dealings with sports agents. Many feel that

schools should not have to forfeit their funds or have players rendered ineligible because of interference by sports agents. As discussed
below, this sentiment is reflected, in part, in agent statutes that grant
educational institutions a statutory private cause of action to seek
damages that reflect losses resulting from agent misconduct.[19]

Another interest that agent statutes seek to protect is that of the student athlete who might unknowingly be drawn into committing violations of NCAA rules by athlete agents. The desire to protect these
interests is expressly recognized in Alabama's agent statute, which
states that "The Legislature finds that dishonest or unscrupulous practices by agents who solicit representation of student-athletes can cause
significant harm to student-athletes and the academic institutions for
which they play. It is the intent of the Legislature to protect the interests of student-athletes and academic institutions by regulating the activities of athlete agents."[20]

Although athlete agent legislation varies among states, the following
characteristics emerge from these statutes.[21]

1. *Registration:* The overwhelming majority of agent statutes require
   agents to register with the state as a prerequisite to conducting
   business as an athlete agent within the state. For example, Alabama's agent statute (prior to that state's adoption of the UAAA)
   provided that "No person shall engage in or carry on the occu-
   pation of an athlete agent either within the state or with a resident of the state without first registering with the commission
   through the Secretary of State."[22] Note that certain registration
   statutes allow an agent to obtain a temporary license while his or
   her registration is being processed.[23] The objective underlying
   these statutes is to establish a certification procedure for individuals entering the field of athlete representation or continuing
   in it.[24] Other states, such as Nevada (prior to its adoption of the
   UAAA), imposed no registration requirement. Nevada's agent
   statute focused principally on delineating proscribed conduct.[25]
   California is noticeably absent from the ranks of states that require agents to register. California's agent statute, the Miller-Ayala Athlete Agents Act, imposes no registration requirement but
   requires agents to file (with the California Secretary of State) detailed information as a prerequisite to "engaging in or carrying
   on the business of athlete agent."[26]

   The degree of information that states require as a part of the
   registration process varies greatly. Some states such as Arkansas
   and Texas seek detailed information from agents regarding

matters such as formal training or practical experience that the applicant has had in contracts, contract negotiations, and complaint resolution. Some statutes require, as a part of the registration process, disclosure of information regarding prior criminal misconduct (for example, whether the agent has pled guilty to crimes involving perjury, taking of a false oath, embezzlement, fraudulent conversion, or misappropriation of funds), and ethical or agent-related misconduct.[27] Such is the case with California's Miller-Ayala Act, which requires the reporting of extensive information regarding the agent's past business relationships, including any misconduct on the part of the agent, and any sanctions imposed on student athletes stemming from interaction with the agent.[28] Other agent statutes, such as Connecticut's, set forth no details regarding the information that an applicant for certification must provide, but authorizes a state official to adopt such regulations.[29]

2. *Payment of Fee:* Agent statutes that require agents to register also tend to require agents to pay fees in varying amounts. For example, North Carolina imposes a $200 fee for the issuance or renewal of a certificate of registration.[30]

3. *Surety Bonds:* As a part of the registration/certification process, some agent statutes require the registered sports agent to post a surety bond or its equivalent (for example, malpractice insurance) that is subject to forfeiture for violations of the statute.[31] The amount of the surety bond that must be posted varies. Georgia and Florida require that an agent post a bond of not less than $10,000 and $15,000, respectively.[32] Several agent statutes, like those for the states of Kansas, North Carolina, and Texas, require the posting of a bond in the amount of $100,000.

4. *Covered Athletes:* Student athletes are included within the scope of all agent statutes. A few statutes bring within their parameters athletes who, although not enrolled in an institution of higher education, remain eligible to participate in intercollegiate sports.[33] Other statutes provide universal protection to all resident athletes engaged in any team sport.[34]

5. *Notification Requirements to Institutions:* Most agent statutes require that an agent provide varying forms of notice to the educational institution attended by the student athlete with whom the agent intends to engage in a contractual relationship or interact in some other manner. The majority of these statutes require that the agent notify the institution that the athlete agent has entered into a contract with one of the school's student athletes. Missouri's statute is illustrative. It provides:

An athlete agent who enters into an agent contract, financial services contract or professional sports services contract with a student athlete who is subject to the rules and regulations of the National Collegiate Athletic Association, the National Association for Intercollegiate Athletics, or the National Junior College Athletic Association must provide written notification to the athletic director or the president of the college or university in which the student athlete is enrolled that the student athlete has entered into such a contract. Written notification of such a contract must be given prior to the student athlete's practicing for or participating in any athletic event on behalf of any college or university or within seventy-two hours after entering into said contract, whichever occurs first. Failure of the athlete agent to provide this notification is a class B misdemeanor.[35]

Some agent statutes go as far as to require that the agent notify certain representatives of a college if the agent intends to have any contact whatsoever with a student athlete enrolled at the particular school.[36] Thus, North Carolina's agent statute provides that "An athlete agent must give prior written notice of his intention to contact an athlete with respect to representing the athlete as an athlete agent to the athletic director of the institution of higher education or to the principal of the high school in which the athlete is enrolled. All such contact shall strictly adhere to the rules of each separate institution with regard to the time, place, and duration of the athlete agent's contact."[37]

Certain agent statutes include within the definition of contact the mailing of written materials by agents to athletes. Therefore, the agent must notify college representatives that such materials have been forwarded to their enrolled athletes.[38] In this regard, Oregon's agent statute provides that "An athlete agent may send a student athlete . . . written materials, provided that the athlete agent has sent an identical copy of the materials to the principal, president or other chief administrator of the educational institutional to which the student athlete has been admitted or in which the student athlete is enrolled."[39]

Athletes are held to similar notification obligations in some states. These statutes typically require student athletes to inform his or her institution, university president, or agent regulatory authority of any contract that the athlete has entered into with an agent. This notification must also occur prior to the athlete's participation in certain athletic-related events such as practicing and/or participation in a contest. Failure to comply with this type of notification requirement constitutes a violation of the statute and may subject the athlete to sanctions, including the payment of fines and criminal liability.

6. *Notification Requirements to Athletes:* Twenty-four states impose obligations on athlete agents to provide written notification appearing in conspicuous type that informs athletes of the consequences (for example, loss of eligibility to compete in intercollegiate athletics) of interactions with athlete agents that violate the rules of conferences and athletic associations. Some statutes also include language that informs athletes of the right to cancel contracts that were improperly entered into. The following language taken from the Alabama pre-UAAA agent statute is illustrative:

> WARNING: IF YOU AS A STUDENT-ATHLETE SIGN THIS CONTRACT, YOU MAY LOSE YOUR ELIGIBILITY TO COMPETE IN INTERCOLLEGIATE ATHLETICS. . . . YOU MAY CANCEL THIS CONTRACT BY NOTIFYING THE ATHLETE AGENT IN WRITING OF YOUR DESIRE TO CANCEL NOT LATER THAN THE 15TH DAY AFTER THE DATE YOU SIGN THE CONTRACT. HOWEVER, EVEN IF YOU CANCEL THIS CONTRACT, THE INTERCOLLEGIATE ATHLETIC ASSOCIATION OR CONFERENCE TO WHICH YOUR COLLEGE OR UNIVERSITY BELONGS MAY NOT RESTORE YOUR ELIGIBILITY TO PARTICIPATE IN INTERCOLLEGIATE ATHLETICS.[40]

7. *Prohibitions on Postdated Contract:* Most statutes prohibit student athletes and athlete agents from entering into postdated contracts. California's statute provides that "no athlete agent shall negotiate or enter into any postdated agent contract, endorsement contract or professional sports services contract . . . that purports to or takes effect at a future time."[41] These provisions are intended to provide protection to institutions since an athlete who improperly enters into a contract with an agent will violate NCAA rules even if the contract is not to take effect until after the student athlete has exhausted his or her athletic eligibility.

8. *Incorporation of Association and Conference Rules:* Many sports agents consider NCAA regulations to be unenforceable against them and therefore routinely ignore their existence. In an attempt to rectify this problem, agent statutes provide that the violation of association and conference rules constitutes a violation of the agent statute. Some agent statutes specifically identify the associations, such as the NCAA and NAIA,[42] while others generally refer to athletic associations.[43] By incorporating the rules of athletic associations, agent statutes impose criminal or civil sanctions on sports agents who violate the rules governing intercollegiate sports.

9. *Recordkeeping:* Another common feature of athlete agent statutes is the inclusion of recordkeeping and reporting requirements; the nature of the obligations imposed varies from state to state.[44] Examples of the records that must be maintained include ex-

penses related to the recruitment of athletes (for example, travel and entertainment expenses), names and addresses of former and current athlete clients, fee schedules (fees charged and received from athletes), and services to be provided.

10. *Sanctions:* The key distinction between the regulations discussed in the Chapter 10 and agent statutes is the ability of state regulators to impose civil and criminal sanctions for noncompliance with the provisions of the statute. Athlete agent statutes impose a range of criminal, civil, and administrative sanctions that may be imposed on agents who engage in prohibitive conduct (Minnesota[45] and Georgia[46] do not classify violations of the statute as criminal actions). Civil and administrative sanctions include:

    a. *Registration Invalidation:* The denial, suspension, or revocation of an athlete agent's license or registration and reprimand or probation may be consequences of an agent's failure to comply with the applicable statutory provisions.[47]

    b. *Invalidation of Agent/Athlete Contracts:* Invalidation of contracts entered into between athlete agents and student athletes that violate the provisions of agent statutes, particularly those requiring adherence to athletic association or conference rules. In some states, such as Alabama, Arkansas, and Florida, such contracts are void.[48] In other states, athlete agent statutes render such contracts voidable at the option of the injured party.[49]

    c. *Fines/Forfeiture:* Violations of agent statutes often require agents to pay fines that range from $10,000 to $100,000, depending on the state.[50] In addition, statutory violations may result in forfeiture of any surety bond that the agent was required to post as a condition to registration or certification.[51] Statutes also mandate that agents must forfeit the right to any repayment for anything that the agent gave to the athlete as an inducement to enter into a contract.[52]

    d. *Private Civil Action:* Some agent statutes afford states' attorneys general the right to pursue an action for injunctive relief against the violating agent.[53] In addition, these statutes may grant injured parties, which may include athletes, agents, colleges, other persons, or any combination thereof, the right to pursue private civil actions against the athlete agent.[54] Certain statutes also give injured parties, principally educational institutions, the right to pursue private causes of action against student athletes.

e. *Criminal Sanctions:* The variation in civil and administrative sanctions is mirrored by criminal penalties that may be imposed upon athlete agents. In some states violations of agent statutes constitute a misdemeanor.[55] It other states, a violation constitutes a felony.[56] Violations may also be punishable by fine, imprisonment, or both, depending on the particular statute.[57]

IMPACT OF AGENT STATUTES

The impact of these statutes has been varied. Many sports agents, including prominent agents, ignore registration and certification requirements. One explanation for this situation is the pervasive lack of enforcement in some states. In 1989, San Francisco attorney Edward King maintained that "one of the most famous football agents in California has not registered as an agent."[58] Apathy toward the lack of registration by popular sports agents provides little incentive for the novice agent to seek certification.

An additional explanation for the lack of sports agent registration is the existence in many agent statutes of language that completely or partially exempts attorneys licensed to practice from the provisions of the statute.[59] It should be noted that other statutes either provide no such exemption, or include an attorney within the purview of agent statutes when he or she negotiates a contract on behalf of an athlete.[60] Requiring all athlete representatives to register, including licensed attorneys, would increase the number of registrants as well as the state's ability to enforce the provisions of the statute effectively.

At one time, the state of Texas seemed to take the most aggressive stance with respect to enforcement of its agent statute. In 1989, the state levied a $10,000 fine against an agent and a firm each for violations of its agent law.[61] Former Heisman Trophy winner Johnny Rodgers and Total Economic Management of America, Inc. were accused of contacting 1989 Heisman Trophy winner Andre Ware of the University of Houston. In addition to the improper contact violation, the alleged violations included offering gifts, cash, and other inducements to Ware's mother.[62]

The $10,000 fine levied against Rodgers and his firm was surpassed a few years later. Agent Jeffrey Newport was fined $16,500 by the Texas Secretary of State.[63] He was also suspended from operating as a sports agent in Texas for two years. These penalties resulted from Newport's violation of provisions of the Texas athlete agent statute that prohibit agents from offering anything of value in attempting to procure athletes as clients. Newport provided a college football player with $5,100 in cash and other improper benefits, including $1,400 toward the purchase of a disability insurance policy.

During the last several years, the state of Florida has taken an aggressive stance in enforcing its agent regulation statute. In 1994, agent Nate Cebrun, who participated in making improper payments to a Florida State University football player, received 30 days in jail and was assessed $2,255 in fines after pleading no contest to the felony charge of refusing to register with the state as a sports agent.[64] Two other individuals who participated in making the improper payments were charged and sentenced for violating Florida's agent registration law statute.[65] In 1999, Florida state authorities charged agents Wesley Carroll and James Ferraro with having contact with a student athlete at the University of Miami, which violated Florida's athlete agent statute. Both agents settled the charges out of court.[66] Also in 1999, Florida authorities charged sports agent Sean Alfortish with funneling money to University of Florida football players in violation of Florida's agent law and practicing sports agency without a license.[67] Alfortish was sentenced to one year of unsupervised probation following a guilty plea to a misdemeanor charge of "attempting to conduct business in Florida without an agent's license."[68] He was also ordered to leave the state of Florida and reimburse the University of Florida's police department the $30,000 it spent on its investigation of his activities.[69]

ACTION BY EDUCATIONAL INSTITUTIONS

Institutions of higher education may be the entities most harmed by sports agent improprieties. As discussed above, colleges and universities may receive stiff sanctions from the NCAA if a player is found to have a relationship with a sports agent in violation of NCAA rules. Since the NCAA has no direct contractual relationship with student athletes, it enforces its regulations by taking action against its member institutions. The NCAA's member institutions generally do not promulgate rules regarding sports agents. Doing so would be futile since, like the NCAA, educational institutions do not have the force of law to enforce any regulations they might institute. Thus, institutions are left to rely on private causes of action such as the tort of interference with a contractual relationship. Such a theory would appear promising given that courts have overwhelmingly recognized the relationship between the student athlete and his or her college as contractual in nature.[70]

In 1995, USC filed an unprecedented lawsuit seeking monetary damages against an athlete agent.[71] USC's suit alleged that agent Robert Caron gave money and other benefits to three of the school's football players. This conduct allegedly violated California's agent statute, which at the time required an agent to be registered and post a $25,000 surety bond.[72] USC also alleged that Caron interfered with the university's contracts with its student athletes by inducing them to engage in conduct that violated NCAA rules. Caron, who denied USC's allegations, agreed to pay the school $50,000 and to a permanent injunction that prohibited him from conferring benefits to amateur USC athletes.[73]

Certain universities have taken a more proactive approach by becoming involved in the agent-selection process. Some have ad hoc systems where coaches or administrators assist student athletes in selecting an agent. Some institutions, such as Temple University, have developed professional sports advisory panels. As it relates to agents, these NCAA-authorized advisory panels are permitted to "Assist the student-athlete in the selection of an agent by participating with the student-athlete in interviews of agents, by reviewing written information player agents send to the student-athlete and by having direct communications with those individuals who can comment about the abilities of an agent (e.g., other agents, a professional league's players' association); and . . . visit with player agents or representatives of professional athletics teams to assist the student-athlete in determining his or her market value (e.g., potential salary, draft status)."[74] Although the effectiveness of such panels in ending the corruption of agents in college sports is limited, they hold the potential to provide valuable information to student athletes regarding agents' qualifications.[75]

Problems with Existing Legislation

Several significant issues—jurisdiction, vagueness, commerce clause, freedom of speech, and quality assurance—impact the legal viability of many of the existing state enacted athlete agent statutes. Certain other weaknesses also characterize much of the present legislation.

JURISDICTION

The first major problem confronting existing athlete agent statutes relates to the jurisdictional authority of states to apply and enforce their laws. This issue arises from the national character of college athletics. For example, may California enforce its registration requirements against an Ohio resident who attempts to represent a student athlete from a California school? Should Ohio's athlete agent law govern the activities of this same agent while he or she "recruits" a client in California? Can a state's athlete agent law be enforced against an agent who has no contact with that state? Two commentators provide the following illustration:

"The Ohio statute provides that 'a court may exercise personal jurisdiction over the athlete agent who resides or engages in business outside [Ohio] as to a cause of action arising from the athlete agent entering into an agent contract with a student-athlete *outside* [Ohio] without complying with section 4771.02 of the Revised Code.' A reading of this one sentence from Ohio's statute demonstrates its obvious unconstitutional stretch of jurisdictional power, attempting to reach athlete agents who have had absolutely no contact with the forum state (i.e., Ohio)."[76] The forgoing questions and illustrations point to a crucial issue: whether and to what extent a state possesses personal jurisdiction over an athlete agent who is not a resident of that state. Thus far, courts have not provided answers to this question.

VAGUENESS

Existing athlete agent statutes have also been criticized for failing to adequately define the conduct that will result in a violation of the statutes. Constitutional law dictates that statutes that suffer from this flaw are unenforceable due to the vagueness doctrine. The notion that underlies the vagueness doctrine is that "[v]ague laws serve as a trap for innocent people by failing to provide them with fair warning. In other words: Statutes that are insufficiently clear are void for three reasons: (1) to avoid punishing people for behavior that they could not have known was illegal; (2) to avoid subjective enforcement of the laws based on 'arbitrary and discriminatory enforcement' by government officers; and (3) to avoid any chilling effect on the exercise of First Amendment freedoms."[77] Several provisions of athlete agent statutes may allow an agent to invoke the vagueness doctrine as a defense. These include unclear definitions (for example, athlete agent and athlete) and provisions that fail to specifically define prohibited conduct.[78]

COMMERCE CLAUSE

Another problem with existing regulations is whether the commerce clause of the United States Constitution would bar the enforcement of any of these state regulations.[79] The commerce clause bars states from regulating affairs of interstate commerce—that is, issues that affect more than one state. Railroads and airlines are two common examples of entities that are regulated by the federal government rather than by individual states. Rather than allowing states to regulate what types of railroad car coupling must be used and thus run the risk of having to change couplings each time a state border is passed, the federal government establishes guidelines for all interstate commerce.

There is precedent for the successful assertion of the commerce clause in barring state regulation of athlete agents based upon judicial decisions involving other sports issues. In *City of Oakland v. Oakland Raiders*, the city of Oakland, California, was barred by the courts from exercising eminent domain rights over a sports franchise because such an action would interfere with interstate commerce.[80] That case was one of several pieces of litigation in the saga of the Raiders NFL franchise in their move from Oakland to Los Angeles. The city of Oakland instituted an action that sought to "condemn" the sports franchise, much in the way municipalities condemn and take homes and other property to construct freeways, parks, or airports. The taking of a sports franchise under this eminent-domain principle was a novel idea that looked like it might prove to be successful. However, instead of reaching its decision on the facts of the case—that whether this was the type of property a city could condemn and keep in the city for the public interest—the court ruled that the commerce clause barred the city from taking such an action. The court reasoned that the sport is an interstate affair and that only the federal government should be able to regulate those activities.

A similar argument could be made that the regulation of sports agents is not a state but a federal affair. A similar defense could be asserted by an athlete agent if a state attempted to prosecute him or her under an athlete agent statute. How successful such a defense might prove remains to be seen.

FREEDOM OF SPEECH

Athlete agent statutes have also been criticized for potentially violating the First Amendment. Provisions that have been subjected to this criticism include those that prohibit contact (including the dissemination of written information) without first notifying certain individuals, such as a university's athletic director. The argument is made that no law should interfere with the constitutional right to free speech.

CONFLICTS OF INTEREST AND EXCESSIVE FEES

Two further areas that any new statute should address are the conflict of interest and excessive fee issues. These matters are discussed in detail in Chapters 5 and 6. Attorneys who represent athletes must conform to a canon of ethics that guards against trying to represent the interests of two clients that might conflict without disclosing the conflict to the respective clients. The scenarios in Chapter 2 where agents represent conflicting interests would properly have to be disclosed by attorneys to their clients. Nonattorneys have no similar requirement absent legislation. Although some states are mindful of this, others have neglected to include an appropriate provision.

Another concern about these state regulations is the excessive fees that sports agents may have to pay to comply with registration in a number of states where they may do business. Not only do agents have to pay registration fees in these states but many states require them to post a bond as well. If all fifty states had a statute requiring this, the cost of entering the sports agent business could be tens of thousands of dollars. Sports agent Craig Fenech maintains that he cannot find an entity that will provide him with a bond for his business. If his experience were typical, such requirements would effectively restrict the number of people to a select category of the well financed. Those excluded would undoubtedly include many talented and conscientious individuals; those admitted might be able to raise enough money for fees but might not make as meaningful a contribution. Moreover, the need for thousands of dollars might in itself be a corrupting factor for agents without enough money who would have to seek financial support from other backers. These "silent partners" might be of questionable integrity.

Vigorous Enforcement of Existing Laws?

That non-sports-agent-specific regulations can be used effectively is illustrated by the pursuit of Tank Black and of Norby Walters and Lloyd Bloom, as well as the state prosecutions of the same parties, and earlier, of Richard Sorkin. As discussed in detail in Chapter 5, fraud or income mismanagement issues can be attacked by utilizing these laws.

But conviction is not necessarily deterrence. In one case, even after conviction, all charges against agent Norby Walters in Alabama were dropped when he paid the University of Alabama a settlement of $200,000.[81] Similarly, Walters' associate Lloyd Bloom received a sentence that required him to serve one week of a one-year sentence washing state trooper cars while staying at the hotel of his choice.[82] Finally, all charges against agent Jim Abernethy were thrown out at the appellate level.[83] The sentences against Bloom and Walters in their federal trial were overturned as well.

Conclusion

The focus of sports agents regulation should be on enforcing these existing laws and not on incorporating outdated concepts of amateurism into new regulations. The focus should be on any illegal activities that occur while recruiting athletes and any violations once an agreement is entered into. These are the types of activities, as with any industry, that public entities should expend their limited resources on, not in seeking to regulate activities where no one is harmed. Many contend that already limited law enforcement resources should not be used to police amateurism. The NCAA appears to have the clearest responsibility in that regard, if amateurism is a goal it chooses to preserve. If the cloak of amateurism is removed, even to a limited degree, then some of the opportunity for agents is removed as well. Law enforcement should focus on the issues addressed in the *Sorkin*, *Abernethy*, and *Walters and Bloom* cases. Individuals with private causes of action must assert their rights as well. For some activities, a private civil suit may be the only manner of regulating the activity. The next chapter focuses on the Uniform Athlete Agents Act.

Chapter 12

A Uniform Approach

The Uniform Athlete Agents Act

The Process of Developing A Uniform Athlete Agents Act

Somewhat anticlimactically, a uniform law regulating sports agents became official in the first year of the new millennium. The future impact of the proposed law is not yet clear. This chapter describes the process undertaken to develop the Uniform Athlete Agents Act, discusses the basic elements of the final product, and provides some analysis of its likely impact.

On August 3, 2000, the National Conference of Commissioners on Uniform State Law (NCCUSL) completed a process begun in 1996 when it passed the long-awaited Uniform Athlete Agents Act (UAAA).[1] The press release issued by NCCUSL identified the purpose of the act as protecting the interests of student athletes and academic institutions by regulating the activities of athlete agents. The promulgation of uniform laws such as the UAAA is not novel.[2] Three familiar examples of the 250 uniform laws drafted by NCCUSL are the Model Penal Code, the Uniform Probate Code, and the Uniform Commercial Code. Before examining the UAAA, we briefly discuss NCCUSL and its function.[3]

The primary function of the NCCUSL is to promote "uniformity in state law on all subjects where uniformity is desirable and practicable."[4] (This purpose certainly brings to mind the sports agent–related dilemmas discussed herein.) The NCCUSL consists of 340 commissioners who are appointed by the governors of the fifty states, the District of Columbia, and Puerto Rico. The process by which commissioners are appointed differs from state to state;[5] however, commissioners most typically are "lawyers, judges, legislators and law school professors."[6]

The process that led to promulgation of the UAAA began when NCCUSL's Committee on Scope and Program, by a narrow three-to-two vote, recommended to the organization's Executive Committee that a drafting committee be established to "draft an act to govern the relationship among sports agents, student athletes and educational institutions."[7] The Executive Committee assigned the UAAA to the Study Committee on Athlete Agents, which it created in 1996.[8] The purpose of the Study Committee was articulated as follows: "The committee was created to study the problem of sports agents contacting college athletes prematurely and affecting their eligibility, in order to determine whether a uniform act should and could be created consistent with National Conference policy, and if so, whether outside funding would be available for the drafting effort."[9]

Thus, early on, the focus of the uniform legislation was on issues relating to recruitment, not sports agent quality control. In July 1996, NCCUSL's Executive Committee approved the creation of a Drafting Committee by a narrow six-to-five vote. The close vote was a manifestation of low support for the proposed act due to "a heavy Conference agenda and concern that drafting a Uniform Athlete Agents Act would have less impact on a national basis than many other topics on the agenda or to be proposed."[10] Following the creation of the Drafting Committee, a search to find funding for the project was successful when the NCAA agreed to "allocate $50,000 for the drafting of an act relating to sports agents."[11] NCAA support seems appropriate considering the legislation's narrow focus on sports agents' recruitment of student athletes. This is a prime concern of the NCAA, and not as urgent a concern for other stakeholders in sports, including the professional leagues and unions. Securing funding along with "including the interests of student-athletes in the drafting process" were conditions imposed by the Executive Committee when it approved the establishment of a Drafting Committee.[12] After funding was obtained, the Drafting Committee proceeded with the development of the UAAA.

At the end of a three-year drafting process that allowed comments by various interested parties including athlete agents; coaches; individuals responsible for administering existing acts; representatives of the players' associations of the NFL, the NHL, and major league baseball; and the NCAA, NCCUSL approved the UAAA during its annual meeting on August 3, 2000.[13] Once a uniform act is passed by the conference and endorsed by the American Bar Association, NCCUSL urges state legislatures to adopt the proposed uniform act.

A uniform federal law might provide the ideal foundation for addressing the problems that exist within the agent industry. A key feature of federal legislation is uniformity. Although a state legislature may adopt a uniform act as proposed by NCCUSL, it may also vary the provisions of the act. As a result, absolute uniformity may not exist even if all fifty states adopt a particular uniform act. In reality, however, a lack of uniformity may not present a significant problem. As of March 12, 2002, eleven states, one district, and one territory had

adopted the UAAA without making any substantively significant variations to it. These are Alabama, Arizona, Arkansas, Delaware, District
of Columbia, Idaho, Indiana, Mississippi, Nevada, Tennessee, Utah,
U.S. Virgin Islands, and West Virginia. As of the same date, the act
had been introduced in an additional fifteen states, including California, Florida, Illinois, and Texas.[14]

A final note is that a uniform act developed by NCCUSL does not
displace all existing law that might be relevant to the subject matter of
the uniform act. For example, principles of law and equity will supplement the provisions of the UAAA. Consequently, legal principles such
as fraud, intentional interference with contractual relations, and
embezzlement remain readily available tools for addressing agent
misconduct.

THE UNIFORM ATHLETE AGENTS ACT

The UAAA was perceived as the means of resolving problems caused
by differences among individual state athlete agent statutes. The
Prefatory Note to the UAAA identifies certain problems resulting from
a lack of uniformity and indirectly articulates the rationale for the
UAAA:

At least twenty-eight States have enacted legislation regulating athlete or
sports agents. The statutes differ greatly. About two-thirds of the statutes impose registration requirements. There are substantial differences in the registration procedures, disclosure required, and requirements relating to record
maintenance, reporting, renewal, notice, warning and security. The term of
the registration is one year in thirteen States, two years in four States, and two
States do not specify a term. Most States require notification to States or educational institutions and athletes of certain matters, but the matters vary
widely. Conscientious agents operating in more than a single State must have
nightmares caused by the lack of uniformity in the existing statutes, the difficulty in compliance and the severity of penalties which may be imposed for
violations.[15]

In attempting to maintain the ability to address the problems that
nonuniform state legislation sought to regulate, the NCCUSL included within the UAAA many of the key provisions of existing state
athlete agent legislation. For example, the UAAA adopts the position
of most statutes by requiring registration of athlete agents.[16] Other
key provisions include the following:

1) *Definitions:* The act provides definitions of key terms such as
   agency contract, athlete agent and student athlete. For example,
   athlete agent is defined to mean "an individual who enters into

an agency contract with a student-athlete or, directly or indirectly, recruits or solicits a student-athlete to enter into an
agency contract."[17] The comment to Section 2 of the UAAA specifically identifies "runners" as falling within the definition of an
athlete agent. The comment also points out that corporations
are not defined as persons and are not required to register, but
individuals working within corporations will be required to register. Finally, attorneys are not excluded from the act if they perform the services of an athlete agent.

2) *Registration:* Agents are required to register before they initiate
contact with a student athlete if the purpose of the contact is to
induce a student athlete to sign an agency contract. The UAAA
further provides that "if the student-athlete initiates contact with
an athlete agent, the athlete agent must apply for registration
within seven days after commencing any effort to induce the
student-athlete to enter into an agency contract."[18]

"Athlete agents are also required to make specific disclosure as
a part of their application for registration."[19] Applications, which
are deemed public records, require disclosure, inter alia, of a
description of formal training as an athlete agent; practical experience as an agent; educational background relevant to athlete agent services; references; the name of each person for
whom the applicant acted as an agent during the five years prior
to submission of the application; criminal convictions involving
acts of moral turpitude and felonies; administrative or judicial
determinations regarding fraudulent acts; any conduct of the
applicant that led to a sanction imposed on a student athlete;
and any denial, suspension, or revocation of a registration or licensure to act as an athlete agent.[20] State authorities responsible
for registration decisions are directed to a list of factors to "consider in determining whether to issue a certificate of registration
or suspend, revoke or refuse to renew a registration."[21]

Consistent with state athlete agent legislation that preceded
the act, it does not develop minimum educational or certification requirements for athlete agents. It was believed that such a
task is best left to players' associations.[22]

Finally, the act allows for each state to determine the amount
of registration and renewal fees.[23] The comment to the relevant
section, however, urges states to adopt reasonable fee structures
to avoid discouraging compliance. It adds that "the wide range
of registration fees imposed by states with existing athlete agent
laws has likely contributed to low registration totals in many
jurisdictions."[24]

3) *Reciprocity of Registration:* The Secretary of State of the state in which an applicant has submitted an application is required to grant reciprocity of registration if the applicant is licensed in another state. The applicant may submit the application and certificate of registration from the other state in which the applicant is registered if certain conditions are met.[25]

4) *Void Contracts:* Section 4(c) provides that any agency contract made in derogation of the registration requirements set forth in the Section is deemed void and the athlete agent is required to "return any consideration received under the contract."[26]

5) *Contract Terms:* The substantive content of agency contracts is also regulated by the Act, which specifies terms that must be included in such contracts."[27] Required terms include provisions relating to the method for calculating the fee to be paid by the student athlete, a warning to the student athlete that signing the contract will result in a loss of any remaining intercollegiate athletic eligibility,[28] and notice that the contract can be canceled within fourteen days after the student athlete signs it.[29]

6) *Notification Requirements:* As was true of some state athlete agent laws, the act imposes obligations on agents and student athletes to notify educational institutions after an agency contract has been consummated.[30] In this regard, athlete agents and student athletes are required to notify the athletic director of the educational institution in which the student athlete is enrolled that they have entered into an agency contract. Notice must be given within 72 hours after entering into an agency contract or before the next scheduled athletic event, whichever occurs first.[31]

7) *Recordkeeping:* Athlete agents must maintain certain records for a minimum of five years.[32] Records include those relating to identities of individuals represented by the athlete agent and the costs incurred by the athlete agent in soliciting and recruiting a student athlete to enter into an agency contract.[33]

8) *Prohibited Conduct:* The act specifies improper conduct by agents. Prohibited conduct includes: furnishing anything of value to a student athlete as an inducement to sign an agency contract, failing to register as required by the act, and intentionally initiating conduct with a student athlete while unregistered.[34]

9) *Criminal Penalties:* The act provides that an athlete agent who engages in the conduct prohibited by Section 14 of the UAAA, may be guilty of a misdemeanor or a felony. Each state is left to determine the extent of criminal penalties for violations of the act.[35]

10) *Civil Penalties:* With respect to civil penalties, the act grants colleges and universities civil remedies against both athlete agents

and former student-athletes for damages resulting from a violation of the Act.[36] Even though institutions are granted a right to
proceed against a student athlete, the comment to Section 16
recognizes that this is likely to occur in only the most egregious
cases.

> It is assumed that educational institutions will be very reluctant to
> bring an action against a former student athlete. Public opinion and the
> desire to be successful in future recruiting of athletes should cause edu-
> cational institutions to carefully consider whether to exercise the right
> established by subsection (a) in most situations. There are, however,
> known instances of extremely egregious conduct by student-athletes
> who receive lucrative professional contracts that caused serious damage
> to education institutions. Subsection (a) keeps open the possibility of a
> civil action against those individuals.[37]

11) *Administrative Penalty:* The Secretary of State of each state may
    assess a penalty against an athlete agent not to exceed $25,000
    for violations of the act.[38]

Conclusion

The UAAA was drafted and promulgated without attempting to tackle
issues beyond the recruitment of athletes by agents at the preprofes-
sional level. Without question, had NCCUSL attempted to grapple
with the full range of concerns beyond recruitment that negatively impact the sports agent business (for example, agent competency, conflicts of interest, fraud, and solicitation), the ensuing controversy would
have delayed or perhaps even precluded the promulgation of the act.
Notwithstanding the limitations of its mission, the UAAA "embodies
most of the principles of the 'aggressive' sports legislation already in
existence" in that it adopts the approach of existing statutes with the
broadest scope and jurisdictional reach.[39]

The UAAA provides a foundational basis for uniformity. Drawing
from a complex and confusing web of existing state legislation, the
UAAA standardizes registration, notice, and disclosure requirements.
Standardization of these and other requirements provides a level of
uniformity that hopefully will encourage agents to comply with the
law in each state without incurring financial hardship and without
having to understand the often confusing matrix of laws that currently exist. Thus the UAAA's uniform registration and reciprocity
provisions are key in effectuating the UAAA's implicit goal of encour-
aging voluntary agent compliance with its requirements.[40]

NCCUSL seeks to deliver two additional messages by virtue of its
approach. The first is that quality control is someone else's responsi-

bility. That someone else is the respective players' union for each league. The other regulator will be the market: as "bad" agents are exposed, prospective customers will get the word from disgruntled customers.

The other message is that existing civil law concepts and criminal legislation are sufficient to address agent misconduct that adversely affects the interests of their athlete clients. All that has been lacking is rigorous enforcement.

Federal legislation might be the preferred approach to regulating athlete agents. However, such legislation will probably never occur. Nevertheless, the UAAA is an important step forward. At a minimum, "the act will establish uniformity and provide for reciprocity among the States adopting it."[41] And while the UAAA or any other legislation is incapable of eradicating all of the problems associated with athlete agents, it will make compliance easier and encourage compliance by providing for reciprocal registration and renewal.[42] As this book goes to press, the likelihood increases that the UAAA will be adopted in close to, if not all, fifty states, the District of Columbia, and U.S. territories. It has thus far been adopted in eleven states, and has been proposed for approval in seventeen jurisdictions, as of December 3, 2001.

The UAAA goes a long way in addressing many of the operational issues that confront the athlete agent who is attempting to comply with the law of each individual state. Uniformity, if adopted by all, makes it easier for those agents who desire to comply to do so. Note two commentators, "The UAAA provides some welcomed relief in that, as a uniform law, it is intended for adoption in all states so that consistent obligations and results can be achieved in any state in which an athlete agent conducts business. Further, its provisions, with . . . [a] few exceptions . . . serve the states well by being relatively straightforward and uncluttered. However, to accept the UAAA as a good thing for states to adopt, one must first believe that athlete agents should be regulated in the first place."[43] As agent Bill Strickland maintains, "conceptually, it is a step in the right direction." Even with a uniform law in place, however, wrongdoing will continue. After the long wait for a uniform attempt to deal with sports agent issues, it took the act itself to crystallize the obvious—that there is no panacea.

Chapter 13

Conclusion
The Absence of a Panacea

This book has attempted to present an overview of the background and the current state of the sports agent business along with the legal principles that impact the industry. In addition, it has touched on efforts undertaken by diverse parties to address the problems that confront the business. For example, the discussion of the Uniform Athlete Agents Act in Chapter 12 illustrates the efforts made by lawmakers to reduce certain aspects of corruption in the industry. In addition, those who control and manage college sports are considering reforms that are intended not only to ameliorate inequities between student athletes and their institutions, but also to remove incentives for agents to engage in dishonest, incompetent, and other forms of inappropriate conduct.

This chapter is written on the premise that although progress has been made, much work remains to be done in attempting to stymie corrupt practices by athlete agents. Thus, efforts must first and foremost be aimed at reducing corruption. In addition, reforms should increase access to information about agents by those most likely, directly or indirectly, to be impacted by agent corruption—athletes, colleges and universities, players' unions, and professional sports leagues. This chapter also proceeds from the premise that a constructive role can be played by each of the principal players most likely to feel the impact of agent irregularities. Finally, reform-minded efforts should be directed toward providing mechanisms to afford relief to victims of agent corruption and to discourage agent conduct that results in unscrupulous behavior.

Reforming College Athletics

We must face the reality that some people will cheat wherever an economic incentive exists for them to do so. In this regard, the future of the sports agent industry, and particularly its regulation, is closely tied to reforms that occur in college sports, a system that still leaves room within which unscrupulous individuals operate.

The relationships in college sports that create incentives for agents to cheat require restructuring. One way to reduce cheating by agents is to lessen the attractiveness of the improper benefits agents offer to student athletes. Several ideas and proposals have been suggested that might indirectly serve as vehicles for accomplishing this objective. These proposals, which seek to balance the inequities that exist in the student athlete/university relationship by providing compensation to athletes, were recently summarized as follows: "There have been a number of models that have been suggested as means of compensating student-athletes in Division I-A men's football and basketball, in response to concerns regarding inequitable treatment of student-athletes at that level. These various models are largely of four types: (1) revenue-sharing; (2) instituting a professional division within the intercollegiate system; (3) a scholarship plus stipend approach; and (4) the reform approach taken by the NCAA."[1] After providing this summary of reform initiatives, Professors Rodney Smith and Robert Walker suggest a fifth model that combines additional grants-in-aid to student athletes with incentives and disincentives depending on an intercollegiate athletics program's success or lack thereof in graduating its student athletes, and economic incentives for student athletes to graduate within six years.[2]

Let us examine how one of the foregoing proposals might indirectly reduce incentives for agents to engage in improper conduct. Some analysts argue that the time is right for colleges and universities to pay student athletes engaged in big-time intercollegiate athletics a stipend in addition to the scholarships that they currently are permitted to receive. The logical entities to provide these increased funds are, first, the member institutions and, if that is not financially feasible, then the NCAA.

The justifications for increased compensation are fairly simplistic. First, from an economic standpoint, should not labor receive a fair share of the contribution they make to the athletic enterprise? As was set forth by two commentators:

> . . . even with figures that do not reflect the full profitability of men's basketball and football programs, seventy-four percent (74%) of Division I-A men's basketball programs earned an average of $2,200,000 of revenues over expenses in 1997, with seventy-one percent (71%) of Division I-A men's football programs making an average of approximately $5,000,000 in 1997. . . .

> Institutions have essentially acknowledged the potential profitability of Division I-A men's basketball and football. Salaries for coaches are the largest single expense at the Division I-A level, whereas grants-in-aid (scholarships for student-athletes) are the major expense at all other levels. Head coaches in Division I-A men's basketball and football are often paid more than $1,000,000 per year in personal income from all sources. . . .

Given that student-athletes at this level do not share in the revenues gener-
ated by "big-time" men's basketball and football in the same unique manner as
the NCAA, conferences, institutions, coaches and administrators, it is not surprising that claims of exploitation and inequitable treatment have arisen.[3]

Second, many of these student athletes actually need additional
compensation either for themselves or, in some instances, for their
families. At a minimum, the additional amount the student athlete receives should be equal to an amount that brings the spending money
available to the student athlete up to that available to the university's
average student. If profits are available, is there a better place for
them to go? If the effect of a modest stipend is a reduction in
unscrupulous payments by others, then all the better for collegiate
sports.

The amateurism reforms that the NCAA is exploring are not overly
dramatic, but they do strive to address the realities of the day. The
dominant belief among NCAA reformers at this point seems to be that
receipt of compensation prior to enrollment at an NCAA institution is
not the evil to be conquered. The current NCAA focus is on advantages that may be gained by an individual athlete from a competitive
standpoint. The concern is in making sure that an individual athlete
does not gain a competitive advantage through the quality of athletic
competition prior to enrollment. The competitive advantage, the reformers have assessed, should be addressed by reducing the years of
NCAA eligibility proportionally with the years spent participating as a
professional prior to enrollment.[4]

Cultural and legal impediments stand in the way of adopting any
form of compensating student athletes. Included among the practical
legal variables that might thwart such a proposal are Title IX, antitrust (if the NCAA imposed a salary cap on or "fixed" the amount of
the stipend), tax, and workers' compensation issues.[5] Assuming that
these legal obstacles can be traversed, the emphasis on the amateurism principle in the NCAA regulatory system and in the mindset
of the public represents a key impediment. Yet the possibility of paying a stipend to student athletes in certain sports should not offend
American sensibilities. As discussed in Chapter 9, the Greek model of
athletics allowed athletes to receive compensation.

Notwithstanding the history described above, it is highly likely that
the NCAA will have taken action to reform its amateurism standards
by the time this book is in print. In 2001, the NCAA's Subcommittee
on Amateurism and Agents presented its final report and recommendations. The report, which was three years in the making, acknowl-

edges at the outset that the NCAA's current amateurism standards are anachronistic and in need of change.

It is important to understand that the notion of amateurism reflected in the current rules is a decidedly un-American notion. This amateurism concept, born in England, was designed to maintain class distinction in competitive sport. . . . Through the adoption of the amateurism proposals now before the membership, the Association has the opportunity to Americanize the concept of amateurism.[6]

This sentiment was echoed by then NCAA president Cedric Dempsey. "The deregulation proposals do not change our philosophy of amateurism but, rather, offer the first true comprehensive evaluation of the amateur status of those who enter our athletics programs as well as our concept of providing competitive equity. . . . The proposals also reflect a common sense of approach to amateurism without compromising our commitment to education."[7]

Three proposals for deregulation of the NCAA's current amateurism rules, which were developed by the subcommittee, were to be presented to the NCAA's Management Council for a vote in April 2002. The three packages present varying levels of deregulation. Under each of the deregulation packages, a prospective student athlete who completed at some organized professional level following graduation from high school without enrolling immediately in college would not be rendered ineligible to compete in intercollegiate athletics. Prospects would, in most cases, "lose one season of eligibility for each year they participated in organized competition."[8] The gist of this rule is that student athletes would be allowed to play for a professional team without losing all of their eligibility to compete at the intercollegiate level in the sport in which they played professionally.

The key remaining components of the three deregulation proposals are as follows.

- Package A would allow a prospective student athlete "to enter a pro draft and be drafted without affecting eligibility." Under current amateurism rules student athletes lose their eligibility if they request to be added to a draft or supplemental draft list.[9] The subcommittee concluded that simply no competitive advantage was gained by an athlete who simply places his or her name on a draft list.[10]
- Package B is the same as Package A but would also allow prospects "to sign a contract or commitment to participate in professional athletics without affecting eligibility." As for rationale, the report

states that "no competitive advantage is gained by signing a contract, and high-school prospects often do not have realistic expec-
tations about their ability to compete at the professional level."[11]
The report adds that prospects who actually play for the professional team with which they signed would be subject to the organized competition rule.

- Package C is the same as Package B but "would allow prospects to
  participate on a professional team without jeopardizing their eligibility."[12] The rationale behind the rule is that it would "help the
  failed professional, the individual who pursues a professional career out of high school but who learns quickly that he or she is not
  succeeding and likely never will succeed as a professional. This
  proposal provides incentive for those individuals to pursue a degree, also knowing they may still compete."[13]

A fourth package would maintain the NCAA's current amateurism
rules.[14]

As it relates to agents, the report emphasizes that the current rules
regarding the relationship between student athletes and agents will
remain in place. The subcommittee proposes three steps aimed at
minimizing the possibility that student athletes will accept money
and other benefits from agents.[15] These include enhancing efforts
at high schools and summer leagues to educate athletes and their
parents, enlarging the role of Professional Sports Counseling Panels
that are currently in place at colleges, and implementing a significant minimum penalty to punish student athletes who violate agent
regulations.[16]

The granting of stipends will not only have principled opposition
but also opposition from those who will merely point to the bottom
line.[17] Not all institutions are financially prosperous, of course; some
lose money. This fact must be borne in mind in any analysis of increased compensation to the student athlete. Some institutions indi-
vidually may not be able to foot the bill to provide the student athlete
with more funds. A reallocation of the entire NCAA budget might
remedy that problem.

Questions also arise concerning a stipend's impact on gender equity
in college sports and on nonrevenue-generating sports.[18] Any resources used to provide greater compensation to presumably revenue-
producing athletes would reduce the availability of funding for the
nonrevenue sports. Legal challenges would likely arise if payments
run afoul of Title IX. The goal of Title IX is so important that any impact it would have on compensation to revenue-generating athletes is
just part of the price that must be paid to bring about equity for

women in collegiate sports. With all of this in mind, one coach noted: "I agree it [payment of stipends] would be wonderful if it could be done, but when you're looking at the number of athletic departments that are running in the red already and the fact that if you are going to do it for revenue-producing sports—football and basketball—you are going to have to do it for a similar number of female athletes . . . I just don't think it's feasible."[19] Such restrictions dampen the enthusiasm for paying stipends to student athletes. Nevertheless, paying stipends at a modest level should be more fully explored.[20]

Related to the idea of allowing student athletes to receive stipends is permitting them to receive endorsement income. This proposal seems more problematic, not because athletes would receive income, but because the sports agent may begin to play an integral role in the athletes' career at a stage that would, again, encourage cheating. It is difficult to imagine a system that would allow an athlete to work with an agent in a financial transaction as a freshman or sophomore without the agent's beginning to utilize the tactics that have been prevalent near the end of the student athlete's career.

But if the receipt of cash for endorsements is not a problem in itself, should student athletes be able to negotiate endorsement contracts on their own? Can an athlete endorse a local automobile dealership if the owner is a booster or alumnus? What happens if the amount received is disproportionate to what is generally perceived as reasonable for such an endorsement? A solution that has some merit is allowing the endorsement of specific products, such as athletic shoes. These companies would not have an independent incentive, as a booster does, to pay more than the athlete's actual market value. Such endorsements would allow the athlete to receive additional revenues from a natural market source. They would also deal with the fairness issue of coaches receiving shoe endorsement income.

Another income-related suggestion is allowing student athletes to take out loans tied to their athletic potential. Such loans go beyond the loans currently allowed for disability insurance and the like. For these loans, the professional leagues, the individual member institutions, and the NCAA are the logical sources. Although none of the possible funding parties is in the banking business, the investment may prove in the long run to be advantageous. In addition to removing the incentive to take money from an agent, a loan provides an incentive for the athlete to stay in school. Critics of this route maintain that the loans could not be made large enough to compete with what some are willing to pay. This postulation may, in the end, be true.

Much like a bank, and as is the case with existing disability insurance loans, the loans can be based on information received from

NCAA or professional scouting sources. Educated guesses are being made every day about a given player's professional prospects. Further, if the professional leagues cooperate, the loan agreement can require automatic repayment to be made to the NCAA from the athlete's salary earned from playing on a professional team. Loans from professional leagues are not as attractive as those from the NCAA because the teams really do not have the same incentive to make the loans that the NCAA does. The ultimate stop for the athlete is the professional league, which may not really care whether the athlete stays in school. Either loan program is viable but the NCAA program, particularly given the NCAA's current prosperity and its desired continued prosperity, seems to be most appropriate. Alternatively, either the NCAA or the pro leagues may be able to develop a relationship with banking institutions that will make loans based on professional athletic potential.

Another proposal that would involve a fundamental change in the structure of college sports is the establishment of professional teams affiliated with colleges and universities. A separate minor league system with home teams centered on campuses seems unattractive. Although it leaves a cleaner taste in the mouths of those who oppose the payment of stipends to amateurs, it removes an incentive from many of our youth to attend college. Predictably, those who would be most negatively impacted would be lower-income individuals. While it is true that some athletes only attend college to participate in sports anyway, the NCAA is striving against that motivation with its ever-evolving initial eligibility measures.

Athlete Agent Regulations

Once monetary incentives to cheat have been lessened, efforts must be directed toward ensuring that only substantively and ethically qualified agents are allowed to practice the trade. The uniform act is a positive development in the evolution of the athlete agent industry in that it achieves uniformity. Yet the focus of the Uniform Athlete Agents Act and other existing state athlete agent laws must be broadened if the athlete agent industry is properly to be policed. Athlete agent acts, including the Uniform Athlete Agents Act, are limited in scope; emphasis is placed on regulating agent conduct that may result in the NCAA taking adverse action against colleges and universities. Protecting the interests of these institutions and tangentially the interests of student athletes is laudable. However, this singularity of focus reveals a major shortcoming of such legislation.

As is true of other professionals such as lawyers and architects, if agents are not qualified, they should not be allowed to fully partici- pate in the industry. Moreover, if agents engage in conduct or pro- duce results that depart from a reasonable level of competence, their right to practice should be suspended or terminated. In short, careful consideration should be given to broadening the scope of regulation of the Uniform Athlete Agents Act (and other state athlete agent laws) so as to incorporate provisions aimed at weeding out incompetent agents. Perhaps the act could establish minimum standards of agent competency. Consequently, a prospective agent who fails to meet the standard cannot become licensed as an agent; an agent whose conduct falls below acceptable standards of competence loses the right to par- ticipate in the industry.

Professional Sports Leagues and Players' Associations

At this time, the professional sports leagues are probably the least ac- tive entities in the regulating of sports agents. They should at least utilize their financial resources for educational purposes. These could include providing information to prospective draftees on the agent se- lection process. By becoming involved in education, they can begin to play a more affirmative role.

As discussed in Chapter 10, the unions have the power to deny unscrupulous agents the right to continue practicing their trade. Con- sistently, the courts have been supportive of the unions when disen- franchised agents have challenged the rights of unions to take such actions.

In addition to the ability to certify and decertify agents, players' unions are the parties with the greatest power to ensure that those who are certified are genuinely qualified. In that regard, whatever test or other instruments that are used to gauge the readiness of a poten- tial agent must have the appropriate level of rigor. In addition to whatever "entry" exam there is, there needs to be adequate continu- ing education and continuous review of an agent's qualifications.

The tide may be turning away, however, from the complacent union that only responds to instances of agent corruption and incompetence after athletes have been victimized. A glimmer of hope is emerging that players' unions will become more proactive in regulating agents. Alarmed by scandals involving corrupt agents and the likelihood that more scandals of the magnitude of that involving Tank Black may arise in the future, the NFLPA is considering whether to adopt a pos- ture more aggressive than it or any players' union has previously taken. In addition to the promulgation of regulations to govern financial advisers discussed in Chapter 5, the players' union is considering initiatives that will focus on the "quality of representation" and the "quality of the oversight [the NFLPA] can provide."[21] Because of the explosion in the number of agents that have gained NFLPA certification, the union will seek to decrease their numbers. NFLPA officials believe a reduction in the number of agents is necessary to weed out incompetent agents and to lessen the burden imposed on its regulatory mechanisms.[22] Specific strategies that the union is considering include significantly increasing the annual dues it charges agents, enhancing the level of difficulty of the examination required for NFLPA certification, and decertifying "an agent who fails to represent a player or negotiate a contract within a certain time period."[23] NFLPA leadership is willing to consider these and other regulatory mechanisms notwithstanding the likelihood that a concerted plan to reduce the number of certified agents will undoubtedly be legally challenged. The likely action would be taken under antitrust laws by an agent who is not able to gain certification and is thus barred from practicing the trade.

Educational Institutions

As discussed in Chapter 11, colleges and universities have much to lose if they become enmeshed in a sports agent scandal. Apart from the harm to the institutions' reputation is the financial cost in legal fees and sanctions an institution must endure. These direct reasons are why these institutions should take action. Educational institutions need to do a better job of policing and educating internally.

Individual institutions need to aggressively take it upon themselves to provide adequate education in this realm to student athletes who will be entertaining this professional option. In years past there was a prominent role at some institutions for an agent-screening panel. If the panels are structured and utilized properly they can be quite valuable. It appears clear, however, that education outside of the formal panels would help further inform the student athlete. Each institution will have to evaluate its own needs. This institutional obligation must be taken seriously.

Conclusion

It is important to recognize that providing student athletes with a student life stipend, loans against future earnings, allowing them to work extensively, or allowing them to endorse products would go strongly against long-standing definitions of amateurism. The NFL faced a similar dilemma regarding the drafting of underclassmen. This same issue is confronting the NBA today with a focus on high-school draftees. But college sports survive as the world changes.

The key parties in this industry—the leagues, NCAA, educational institutions, and legislators—need to work more closely together. The communication between the diverse entities involved is the overall key. From the empirical experience over the past several years it is evident that no entity acting alone can resolve the problems of the sports agent industry. Communication between sectors is the initial step. Once that communication is in place, constructive change is almost certain.

Even with these changes in place, the problems typified by Walters and Bloom and now Tank Black will continue to occur to some degree. Where such incidents do occur, or where other laws are broken, the applicable laws must be vigorously enforced. The U.S. Attorney in the Walters-Bloom trial expressed concern over the influence organized crime could have over collegiate and professional sports if rules violations such as payments to athletes continue. He cited the fact that Michael Franzese, a member of the Columbo crime family, was a financier of the Walters-Bloom firm World Sports & Entertainment. Regarding this financing, Franzese told *Sports Illustrated* reporter Bruce Selcraig, "Look, we were business associates. I'm not going to lie and say we weren't. But to say I had anything to do with his sports business, that I controlled it or called the shots, is ridiculous."[24] The district attorney, Anton Valukas, feared that an organized crime connection of this nature could place pressure on players to shave points or otherwise throw sporting events to serve the purposes of their underworld benefactors.[25] In a similar fashion, the convictions of the like of Tank Black and Myron Piggie should set off a warning signal regarding the types of influences that need to be guarded against.

The problems in college sports certainly go way beyond sports agents.[26] The reality is that sport has become more than an extracurricular activity: sport is now a global business. With the elevation of sports to this higher level, a reevaluation of all the surrounding circumstances must be made, not just in terms of sports agents but in terms of college sports in general and the level of education that the student athletes are receiving.

Reforming college sports should not be feared. It may be the transition itself that is the most difficult step to take. For a long time the tennis world regarded professional athletes as manual laborers. It took "Cash and Carry" Pyle to help change that perception. When he finally convinced the female sensation of the day, Suzanne Lenglen, to accept his offer to turn professional, the press acknowledged that she "was not denigrating herself but uplifting the world of sport."[27]

The alternative and probable outcomes of not taking action make the rationale for placing the appropriate level of regulatory focus on the sports agent industry clear. The passage of the Uniform Athlete Agents Act is certainly a milestone, but much more remains to be done.

Notes

Introduction

1. *Palmer Adds New Charges Against Walters, Bloom,* Sports Industry News 239 (July 29, 1988).
2. See, e.g., Steve Fiffer, *Two Sports Agents Convicted of Fraud and Racketeering,* New York Times A-I, col. 1, A-31, col. 3 (April 14, 1989).
3. Rick Morrissey, *Agent's Penalty Would Suit Auburn,* Chicago Tribune 11C (March 5, 2000).
4. *Congress Should Take Action to Regulate Agents Who Represent Athletes and Other Gullible Stars,* San Antonio Express News 2G (March 12, 2000).
5. William Oscar Johnson & Ron Reid, *Some Offers They Couldn't Refuse,* Sports Illustrated 35 (May 21, 1979).
6. Ronald D. Mott & Stephen R. Hagwell, *Student-Athletes: NCAA Rules No Deterrent for Agents,* NCAA News 1 (October 2, 1995).
7. Harvey Araton, *In an Often Shady and Dirty Business, It Is Business as Usual,* New York Times § 8, p. 2, col. 1 (April 2, 2000).
8. Ted Gup, *Playing to Win in Vegas,* Time 56 (April 3, 1989).
9. Josh Gotthelf, *Linebacker: Agent Paid Me Cash,* SportsBusiness Journal 1 (July 26, 1999).
10. Phil Taylor & Don Yaeger, *Tangled Web; Marcus Camby Was Both Victim and Villain in His Illicit Dealings with Agents While at UMASS,* Sports Illustrated 66 (September 15, 1997).
11. John Gorman, *"Agent Threatened Me": Bears' Douglass,* Chicago Tribune § 4, p. 1, col. 3 (March 16, 1989). See discussion in next chapter.
12. Oliver Williamson, *Markets and Hierarchies* 7 (The Free Press, 1975).
13. John Bannon, *Ex-Agent: "No Clean Programs,"* USA Today C-1, col. 4 (December 17, 1987).
14 Mike Freeman, *Pro Football: Protecting Players from Their Agents,* New York Times § 8, p. 1 col. 1 (July 26, 1998).
15. Bill King, *Playing on the Edge,* SportsBusiness Journal 28 (May 15–21, 2000).
16. See Chapter 9.
17. Liz Mullen, *Black Hit with Criminal, Civil Charges,* SportsBusiness Journal 7 (March 6–12, 2000).
18. *Id.*
19. Scott Edelman, *College Can Take Action Against Agents,* New York Times § 8, p. 11, col. 1 (October 15, 1995).
20. David Pickle, *Experience-Based Amateurism Model Presented to Division II Membership,* NCAA News C1 (January 17, 2000).

21. Welch Suggs, *Divisions I and II Diverge on Amateurism Proposals*, Chronicle of Higher Education A-38 (January 19, 2001).

22. See discussion in Chapter 2.

Chapter 1. Historical and Legal Foundations

1. Gerald Eskenazi, *Red Grange, Football Hero of 1920's Dead at 87*, New York Times B-5, col. 1 (January 29, 1991); Robert C. Berry, William B. Gould, & Paul D. Staudohar, *Labor Relations in Professional Sports* 10 (Auburn House, 1986) *("Labor Relations")*; Marc Pachter, *Champions of American Sport* 265–266 (Abrams, 1981).

2. Berry, et al, *Labor Relations* at 10 (cited in note 1).

3. *Id*. There were also reports that tennis great Bill Tilden signed with Pyle, which Tilden denied (*Davis Cup Men Deny Signing with Pyle*, New York Times 8 (August 28, 1926)), indicating that even in the beginning there were some negative connotations to being associated with an agent.

4. Arlene Schulman, *Life of the Touring Pro*, New York Times C-2, col. 3 (September 11, 1989).

5. Craig Neff, *Den of Vipers*, Sports Illustrated 76 (October 19, 1987).

6. *See Double Play*, Time 61 (March 25, 1966); Jack Mann, *The $1,000,000 Holdout*, Sports Illustrated 26 (April 4, 1966). *See also All-Star Agent Is a High Scorer*, Business Week 153 (September 20, 1969); *Playing the Money Game*, Time 94 (March 21, 1969).

7. *Double Play*, Time at 61 (cited in note 6).

8. Mann, Sports Illustrated at 26, 28 (cited in note 6).

9. *Double Play*, Time at 61 (cited in note 6).

10. George W. Schubert, Rodney K. Smith, & Jess C. Trentadue, *Sports Law* 123–127 (West, 1986).

11. *See, e.g., Mackey v NFL*, 407 F Supp 1000 (D Minn 1975), aff'd in part & rev'd in part, 543 F2d 606 (8th Cir 1976).

12. *See, e.g., Robertson v NBA*, 389 F Supp 867 (SDNY 1975), aff'd, 556 F2d 682 (2d Cir 1977); *Denver Rockets v All-Pro Management Inc.*, 325 F Supp 1049 (CD Cal 1971).

13. *McCourt v California Sports, Inc.*, 460 F Supp 904 (ED Mich 1978), vacated 600 F2d 1193 (6th Cir 1979).

14. *Mackey*, 543 F2d at 606.

15. *Id*. at 609.

16. *Id*. at 622.

17. Roger Noll, *Economics of Sports Leagues*, in Gary A. Uberstine, ed., *Law of Professional and Amateur Sports* § 17.03[4] (Clark Boardman Company Ltd., 1988).

18. *Id*.

19. Roger Kahn, Introduction to Woolf, *Behind Closed Doors* vii–xiii (New American Library, 1976).

20. *Id*.

21. Mike Trope with S. Delsohn, *Necessary Roughness* (Contemporary Books, 1987).

22. Johnson & Reid, *Some Offers They Couldn't Refuse*, Sports Illustrated 28 (May 21, 1979).

23. Mark H. McCormack, *What They Don't Teach You at Harvard Business*

School 1 (Bantam, 1984); Donald L. Dell, *Minding Other People's Business: Winning Big for Your Clients and Yourself* 1 (Villard, 1989).

24. John Saraceno, *King Forges NBA Link*, USA Today § 3-C, col. 3 (January 16, 1990).

25. Bryan Burwell, *Think Williams Got Bad Deal? Don't Try to Tell Him That*, SportsBusiness Journal 54 (October 11–17, 1999).

26. Jarrett Bell, *Rookie Works Hard for His Money Willams' Deal Is Stuffed with Controversial Incentives*, USA Today 3C (November 24, 1999).

27. For a discussion of these and other examples of common agency relationships, *see* Leonard Lakin & Martin Schiff, *The Law of Agency* 2 (Kendall/Hunt, 2d ed 1996).

28. Restatement (Second) of Agency, § 1(1) (1958).

29. *Id*. at § 1(2).

30. *Id*. at § 1(3).

31. Lakin & Schiff, *The Law of Agency* at 1 (cited in note 27).

32. National Conference of Commissioners on Uniform State Laws, *Uniform Athlete Agents Act*, p. 2 (2000).

33. Harold G. Reuschlein & William A. Gregory, *The Law of Agency and Partnership* 11 (West Publishing, 2d ed 1990).

34. Lakin & Schiff, *The Law of Agency* at 97 (cited in note 27).

35. Reuschlein & Gregory, *The Law of Agency and Partnership* at 35 (cited in note 33).

36. *Id*.

37. Lakin & Schiff, *The Law of Agency* at 97–98 (cited in note 27).

38. *Id*. at 124.

39. Lakin & Schiff, *The Law of Agency* at 98 (cited in note 27).

40. *Id*.

41. Interview of Michael B. Siegel, May 17, 2001, Philadelphia, PA.

42. *Id*.

43. *Id*.

44. Lakin & Schiff, *The Law of Agency* at 100 (cited in note 27).

45. *Id*. at 27.

Chapter 2. The Business

1. Leigh Steinberg, *Time to Revise Game Rules*, Sporting News 10 (November 16, 1987).

2. *New Role, New Model*, SportsBusiness Journal (May 15–21, 2000).

3. Interview of Reginald Wilkes, September 11, 1989, Philadelphia, PA.

4. Mike Freeman, Pro Football: Notebook, New York Times, § 8, p. 6 (July 30, 2000).

5. Teresa M. Walker, *Titans Land Pickens: "Misunderstood" Ex-Bengal Receiver Signs Five-Year Deal*, Chattanooga Times/Chattanooga Free Press D1 (July 27, 2000); *NFL Update*, Dallas Morning News 9B (August 1, 2000).

6. Jeffrey Z. Rubin & Frank E. A. Sander, *When Should We Use Agents? Direct vs. Representative Negotiation*, Negotiation Journal 401 (October 1988).

7. Greg Hansen, *NFL See Northcutt as Cornerback*, Arizona Daily Star 10C (March 26, 2000); Nick Cafardo, *Don't Count Out Holmes Run Ravens Free Agent Still May Be Targeted*, Boston Globe D2 (March 31, 2000).

8. Robert H. Ruxin, *An Athlete's Guide to Agents* 18 (Stephen Green, 1989) (*Athlete's Guide*). *See also* Dan Weil, *NBA Do-It-Yourselfers Rare*, SportsBusiness Journal (January 31–February 6, 2000) p. 44.

9. Rick Hummel, *Morris Says Cards Were Fair in Negotiations on Contract*, St. Louis Post–Dispatch 18 (January 5, 2002).

10. *Id.*

11. *Id.*

12. *Id.*

13. Sid Hartman, *Tice: McDaniel Won Most Battles*, Star-Tribune 3C (February 11, 2000).

14. Alan Breznick, *Court Coup for Local Lawyer*, Washington Post F18 (May 17,1999).

15. *Allen's Method Bad Deal for Agents*, Capital Times 2B (February 11, 1999).

16. Patrick Hruby, *Free Agent? New NBA Rules Alter Player Reprs' Roles*, Washington Times B1 (June 29, 1999).

17. *Allen's Method Bad Deal for Agents*, Capital Times 2B (February 11, 1999).

18. Thomas Heath, *NBA Stars Find Babby Cheaper by the Hour; D.C. Lawyer Bucks Tide of Agent Representation*, Washington Post D4 (May 10, 2000).

19. *Id.;* Liz Mullen, *Babby Signs Battier*, SportsBusiness Journal 5 (May 14–20, 2001).

20. *Id.*

21. *Id.*

22. Richard M. Nichols, *Agent, Lawyer, Agent/Lawyer . . . Who Can Best Represent Student Athletes?* 14 Ent & Sports L 1 (1996).

23. *Id.*

24. Stacey M. Nahrwold, *Are Professional Athletes Better Served by a Lawyer-Representative Than an Agent? Ask Grant Hill*, 9 Seton Hall J Sport L 431, 441–42 (1999).

25. *Id.* at 445.

26. Inquiry into Professional Sports, Final Report, HR Rep No 1786, 94th Cong, 2d Sess 70 (1977).

27. John Culver, Speech to Sports Lawyers Association, Washington, D.C. (May 12, 1989).

28. Len Elmore, *Turn Out the Lights, Agents' Party Is Over*, SportsBusiness Journal 54 (July 9–15, 2001).

29. *Follow the Bouncing Basketball News, Question of the Day—Do NBA Draft Picks Need Agents?* Sports Business News, July 19, 2001. <http://www.sportsbusiness news.com/basketball/index.asp?sStoryId=1451>.

30. *Id.*

31. Alan Abrahamson, *Sports and the Agent: Endangered Species?* Los Angeles Times D1 (March 3, 1999).

32. Hruby, Washington Times at B1 (cited in note 16).

33. Interview of William Strickland, May 17, 2001, Philadelphia, PA.

34. Hansen, Arizona Daily Star at 10C (cited in note 7).

35. Bryan Burwell, *Think Williams Got a Bad Deal? Don't Try to Tell Him That*, SportsBusiness Journal 54 (October 11–17, 1999).

36. Steve Davis, *This Pronunciation Thing Isn't Exactly Sparking a Controversy*. Dallas Morning News 2B (September 7, 2000).

37. *See* Donald E. Biederman, et al, *Law and Business of the Entertainment Industries* 471 (Auburn House, 1987).

38. *Id.*

39. Kashif, Speech to Black Entertainment and Sports Lawyers Association, Antigua, British West Indies (November 3, 1989).

40. There have been a number of scholarly articles examining various aspects of this field. All give an overview of the role of the athlete agent. Examples of recent scholarship include Thomas J. Arkell, *Agent Interference with College Athletics: What Agents Can and Cannot Do and What Institutions Should Do in Response,* 4 Sports Lawyers J 147 (1997); Jamie E. Brown, *The Battle the Fans Never See: Conflict of Interest for Sports Lawyers,* 7 Georgetown J Legal Ethics 813 (1994); Walter T. Champion, Jr., *Attorneys Qua Sports Agents: An Ethical Conundrum,* 7 Marquette Sports L J 349 (1997); Phillip J. Closius, *Hell Hath No Fury Like a Fan Scorned: State Regulation of Sports Agents,* 30 U Toledo L Rev 511 (1999); Bryan Couch, *How Agent Competition and Corruption Affects Sports and the Athlete-Agent Relationship and What Can Be Done to Control It,* 10 Seton Hall J Sport L 111 (2000); Robert P. Garbarino, *So You Want to Be a Sports Lawyer, or Is It a Player Agent, Player Representative Sports Agents, Contract Advisor, Family Advisor, or Contract Representative?* 11 Villanova Sports & Ent L Forum 11 (1994); Edward V. King, *Practical Advice for Agents: How to Avoid Being Sued,* 4 Marquette Sports L J 89 (1993); James Malone & Daren Lipinsky, *The Game Behind the Games: Unscrupulous Agents in College Athletics & California's Miller-Ayala Act,* 17 Loyola Ent L J 413 (1997); Nahrwold, 9 Seton Hall J Sport L 431 (cited in note 24); Nichols, 14 Ent & Sports L 1 (cited in note 22); Alec Powers, *The Need to Regulate Sports Agents,"* 4 Seton Hall J Sport L 253 (1994); Rob Remis & Diane Sudia, *Statutory Regulation of Agent Gifts to Athletes,* 10 Seton Hall J Sport L 265 (2000); Rob Remis & Diane Sudia, *Athlete Agent Contracts: Legislative Regulation,* 10 Seton Hall J Sport L 317 (2000); Rob Remis & Diane Sudia, *Escaping Athlete Agent Statutory Regulation: Loopholes and Constitutional Defectiveness Based on Tri-Parte Classification of Athletes,* 9 Seton Hall J Sport L 1 (1999); Jan Stiglitz, *A Modest Proposal: Agent Deregulation,* 7 Marquette Sports L J 361 (1997).

Other articles include Jeffrey P. Crandall, *The Agent-Athlete Relationship in Professional and Amateur Sports: The Inherent Potential for Abuse and the Need for Regulation,* 30 Buffalo L Rev 815 (1981); James J. Giulietti, *Agents of Professional Athletes,* 15 New England L Rev 545 (1980); Adam B. Nimoy & Jackson D. Hamilton, *Attorneys and the California Athlete Agencies Act: The Toll of the Bill,* 7 Hastings Comm & Ent L J 551 (1985); Miriam Benitez, *Of Sports, Agents, and Regulations—The Need for a Different Approach,* 3 Ent & L J 199 (1986); Craig Massey, *The Crystal Cruise Cut Short: A Survey of the Increasing Regulatory Influences over the Athlete-Agent in the National Football League,* 1 Ent & Sports L J 53 (1984); Len Elmore, *The Agent's Role in Professional Sports: An Athlete's Perspective,* 31 Boston Bar J 613 (1987); Gary Uberstine & Richard J. Grad, *Enforceability of Sports Contracts: A Practitioner's Playbook,* 7 Loyola Ent L J 1 (1987); Dana Alden Fox, *Regulating the Professional Sports Agent: Is California in the Right Ball Park?* 15 Pac L J 1231 (1984); Gary Kohn, *Sports Agents Representing Professional Athletes: Being Certified Means Never Having to Say You're Qualified,* 6 Ent & Sports Lawyer 1 (Winter 1988); Lori J. Lefferts, *The NFL Players Association's Agent Certification Plan: Is It Exempt from Antitrust Review?* 26 Arizona L Rev 699 (1984); Lloyd Z. Remick & David S. Eisen, *The Personal Manager in the Entertainment and Sports Industries,* 3 Ent & Sports L J 57 (1986); Gary Roberts, *Protecting the College Athlete from Unscrupulous Agents,* 5 Sports Lawyer 8 (Fall 1987); Lionel Sobel, *The Regulation of Sports Agents: An*

Analytical Primer, 39 Baylor L Rev 701 (1987); Michael J. Sullivan, *Remedying Athlete-Agent Abuse: A Securities Law Approach*, 2 Ent & Sports L J 53 (1984); Bill Winter, *Is the Sports Lawyer Getting Dunked? (Non-Lawyer Agents in Professional Sports)*, 66 ABA J 701 (June 1980); *Regulation of Sports Agents: Since at First It Hasn't Succeeded, Try Federal Legislation*, Sports Inc. 42 (May 30, 1988). *See also* John Weistart & C. Lowell, *The Law of Sports* § 3.17 (Michie, 1979).

41. Champion (cited in note 40).

42. *See, e.g.*, Bulkeley, *Sports Agents Help Athletes Win—and Keep—Those Super Salaries*, Wall Street Journal 31, § 2, col. 4 (March 25, 1985); HR Rep No 1786 at 71 (cited in note 26).

43. David Ware, Speech to the National Football League Players Association agent certification meeting, Washington, DC (April 19, 1989).

44. Abrahamson (cited in note 31).

45. Hruby, Washington Times at B1 (cited in note 16)

46. Kent Somers, *NBA Example May Diminish Agents' Power*, Arizona Republic C1 (March 24, 1999).

47. Daniel Kaplan, *Lofty Mission or Signing Tool? IMG's Academy Develops Athletes, Facilities and Controversy*, SportsBusiness Journal 3, 42 (March 19–21, 2001).

48. David Falk, Speech at the Seton Hall Sports Law Symposium in Newark, NJ, (April 28, 1989).

49. Wayne Henniger, *Octagon Puts Together Many-sided Vick Strategy*, SportsBusiness Journal 13 (Sept. 17–23, 2001).

50. Interview of Reginald Wilkes (cited in note 3).

51. Telephone Interview of Edward V. King, Jr., September 3, 1989.

52. Interview of Merle Scott, November 1, 2000, Philadelphia, PA.

53. *Follow the Bouncing Basketball News, Question of the Day—Do NBA Draft Picks Need Agents*, Sports Business News, July 19, 2001. <http://www.sportsbusinessnews.com/basketball/index.asp?sStoryId=1451>.

54. Abrahamson (cited in note 31).

Chapter 3. Consolidation

1. *See, e.g.*, Liz Mullen, *Steinberg Case: Secret Agent's Tale*, SportsBusiness Journal 1 (June 18–24, 2001), (outlining the dispute between David Dunn and his former firm, Steinberg, Moorad and Dunn).

2. As of 1999–2000 season, the NBA, NFL, NHL and MLB are comprised of 29, 31, 28, and 30 teams, respectively. As of the 1989–90 seasons, these leagues contained 27, 28, 21, and 26 teams, respectively. The growth in the leagues over the past decade was 7.4 percent, 10.7 percent, 33.3 percent, and 15.4 percent, respectively. This data was compiled based on information obtained from the official website for each league.

3. Bob Woolf, *Agents on Campus*, in Richard Lapchick & John Slaughter, eds., *The Rules of the Game: Ethics in College Sport* 108 (Macmillan for the American Council of Education, 1989).

4. Telephone interviews with respective players' association representatives, (February 22, 2001).

5. Timothy Davis, Alfred D. Mathewson, and Kenneth L. Shropshire, eds., *Sports and the Law* 145 (Carolina Academic Press, 1999).

6. *Q & A: David Falk*, SportsBusiness Journal 30 (May 17–23, 1999).

7. Assante Corporation website, visited February 3, 2001, <http://www.assante.com/main/sportsEntertainment/>.

8. SFX website, visited February 3, 2001, <http://www.clearchannel.com/Entertainment/ent_sfxsg.php>.

9. Octagon website, visited February 5, 2001, <http://www.octagon.com/athlete_representation.html>.

10. Liz Mullen, *Assante Close to Deal with Hoops Agent Fegan,* SportsBusiness Journal 1, 47 (July 3–9, 2000).

11. News releases, *Assante Strengthens Athlete Representation with Purchase of Leading Basketball Agent,* Assante website, visited February 3, 2001. <http://www.assante.com/main/aboutAssante/press.cfm?nr_id+nr45.cfm>.

12. Peter Spiegel, *Flesh Peddlers Go Global,* Forbes 189 (March 9, 1998).

13. Richard Alm, *Some Small Sports Marketers Join Big Teams, Others Cherish Control,* Dallas Morning News (December 28, 1999).

14. *Id.*

15. *Id.*

16. Jim Sullivan, *When It Comes to Pop Concerts, He Is the Player,* Boston Globe N1 (May 16, 1999).

17. *eSuperstars.com Offers a Super Bowl Dream Come True,* Business Wire (December 15, 1999).

18. Michael F. Legg, *SFX Entertainment Company Update,* Prudential Securities Equity Research 4 (December 6, 1999).

19. *eSuperstars.com Offers a Super Bowl Dream Come True,* Business Wire (December) cited in note 17.

20. Richard Sandomir, *Sale of Agency Opens New Doors for Falk and Clients,* New York Times C-6 (May 6, 1998).

21. *SFX Shares Drop After Buying Streak Attracts Antitrust Scrutiny,* Dow Jones Business News (September 22, 1998).

22. Sandomir, New York Times at C-6 (cited in note 20).

23. Spiegel, Forbes at 189 (cited in note 12).

24. Patrick Haverson, *Shake-up Creates Powerful Players Agents,* Financial Times 14 (September 25, 1998).

25. Sandomir, New York Times at C-6 (cited in note 20).

26. *Id.*

27. *SFX Renames Agents' Business,* Associated Press (December 13, 1999).

28. *SFX Steals the NBA Draft,* Sports Business News, visited August 30, 2001, http://www.sportsbusinessnews.com/basketball/index.asp?sStoryId=989.

29. Liz Mullen, *Falk-Tellem Combo Trumpets NBA Draft Day Numbers for SFX Sports,* SportsBusiness Journal 21 (July 24–30, 2000).

30. *Id.*

31. *SFX Entertainment Acquires SME,* Business Wire (November 24, 1999).

32. Liz Mullen, *SFX Buys Golf Agency Signature,* SportsBusiness Journal 41 (July 2–8, 2001).

33. Mark Fainaru-Wada & Ron Kroichick, *Agents of Influence,* San Francisco Chronicle C1 (March 11, 2001).

34. Bryan Burwell & Liz Mullen, *SFX: Falk Nearly Walked,* SportsBusiness Journal 4, 43 (April 23–29, 2001).

35. E. Scott Reckard, *Steinberg to Sell Firm for $120 Million,* Los Angeles Times C-1 (October 28, 1999).

36. Kevin Dougherty, *DPM Now Part of Assante,* Montreal Gazette D-2 (January 13, 2000).

37. Interview of Rand Sacks, January 20, 1999, Philadelphia, PA.

38. Reckard, Los Angeles Times at C-1 (cited in note 35).

39. *Id.* at C-1.

40. *Id.*

41. Assante website, "Assante strengthens athlete representation with purchase of leading basketball agent," visited February 3, 2001, <http://www.assante.com/main/aboutAssante/press.cfm?nr_id=nr45.cfm>.

42. *Id.*

43. *Id.*

44. Spiegel, Forbes at 189 (cited in note 12).

45. *Id.* at 189.

46. Alm, Dallas Morning News (cited in note 13).

47. Fainaru-Wada & Kroichick, San Francisco Chronicle at C1 (cited in note 33); Liz Mullen, *Final Score from NFL Draft Day's First Round: IMG 6, Assante 5,* SportsBusiness Journal 22 (April 31–May 6, 2001).

48. Michael J. Pachuta, *Interpublic Sees Acquisitions,* Global Rebound Aiding Sales, Investor's Business Daily A-22 (June 1, 1999).

49. *Id.* at A-22.

50. *Id.*

51. Andrew Ross Sorking, *Some Reshuffling in Sports Marketing,* New York Times D-7 (February 12, 1998).

52. *Interpublic's Offer for Brands Hatch Declared Unconditional,* PR Newswire (December 1, 1999).

53. Stuart Elliot, *Lowe Group Creates the Octagon Brand,* New York Times C-11 (September 27, 1999).

54. *Octagon Announces Unification of Group Branding,* Business Wire (September 27, 1999).

55. *Id.*

56. *Octagon Announces Major Move in Golf Representation Through Partnership with Pros Inc.,* Business Wire (March 3, 1999).

57. *Octagon Announces Unification of Group Branding* (cited in note 54).

58. Liz Mullen, *Octagon's NFL Buy Fills Out the Ticket,* SportsBusiness Journal 9 (December 18–24, 2000).

59. *Octagon Solidifies Baseball Unit with Woolf Associates Baseball Acquisition,* visited February 3, 2001, <http//:www.octagon.com/001214_woolf.html>.

60. Liz Mullen, *Octagon Pushes Its Boundaries with Carlisle Sports Acquisition,* SportsBusiness Journal 10 (August 27–September 2, 2001).

61. Liz Mullen, *And 1 Signs Isaiah Rider; Wilhelmina Corners Golfer Kuchar,* SportsBusiness Journal 15 (November 27–December 3, 2000).

62. Liz Mullen, *George Looks to Wilhelmina for Face Time,* SportsBusiness Journal 5 (January 1–27, 2002).

63. Liz Mullen, *With Marbury Signing, Wilhelmina Becoming Fashionable in Sports World,* SportsBusiness Journal 21 (September 25–October 1, 2000).

64. *Id.*

65. Liz Mullen, *Hollywood Connection Changes the Game for Agents,* SportsBusiness Journal 1, 46 (August 16–22, 1999).

66. *Id.*

67. Liz Mullen, *NHL Union Also Worried About Old Setup at SFX, Source Says,* SportsBusiness Journal 15 (January 8–14, 2001).

68. *Id.*

69. *Josh Gotthelf, SFX Deal Would Link Tellem, Falk*, SportsBusiness Journal 1, 46 (August 23–29, 1999).

Chapter 4. The Basics

1. *Q & A: David Falk*, Sports Business Journal 30, 31 (May 17–23, 1999).
2. Robert H. Ruxin, *An Athlete's Guide to Agents* 34 (Stephen Greene, 1989) ("*Athlete's Guide*").
3. Interview of Dr. Michael Jackson, September 11, 1989 in Philadelphia, PA.
4. Bucky Woy, *Sign 'em Up Bucky: The Adventures of a Sports Agent* 46 (Hawthorn, 1975).
5. Bob Woolf, *Behind Closed Doors* 300 (New American Library, 1976).
6. Edward V. King, Jr., *Agents: Do They Help or Hurt the Athlete? Dependency Leads to Abuse*, New York Times S-9, col. 2 (March 5, 1989).
7. Agents generally charge athletes on a percentage basis. The rate varies, but for contract negotiations it is generally less than 5 percent. *See also* George W. Schubert, Rodney K. Smith, & Jess C. Trentadue, *Sports Law* 30 (West, 1986), which notes that flat-rate fees or some combination may be used.
8. National Collegiate Athletic Association, *A Career in Professional Sports: Guidelines That Make Dollars and Sense* 6 (NCAA, 1984) ("*Guidelines*").
9. Powers, *Coaches, Athletes Are Artful Hustlers, Too*, Sporting News 12 (November 16, 1987).
10. Lawrence Taylor & David Falkner, *L.T. Living on the Edge* 74 (Warner, 1987).
11. Richard B. Schmitt, *Suit Spotlights Changed World of Sports Agents*, Wall Street Journal B1–6 (December 15, 1999).
12. Bruce Selcraig, *The Deal Went Sour*, Sports Illustrated 32 (September 15, 1988).
13. John Bannon, *Ex-Agent: "No Clean Programs,"* USA Today C-1, col. 4 (December 17, 1987).
14. *Guidelines* at 4 (cited in note 8).
15. Jack McCallum & Richard O'Brien, *Singled Out*, Sports Illustrated 18 (July 25, 1994).
16. Earl Gustkey, *Riding Out the Storm*, Los Angeles Times C1 (August 14, 1996).
17. Craig Neff, *Agents of Turmoil*, Sports Illustrated 36 (August 3, 1987).
18. Michael O'Keefe, *Show Them the Trouble: Players Stuck in the Middle as NCAA Attacks Agents*, New York Daily News 69 (March 5, 2000).
19. *Ex Agent for Enis Banned for 2 Years*, New York Times D-7 (October 23, 1998).
20. Craig Neff, *In Hot and Heavy Pursuit*, Sports Illustrated 84, 85 (October 19, 1987).
21. *Agent's Arrest Ordered by Judge*, Atlanta Journal Constitution 9 (September 1, 1999).
22. *Agent: Players' Contracts Had Bonuses of $75 to $100*, USA Today 9-C, col. 2 (December 16, 1987).
23. *Id.*
24. *Bloom v Harmon*, No. 11059-014 (1987) (Culver, Arb.) at 2.
25. *Id.* at 5.

26. *See* John Gorman, *Sports Agent Case Puts Iowa on Trial, Too,* Chicago Tribune § 4, p. 9, col. 1 (March 8, 1989).

27. Brian Bosworth with Rick Reilly, *The Boz: Confessions of a Modern Antihero* 229 (Charter, 1989).

28. *See* Danny Robbins and Manny Topol, *Influence on the Bench,* Newsday 5 (April 3, 1988).

29. *Id.*

30. L. Jon Wertheim, *Web of Deceit,* Sports Illustrated 80 (May 29, 2000)

31. Michael O'Keefe, *Show Them the Trouble: Players Stuck in Middle as NCAA Attacks Agents,* New York Daily News 69 (March 5, 2000).

32. *Id.*

33. Maryanne Hudson & Elliott Almond, *They Play by Their Own Rules: Colleges: Sports Agents Are Everywhere, and the NCAA Estimates 70% of Current Athletes Have Had Contact with Them,* Los Angeles Times C1 (October 13, 1995).

34. Michael O'Keefe, *This Piggie Went to Jail: Street Agent Awaits Sentencing for Sins Many Have Committed,* New York Daily News 94 (January 21, 2001); *Piggie Sentenced,* http://sportsillustrated.cnn.com/basketball/college/news/2001/05/30/piggie_sentencing_ap/.

35. John Gorman, *"Agent Threatened Me": Bears' Douglass,* Chicago Tribune § 4, p. 1, col. 3 (March 16, 1989).

36. *Id.*

37. *Id.*

38. *See* Ruxin, *Athlete's Guide* at 35–40 (cited in note 2), which outlines the procedure used by UCLA athletes.

39. Phil Taylor & Don Yaeger, *Tangled Web: Marcus Camby was Both Victim and Villain in His Illicit Dealings with Agents While at UMass,* Sports Illustrated 66 (September 15, 1997).

40. *Id.*

41. *Id.*

42. Rick Hornung, *Hoop Schemes: Toronto Raptors Basketball Player Marcus Camby,* Saturday Night 69 (February 1998).

43. *Id.*

44. *Id.*

45. *Id.*

46. *Id.*

47. *Id.*

48. Dan Shaughnessy, *Regrettably, Camby Expresses No More Regrets,* Boston Globe G1 (November 15, 1997).

49. *Lounsbury Penalized,* Boston Globe F2 (December 3, 1997).

50. Steve Fiffer, *Two Sports Agents Convicted of Fraud and Racketeering,* New York Times A–1, col. 1, A–31, col. 2 (April 14, 1989).

51. Ruxin, *Athlete's Guide* at 29 (cited in note 2).

52. Kenneth L. Shropshire, *In Black and White: Race and Sports in America,* ch 6 (New York University Press 1996); James G. Sammataro, *Business and Brotherhood, Can They Coincide? A Search into Why Black Athletes Do Not Hire Black Agents,* 42 Howard L J 535 (Spring 1999)

53. See the story recounted in Barry Cooper, *Black Sports Agents Beat Odds with Top Clients,* New Pittsburgh Courier A10 (July 13, 1994).

54. Quoted in Phillip M. Hoose, *Necessities: Racial Barriers in American Sports* 29 (Random House, 1989).

55. Interview of William Strickland, May 17, 2001, Philadelphia, PA.

56. Dan Weil, *For Longtime Partners, Teamwork Pays on the Court, at the Office,* SportsBusiness Journal 24, 25 (February 24–25, 2000).

57. *Id.* at 25.

58. *By the Numbers 2002,* SportsBusiness Journal 55, December 31, 2001.

59. Weil, *For Longtime Partners* at 25 (cited in note 56).

60. Liz Mullen, *Women Agents? So Far, Only a Handful,* SportsBusiness Journal (October 12, 1998), visited May 2, 2002, http://www.sportsbusinessjournal. com/article.cms?articleId=19126&s=1.

61. *Id.*

62. *Id.*

63. Telephone interview with Wendi Huntley, March 28, 2002.

64. *Id.*

65. Mullen (cited in note 1).

66. *Id.* (quoting the comments of Linda Joplin, who at the time of the report was the chair of the California National Organization for Women's Gender Equity Committee).

67. Huntley interview (cited in note 63).

68. Michael O'Keefe, *Show Them the Trouble: Players Stuck in Middle As NCAA Attacks Agents,* New York Daily News 69 (March 5, 2000).

69. Mike Freeman, *Pro Football: Protecting Players from Their Agents,* New York Times § 8, p. 1 (July 26, 1998).

70. Joan M. O'Connell & Brenton Welling, *How Leigh Steinberg Rises Above His "Sleazoid Profession,"* Business Week 62 (January 14, 1985).

71. Lee Smith, *Scott Boras Saves Baseball,* Men's Journal 86 (April 2001).

72. *Id.* at 89.

73. *Id.*

74. Len Elmore, *Turn Out the Lights, Agents' Party Is Over,* SportsBusiness Journal 54 (July 9–16, 2001).

75. David Ware, Speech to the National Football League Players Association agent certification meeting, Washinton DC (April 19, 1989)

76. John Culver, Speech to the Sports Lawyers Association in Washington, DC (May 12, 1989).

77. Bob Woolf, *Agents on Campus,* in R. Lapchick & J. Slaughter, eds., *The Rules of the Game: Ethics in College Sport* 108 (Macmillan for the American Council of Education, 1989).

78. Ware, Speech (cited in note 75).

79. Interview of Stanley O. King, March 15, 2001 in Philadelphia, PA.

80. Transcript of Interview of Kevin Robinson, May 17, 2001, at 2.

81. *Id.* at 4.

82. *Id.* at 6.

83. *Id.* at 4.

84. Freeman, New York Times (cited in note 69).

Chapter 5. Unscrupulous and Criminal

1. Fla Stat § 468.45 (West Supp 1990).

2. See Chapter 4.

3. See Chapter 11.

4. Craig Neff, *Den of Vipers,* Sports Illustrated 76 (October 19, 1987).

5. Bobby Clay, *Black Agents Compete for Blue Chip Athletes,* Black Enterprise, July 1992, at 54.

6. Melissa Isaacson, *New Villain: Financial Adviser,* Chicago Tribune (March 5, 2000).

7. *Id*. at 36.

8. *Id*.

9. Edward T. Pound & Douglas Pasternak, *Money Player: How Some of the NFL's Biggest Stars Got Taken for Millions,* at 30 (February 11, 2002).

10. *Id*. at 33.

11. ¶1, Complaint, *Securities and Exchange Commission v. Donald D. Lukens.*

12. ¶2. Complaint.

13. *Id*. at 8, ¶20.

14. Pound & Pasternak, at 31 (cited in note 9)

15. *Id*. at 30.

16. ¶1, Complaint, *Securities and Exchange Commission v. Dunyasha M. Yetts, et al.*

17. *Id*., at ¶¶10 and 11.

18. *Id*.

19. *Id*., at ¶¶18.

20. Pound & Pasternak, at 35 (cited in note 9).

21. *Id*. at 36.

22. *Id*.

23. Bob Cohn, *Caught in the Con Game,* The Washington Times (October 10, 2001), at C1.

24. Pound & Pasternak, at 30 (cited in note 9).

25. *Id*. at 32.

26. *Id*. at 34.

27. *Id*. at 32.

28. For the most complete discussion on this case prior to adjudication, *see* L. Jon Wertheim, *Web of Deceit,* Sports Illustrated 80 (May 29, 2000).

29. *Id*.

30. *Id*.

31. *Id*.

32. *Tank Black Ordered to Prison on Money-Laundering Case,* Chattanooga Times D6 (June 15, 2001).

33. See *Former NFL Agent "Tank" Black Pleads Guilty to Money Laundering,* visited January 17, 2001, <http://www.cbs.sportsline.com/u/wire/stories.0,11 69,3373398_59,00.html.

34. Judy Mathewson, *NFL Former Agent "Tank" Black Conspired to Defraud, Jury Says,* Bloomberg News (February 12, 2002).

35. " 'Tank' Black sentenced for money-laundering." <http://www.fox sports.com/nfl/home/nfl_news.cfm?cont-_id=17837&table_name=ap_cont_ text&table_cd=a&>.

36. David Newton, *High-profile Stars Defrauded, Indictment Says,* The State (Lexis January 11, 2001).

37. *Id*.

38. Michael Goodwin & Sam Goldaper, *Enmeshed in a Tangled Web,* New York Times § 5, p. 1, col. 2 (March 15, 1987); Greg Papanek, *A Lot of Hurt,* Sports Illustrated 89 (October 19, 1987).

39. Tom Collins, Address to the Sports Lawyers Association (May 5, 1990).

40. See William Nack, *Thrown for Heavy Losses*, Sports Illustrated 40, 41 (March 24, 1986).

41. *Id.*

42. *Rodri Faces Lawsuits as Investments Fail*, Sports Industry News 182 (May 22, 1987).

43. *Kelly Is Suing His Former Agents*, New York Times D-20, col. 1 (April 27, 1989).

44. Stacey M. Nahrwold, *Are Professional Athletes Better Served by a Lawyer-Representative Than an Agent? Ask Grant Hill*, 9 Seton Hall J Sport L 431, 433 (1999) (citations omitted).

45. Steve Fiffer, *Money Misspent, Witness Says*, New York Times B-11, co. 5 (March 24, 1989).

46. *Id.*

47. *United States v Marion Darnell Jones, James E. Brown, Willie Williams, Jr. and Andre Lewis*, Indictment, Criminal No 3701-114 (US Dist Ct, D SC January 10, 2001).

48. Newton, The State (cited in note 36).

49. *United States v Marion Darnell Jones, James E. Brown, Willie Williams, Jr. and Andre Lewis*, Indictment, Criminal No. 3701-114 (US Dist Ct, D SC January 10, 2001).

50. *Id.* Newton (cited in note 36).

51. *Four Plead Innocent in Alleged Scheme to Defraud Athletes*, The Herald, Rock Hill 2B (January 26, 2001).

52. Don Dronin, *Carruth's Lawyers Goes on Offensive*, USA Today 11C (November 29, 2000).

53. *Rios Out for 2-3 Months Because of Ankle Injury*, Los Angeles Times part 4, p. 7 (June 19, 2001).

54. *Adviser to the Stars Gets 12 Years*, Sporting News 35 (January 23, 1989).

55. *Id.*

56. *People v. Sorkin*, 407 NY S 2d 772 (App. Div 1978) and Pete Axthelm. *The Guy with the Edge*, Newsweek (October 3, 1977), at 57.

57. *Id.*

58. *Id.*

59. *Baseball Notebook*, Dayton Daily News 3D (February 2, 2001).

60. Newton, The State (cited in note 36).

61. *Wilson Wins*, Associated Press (February 1, 2001).

62. *Id.*

63 Mike Dodd, *Madlock's Ex-agent Claims Legal Victory*, USA Today 6C (August 7, 1991).

64. *Greenberg's Side of the Madlock Suit*, Sporting News 13 (September 2, 1991).

65. Dodd, USA Today at 6C (cited in note 63).

66. *Hernandez v Childers*, 806 F Supp 1368 (ED Ill 1992). Other cases involving alleged mismanagement resulting in tax problems for athletes include *Wilson v Commissioner of Internal Revenue*, 1995 WL 649897; *Willoughby v Commissioner of Internal Revenue*, 1994 WL 444427.

67. *Hilliard v Black*, 125 F Supp 2d 1071, 1074 (ND Fla 2000).

68. *Id.* at 1073.

69. *Williams v CWI, Inc.*, 777 F Supp 1006 (DC 1991).

70. *Id.* at 1007.

71. *Id.*

72. *See Willoughby,* 1994 WL 444427 (US Tax Ct) (cited in note 66) for a discussion of the player's case against his agent.

73. *Blatt v Farley,* 276 Cal Rptr 612 (1990).

74. 973 SW2d 348 (Tex App 1999), submitted October 16, 1997; opinion delivered June 25, 1998.

75. *Terrell v Childers,* 920 F Supp 854 (ND Ill 1996).

76. *Blatt,* 276 Cal Rptr 612 (cited in note 73).

77. *Clark v Weisberg,* 1999 US Dist LEXIS 11341 (ND Ill 1999).

78. *Id.* at 4.

79. *Clark v Robert W. Baird Co., Inc.,* 2001 US Dist Lexis 6275 (ND Ill 2001).

80. Jill Lieber, *And One Who Prospered,* Sports Illustrated 96 (October 19, 1987); Earl C. Gottschalk Sr., *Orel Hershiser Sees a Lot of Pitches Related to Money,* Wall Street Journal p. 1, col. 4 (March 15, 1989).

81. *Brown v Woolf,* 554 F Supp 1206 (SD Ind 1983).

82. *Id.* at 1207.

83. *Id.*

84. *NFLPA Regulations Governing Contract Advisors,* § 4: Agreements Between Contract Advisors and Players; Maximum Fees, p. 9.

85. *Id.* at § 4(B)(3), p. 10.

86. Martin J. Greenberg & James T. Gray, Sports Law Practice, 2d ed. (Lexis, 1998) at 975.

87. *NFLPA Regulations Governing Contract Advisors,* § 4(B)(4), p. 10.

88. *Id.*

89. *MLBPA Regulations Governing Player Agents,* § 4(F).

Chapter 6. Conflicts of Interest

1. See Chapter 1.

2. Leonard Lakin & Martin Schiff, *The Law of Agency* 97 (Kendall/Hunt, 2d ed. 1996).

3. *Id.* at 27.

4. *Reggie White's $1.5 Million Suit,* Sports Industry News 229, (July 28, 1989). The suit served as leverage in White's bid for a contract renegotiation.

5. Ron Borges & Larry Tye, *Patriots VP Faces Charges,* Boston Globe, April 4, 1992.

6. *Detroit Lions, Inc. v Argovitz,* 580 F Supp 542 (ED Mich 1984).

7. *Id.* at 546.

8. *Id.* at 547.

9. *Detroit Lions,* 580 F Supp at 547–48; *see generally,* Lakin & Schiff, The Law of Agency at 98 (cited in note 2).

10. Glen Macnow, *Chief of NHL Union Is on Thin Ice,* Philadelphia Inquirer, D-1, col. 1 (July 16, 1989).

11. Craig Neff, *Den of Vipers,* Sports Illustrated 84 (October 19, 1987).

12. This hypothetical is based on a situation involving athletes who played for the Kansas Royals major league baseball team in 1981. It is discussed in Jamie E. Brown, *The Battle the Fans Never See: Conflicts of Interest for Sports Lawyers,* Note, 7 Georgetown J of Legal Ethics, 813 (1994).

13. *Id.* at 817.

14. *Id.*

15. Rob Remis, *Analysis of Civil and Criminal Penalties in Athlete Agent Statutes and Support for the Imposition of Civil and Criminal Liability Upon Athletes*, 8 Seton Hall of Sports L1, 31 n. 121 (1998).

16. Brown, at 813 (cited in note 12).

17. Restatement (Second) Agency § 387 (1958).

18. *NBPA Regulations Governing Player Agents* 5–6 (as amended June 1991).

19. *MLBPA Regulations Governing Player Agents*, in Martin J. Greenberg & James T. Gray, Sports Law Practice 943–44 (2d ed. 1998).

20. Andy Bernstein, *IMG Cuts Ties to NHL After Conflict Alleged*, SportsBusiness Journal 1, 41 (April 16–22, 2001).

21. *Id.*

22. Andy Bernstein, *Structure Still Shifting at SFX*, SportsBusiness Journal 10, (June 4–10), 2001.

23. Liz Mullen, *Union Attorneys Giving SFX's New Baseball Company a Good Going-over*, SportsBusiness Journal 19 (April 9–15, 2001).

24. Liz Mullen, *Fired Agents Blame Losses on SFX Merger*, SportBusiness Journal 1, 31 (February 12–18 2001).

25. Mark Ynman & Skip Rozin, *Sparks Fly at SFX*, Business Week 68 A4 (June 25, 2001).

26. See Jack McCallum, *I Own You*, Sports Illustrated 50 (February 14, 2000).

27. *NBPA Regulations Governing Player Agents* 5–6 (as amended June 1991).

Chapter 7. Ethics

1. Walter T. Champion, *Attorneys qua Sports Agents: An Ethical Conundrum*, 7 Marquette Sports L J 349, 359 (1997).

2. Robert E. Fraley & F. Russell Harwell, *Ethics and the Sports Lawyer: A Comprehensive Approach*, 13 J of the Legal Profession, 9, 53 (1988).

3. *Id.*

4. Comment, *The Agent-Athlete Relationship in Professional and Amateur Sports: The Inherent Potential for Abuse and the Need for Regulation*, 30 Buffalo L Rev 815, 823, n. 37 (1981).

5. John A. Walton, *Conflicts for Sports and Entertainment Attorneys: The Good News, the Bad News and the Ugly Consequences*, 5 Villanova Sports & Ent L J 259, 261 (1998).

6. *Id.* at 264.

7. *Id.* at 261.

8. *Id.* at 263.

9. Fraley & Harwell, 13 J Legal Prof at 74–75 (cited in note 2).

10. Walton, 5 Villanova Sports & Ent L J at 273 (cited in note 5).

11. Annotated Model Rules Rule 1.7 (commentary at 11) (1983).

12. Fraley & Harwell, 13 J Legal Prof at 73–74 (cited in note 2).

13. *NBPA Regulations Governing Player Agents* 5–6 (as amended June 1991).

14. Fraley & Harwell, 13 J Legal Prof at 74–76 (cited in note 2).

15. Jamie E. Brown, *The Battle the Fans Never See: Conflicts of Interest for Sports Lawyers*, 7 Georgetown J Legal Ethics, 813, 818, (1994).

16. Walton, 5 Villanova Sports & Ent L J at 263 (cited in note 5).

17. *Detroit Lions, Inc. v Argovitz*, 580 F Supp 542 (ED Mich 1984).

18. *Id.* at 548.

19. *Id.*

20. John C. Weistart & Cym H. Lowell, The Law of Sports 53 (1985 Supplement).

21. *Id.* at § 3.19, at Supp. 53 (1985).

22. Fraley & Harwell, 13 *J of Legal Prof* at 19 n. 23 (cited in note 2).

23. *Id.* at 19 n. 24.

24. ISBA Advisory Opinion on Professional Conduct, Opinion No. 700 (November 4, 1980).

25. *Cuyahoga County Bar Association v. Glenn,* 649 NE2d 1213 (Ohio 1995).

26. *In the Matter of Fredrick J. Henley, Jr.* 478 SE2d 134 (Ga 1996).

27. Paul T. Dee, *Ethical Aspects of Representing Professional Athletes,* 3 Marquette Sports L J 111, 113 (1992).

28. In the Matter of a Member of the State Bar of Arizona, James J. Dwight. 573 P2d 481 (Ariz 1977).

29. *Id.* at 484.

30. *Id.*

31. *Kelly v State Bar,* 808 P2d 808 (Cal 1991).

32. *Id.* at 517.

33. *Id.*

34. *In re Pappas,* 768 P2d 1161, 1166 (Ariz 1988).

35. Michael A. Weiss, *The Regulation of Sports Agents: Fact or Fiction?* 1 Sports L J 329, 349 (1994); Curtis D. Rypma, Note, *Sports Agents Representing Athletes: The Need for Comprehensive State Legislation,* 24 Valparaiso Univ L Rev 481, 407 (1990).

36. Fraley & Harwell, J Legal Prof at 41–42 (cited in note 2).

37. *In the Matter of the Application of Steven B. Jackman for Admission to the Bar,* 761 A2d 1103, 1106 (NJ 2000).

38. *Id.*

39. *Birbrower, Montalbano, Condon & Frank P.C. v The Superior Court of Santa Clara County,* 949 P2d 1 (Cal 1998).

40. *Id.* at 6.

41. ISBA Advisory Opinion on Professional Conduct, Opinion No. 700 (November 4, 1980).

42. Model Rules of Professional Conduct, Rule 7.3(a).

Chapter 8. Agent Wars

1. Leonard Lakin & Martin Schiff, *The Law of Agency* at 101 (Kendall/Hunt, 2d ed 1996).

2. *Id.*

3. Mike Freeman, *Pro Football, Protecting Players from Their Agents,* New York Times § 8, p. 1 (July 26, 1998).

4. *Gandler v Nazarov,* 1995 WL 363814 (SDNY).

5. *Id.*

6. 898 SW2d 98 (Mo Ct App 1995).

7. Lakin & Schiff, *The Law of Agency* at 109 (cited in note 1).

8. *Id.* at 124.

9. *Id.*

10. *Zinn v Parrish,* 644 F2d 360 (7th Cir 1981).

11. *Id*. at 361.

12. *Id*. at 362.

13. *Id*. at 364.

14. *Id*. at 366.

15. *Athletes and Artists, Inc. v Millen*, 1999 US Dist LEXIS 11991 (SDNY).

16. *Id*. at 16.

17. *Id*. at 8.

18 National Football League Players Standard Representation Agreement § 12.

19. *Id*.

20. *Pro Tect Management Corp. v Worley*, 1991 US Dist LEXIS 13058 (SDNY).

21. *Speakers of Sports, Inc. v ProServ, Inc.*, 178 F3d 862 (7th Cir 1999).

22. *Id*. at 864.

23. *Id*.

24. *Id*. at 865.

25. *Wright v Bonds*, 117 F3d 1427, 1997 US App LEXIS 24340 (9th Cir 1997) (unpublished opinion).

26. Bryan Couch, *How Agent Competition and Corruption Affects Sports and the Athlete-Agent Relationship and What Can be Done to Control It*, 10 Seton Hall J Sport L 111, 119 (2000). Other examples of allegations by an agent that another agent improperly interfered with his or her client include *Roundball Enterprises, Inc. v Richardson*, 616 F Supp 1537 (SDNY 1985) (sports representation firm alleged that agent Patrick Healy improperly persuaded basketball player Michael Ray Richardson to terminate his contract with Roundball and sign a representation agreement with Healy's sports management firm).

27. *Manton v California Sports, Inc.*, 493 F Supp 496 (ND Ga 1980).

28. *Faigin v Kelly*, 184 F3d 67, 74 (1st Cir 1999).

29. *Id*. at 73.

30. *Id*. at 74.

31. *Weinberg v Silber*, 140 F Supp 2d 712 (ND Tex 2001).

32. *Jacobs v ProSports Management of the South, Inc.*, 243 BR 836, 845 (MD Fla 2000).

33 Liz Mullen, *Steinberg Case: Secret Agent's Tale*, SportsBusiness Journal 1 (June 18–24, 2001).

34. Liz Mullen, *Agent Lawsuit File Kept Open*, SportsBusiness Journal 6 (July 16–22, 2001).

35. *Id*.

36. *See* Liz Mullen, *Union Claims Role in Agency Lawsuit*, SportsBusiness Journal 1 (July 9–15, 2001).

37. *Id*. at 52.

38. Liz Mullen, *Restraining Order Issued Against Dunn*, SportsBusiness Journal 42 (August 20–26, 2001).

39. Liz Mullen, *21 Players Back Dunn in Fight with Steinberg*, SportsBusiness Journal 3 (Aug. 27–Sept. 2, 2001).

Chapter 9. The Last Amateurs on Earth

1. David C. Young, *The Olympic Myth of Greek Amateur Athletics* 7 (Ares, 1985). For a critical view of the amateurism ideal in intercollegiate athletics *see* Walter

Byers, *Unsportsmanlike Conduct: Exploiting College Athletes* (Univ. of Michigan Press, 1995). Byers served as executive director of the NCAA from 1951 to 1987. Another critical assessment of the incorporation of the amateur ideal into American intercollegiate athletics as manifested in the NCAA regulatory system can be found in Allen L. Sack & Ellen J. Staurowsky, *College Athletes for Hire: The Evolution and Legacy of the NCAA's Amateur Myth* (Praeger, 1998).

2. John C. Weistart & Cym H. Lowell, *The Law of Sports* p. 7, § 1.04 (Michie, 1979).

3. National Collegiate Athletic Association, 2000–2001 Manual art. 2.9 [hereinafter NCAA Manual].

4. NCAA Manual art. 12.1.1(a)–(f).

5. Weistart & Lowell, *The Law of Sports* at 7, § 1.04 (cited in note 2).

6. NCAA Manual art. 12.1.1(a) & (b).

7. Howard J. Savage, *American College Athletics* (Carnegie Foundation for the Advancement of Teaching, 1929).

8. *Id.* at 34.

9. Young, *Olympic Myth* at 7 (cited in note 1).

10. *Id.* at 1. Young notes later that in a single running event the winner received enough money to buy six or seven slaves, one hundred sheep, or three houses. *Id.* at 127.

11. *Id.* at 7.

12. Eugene A. Glader, *Amateurism and Athletics* (Leisure Press, 1978).

13 Young, *Olympic Myth* at 7 (cited in note 1).

14. *Id.* at 8.

15. *Id.*

16. *Id.* at 9, n. 3. Young maintains further that this was not, in fact, the first revival of the Olympics. He writes that as early as 1870 a modern Olympiad took place in Athens and cash prizes were awarded. *Id.* at 31.

17. *Id.* at 9.

18. *Id.* at 10.

19. *Id.* at 9.

20. *Id.* at 12.

21. *Id.* at 12–13.

22. *Id. at* 13.

23. *Id.* at 14.

24 Marc Pachter, *Champions of American Sport* 195 (Abrams, 1981).

25. *Id.*

26. Young, *Olympic Myth* at. 87 n. 84 (cited in note 1).

27. *Id.* at 86, citing Avery Brundage, "Why the Olympic Games?" in United States Olympic Committee, *Report: Games of the XI Vth Olympiad, London, England* 23ff. (1948).

28. Young, *Olympic Myth* at 87 n. 84 (cited in note 1).

29. *Id.*

30. *Id.* at 100, citing H. Hewitt Griftin, *Athletics* 13–14 (George Bell, 1891), and H. F. Wilkinson, *Modern Athletics* 16 (Frederick Warne, 1868).

31. Young, *Olympic Myth* at 19 (cited in note 1).

32. Glader, *Amateurism and Athletics* at 15 (cited in note 12); Ronald A. Smith, *Sports and Freedom: The Rise of Big-Time College Athletics* 166 (Oxford University Press, 1988).

33. Smith, *Sports and Freedom* at 166 (cited in note 32).

34. Glader, *Amateurism and Athletics* at 17 (cited in note 12).

35. Smith, *Sports and Freedom* at 165–66 (cited in note 32).

36. Savage, *American College Athletics* at 36 (cited in note 7).

37. Young, *Olympic Myth* at 22 (cited in note 1).

38. Smith, *Sports and Freedom* at 169 (cited in note 32), citing Alexander Agassiz, *Rowing Fifty Years Ago*, Harvard Graduates Magazine 458 (March 1907); Charles W. Eliot, *In Praise of Rowing*, 15 Harvard Graduates Magazine 532 (March 1907); and B. W. Crowninshield, "Boating," in F. O. Vaille and H. A. Clark, *The Harvard Book* vol. 2, p. 263 (Welch, Bigelow, 1875).

39. Smith, *Sports and Freedom* at 171 (cited in note 32).

40. *Id*. at 188.

41. *Id*.

42. *Id*.

43. *Id*. at 174.

44. Savage, *American College Athletics* at 42 (cited in note 7).

45. "Eligibility Rules," NCAA Constitution (1906), art. VII.

46. Paul Lawrence, *Unsportsmanlike Conduct: The National Collegiate Athletic Association and the Business of College Football* 24 (Praeger, 1987).

47. *Id*. at 43.

48. *Walters and Bloom v. Fullwood and Kickliter,* 675 F Supp 155 (SDNY 1987).

49. *Id*. at 163.

50. *National Collegiate Athletic Association v Board of Regents of the University of Oklahoma,* 468 US 85 (1984).

51. *Id*. at 96 (emphasis added).

52. *Gaines v NCAA,* 746 F Supp 738 (MD Tenn 1990).

53. *Id*. at 744 (emphasis added).

54. *Banks v NCAA,* 977 F2d 1081 (7th Cir 1991).

55. *Id*. at 1091 (emphasis added).

56. *Id*.

57. NCAA Manual art. 12.1.1.

58. NCAA Manual art. 12.1.1.1.1.

59. NCAA Manual art. 12.3.1.2.

60. NCAA Manual art. 12.1.1(f).

61. NCAA Manual art. 15.02.4.

62. NCAA Manual art. 15.02.4.

63. NCAA Manual art. 15.02.04.

64. NCAA Manual art. 15.02.4.

65. NCAA Manual art. 15.02.4(d).

Chapter 10. Knights of Columbus Rules?

1. Jack Falla, *NCAA: The Voice of College Sports* at 13 (NCAA, 1981).

2. Richard D. Schultz, Speech to Sports Lawyers Association, Washington, DC, (May 12, 1989).

3. 2000–01 NCAA Division I Manual, § 12.3.1 at 77.

4. *Id*.

5. Mike Sullivan & Craig Neff, *Shame on You, SMU,* Sports Illustrated 18 (March 19, 1987).

6. *$1.8 Million in Losses Faced by Kentucky Under Probation,* Sports Industry News 157 (May 26, 1989).

7. Schultz, Speech (citied in note 2).

8. NCAA, *Memorandum to Individuals Acting in the Capacity of Player Agents* (September 2, 1988) (hereafter cited as NCAA memorandum).

9. Mike Trope with Steve Delsohn, *Necessary Roughness* at 68 (Contemporary Books, 1987).

10. Bruce Selcraig, *Agents of Violence,* Sports Illustrated 25 (April 6, 1987).

11. Ben Brown, *Jury Selection Begins in Agents' Trial,* USA Today 1C, col. 2 (March 1, 1989).

12. Diana Sudia & Rob Remis, *The History Behind Athlete Agent Regulation and the "Slam Dunking of Statutory Hurdles,"* 8 Vill Sports & Ent L J 67, 72 (2001).

13. Schultz, Speech (cited in note 2).

14 29 USC § 141 *et seq.* (1982). For discussion of the applicability of the NLRA to sports, *see* Robert C. Berry, William B. Gould, & Paul D. Staudohar, *Labor Relations in Professional Sports* at 31–34 (Auburn House, 1986).

15. NFLPA Regulations Governing Contract Advisors (hereafter cited as NFLPA Regulations); MLBPA Regulations Governing Player Agents (hereafter MLBPA Regulations); and National Basketball Players Association Regulations Governing Player Agents (hereafter NBPA Regulations).

16. MLBPA Regulations at 3.

17. In 1988 the NBPA decertified one agent for improprieties and declared all basketball-related contracts negotiated by that agent void. *See Agent Has His Certification Suspended by NBA Union,* Philadelphia Inquirer E-5, col. 4 (May 31, 1988). Similarly, the *Philadelphia Inquirer* reported that the NFLPA had decertified a sports agent for alleged problems in "the handling of clients' funds." *See* Glen Macnow, *Becoming an Agent,* Philadelphia Inquirer A-12, col. 2 (August 23, 1987). Robert Ruxin also writes that the NFLPA refused to renew an agent's certification because he forged a power of attorney. *See* Robert H. Ruxin, *An Athlete's Guide to Agents* at 86 (Stephen Greene, 1989). The NFLPA maintains that confidential hearings have been held regarding other agents as well.

18. *Collins v National Basketball Players Association,* 850 F Supp 1468 (D Colo 1991).

19. *Collins v National Basketball Players Association,* 976 F2d 740 (10th Cir 1992) (unpublished opinion).

20. *Collins,* 850 F Supp 1468.

21. Lionel Sobel, *The Regulation of Sports Agents: An Analytical Primer,* 39 Baylor L Rev 727 (1987). The agreement is enforced with teams in collective bargaining agreements.

22. MLBPA Regulations at 2, citing 29 USC § 141 *et seq.* (1982).

23. *Id.* at 2, citing MLB Collective Bargaining Agreement, art. II.

24. *Id.* at 2, citing MLB Collective Bargaining Agreement, art. IV. One agent publicly decertified under the program was Jerry Kapstein, not for any improprieties but because he took a management position within the San Diego Padres organization. *Kapstein Decertified,* New York Times A-28, col. 2 (November 3, 1989). Gene Orza of the MLBPA noted that in the first nine months only one team had negotiated with an agent that was not certified, and in that case the team official admitted that negotiating with the uncertified agent had been unintentional. See Gene Orza, Speech to Sports Lawyers Association, Washington, DC, May 12, 1989.

25. 1992 US App LEXIS 24069 (10th Cir 1992) (unpublished opinion).

26. *Id.* at 7.

27. 87 F Supp 2d 1 (DDC 2000).

28. 92 F Supp 2d 918 (D Minn 2000).

29. *NFL Notes*, Washington Post, December 11, 1996.

30. *Id.*

31. D. Orlando Ledbetter, *Show Me the Clients*, Houston Chronicle, April 25, 1999.

32. *Id.* at 36.

33. Liz Mullen, *Tank Fires Back: Black Claims Players He Defrauded Owe Him Money*, SportsBusiness Journal (February 11, 2002).

34 Nate Allen, *Agent Resigns Under Pressure from NBA Players Association*, Mark's Sports Law News, www.sportslawnews.com/archive/Articles%202000/defaziodecert.htm (March 14, 2001).

35. Sobel, *Regulation of Sports Agents* at 732 (cited in note 21).

36. Doug Allen, Memorandum to NFLPA contract advisers, November 1988.

37. Sobel, *Regulation of Sports Agents* at 735 (cited in note 21).

38. Orza, Speech (cited in note 24).

39. NFLPA Regulations and Code of Conduct Governing Registered Player Financial Advisors 3 (2002).

40. Introduction, NFLPA Regulations and Code of Conduct Governing Registered Player Financial Advisors, at 2 (2002).

41. *Id.*

42. *Id.* at 5.

43. *Id.* at 8-9.

44. *Id.* at 9, § II(C)—Professional Qualifications.

45. *Id.* at 10, § II(D)—Legal Standing.

46. *Id.* at 10, § III(A)—Criminal Record.

47. *Id.* at 11, § III(D)—Civil Judgments.

48. *Id.* at 12, § III(I).

49. *Id.* at 13, § III(G).

50. *Id.* at 13, § IV

51 *Id.* at 14, § IV(B)(II).

52. *Id.* at 15 § IV(B)(II).

53. *Id.* at § II(D)—Insurance.

54. See Gene Rosenblatt, *Agent Interests: Can ARPA Do the Job?* Sports Inc. 98 (November 16, 1987).

Chapter 11. The Laws

1. Katherine Waugh, *Shake 'em Hard in the Sports Side*, National Law Journal 8 (April 3,1989).

2. Uniform Athlete Agents Act (2000).

3. 18 USC 1961 *et seq.* (1988).

4. John Gorman, *Lawyers Testify They Gave Lawyers Wrong Information*, Chicago Tribune § 4, p. 2, col. 5. March 30, 1989.

5. Waugh, National Law Journal at 8 (cited in note 1).

6. *Criminal Penalties Imposed in Agent Contract Case*, Sports Industry News 125 (April 28, 1989).

7. *Clark v Robert W. Baird, Co.*, 142 F Supp 2d 1065 (N D Ill 2001).

8. 18 F3d 899 (11th Cir 1994).

9. *Id.* at 914.

10. Robert H. Ruxin, *An Athlete's Guide to Agents,* 90 (Stephen Greene, 1989).

11. Glenn Burleigh, *Sports Law and Representation: More Agents Than Players in Lucrative Field?* 133 Chicago Daily Law Bulletin (October 7, 1987). See, e.g., Robert C. Berry, William B. Gould, and Paul D. Stadohar, *Labor Relations in Professional Sports* at 255–56 (Auburn House, 1986), which notes that, regarding franchise relocations, "Congress will not at length do nothing and leave the disposition of the antitrust problems to the courts under existing law."

12. Bill Sing, *Despite Reforms, Abuses Still Suspected on Wall St.,* Los Angeles Times, p. 1, col. 3 (December 24, 1988).

13. *Former Agent Convicted,* New York Times, B-87, col. 6 (March 2, 1978); *Abernethy v State,* 545 So 2d 185 (Ala Crim App 1988).

14. See discussion in Chapter 5.

15. *Ala Code* §§ 8-26-1 to –41 (2000); *Ariz Rev Stat* §§ 15-1761 to –1765 (2000); *Ark Code Ann* §§ 17-16-101 to –207 (Lexis 1999); *Cal Bus & Prof Code* §§ 6106.7, 18895 to 18897.97 (West 2000); *Colo Rev Stat Ann* §§ 23-16-101 to –108 (2000); *Conn Gen Stat.* §§ 20-553 to -569 (1999); *Fla Stat Ann* §§ 468.451 to .457 (West 2001); *Ga Code Ann* §§ 43-4A-3 to -20 (Supp 2001); *Ind Code Ann* §§ 35-46-4-1 to -4 (1998); *Iowa Code Ann* § 9A.1 to .12 (1995); *Kan Stat Ann* §§ 44-1501 to -1515 (2000); *Ky Rev Stat Ann* §§ 164.680–.689 (Michie 1999); *La Rev Stat Ann* §§ 4.420-433 (West 2001); *Md Code Ann Bus Reg* 4-401 to -426 (1999); *Mich Comp Laws* § 750.411e (Lexis 2001); *Minn Stat* § 325E.33 (1995); Miss *Code Ann* §§ 73-41-1 to -23 (2000); *Mo Rev Stat* §§ 317.018, 436.200 – .212 (Supp 2001); *New Rev Stat* 398.065 – .255 (2000); *NC Gen Stat* §§ 78C-71 to -81 (1999); *ND Cent Code* §§ 9-15-01 to -05 (2001); *Ohio Rev Code Ann* §§ 4771.01–.99 (Anderson 2000); *Okla Stat Ann* tit 70, §§ 821.61 – .71 (1997); *Ore Rev Stat* tit 52, §§ 702.005 – .057 (1999); 5 *Pa Cons Stat* §§ 3301 – 3312 (2000); *SC Code Ann* §§ 16-1-90, 16-1-100, 59-102-10 to -50 (2000); *Tenn Code Ann* §§ 49-7-2112 to -2121 (2000); *Tex Occ Code Ann* §§ 2051.001 – .553 (Vernon 2000).

16. HB 1251, 56th Leg, 1st Reg Sess (Wash 1999).

17. Miss Code Ann § 73-67-1 (2001) (repealing existing agent statute and replacing it with the Uniform Athlete Agents Act).

18. *Alabama to Forfeit $250,000 to N.C.A.A.,* New York Times, B-l, col. 5 (December 16, 1987).

19. Richard P. Woods & Michael R. Mills, *Tortious Interference with an Athletic Scholarship: A University's Remedy for the Unscrupulous Sports Agent,* 40 Alabama L Rev (1988).

20. Ala Code, § 8-26-1.1.

21. The following series of articles provide detailed analysis of athlete agent statutes: Rob Remis, *Analysis of Civil and Criminal Penalties in Athlete Agent Statutes and Support for the imposition of Civil and Criminal Liability Upon Athletes,* 8 Seton Hall J of Sport L 1 (1998); Rob Remis, *The Art of Being a Sports Agent in More than One State: Analysis of Registration and Reporting Requirements and Development of a Model Strategy,* 8 Seton Hall J of Sport L 419 (1998); Rob Remis & Diane Sudia, *Escaping Athlete Agent Statutory Regulation: Loopholes and Constitutional Defectiveness Based on Tri-Parte Classification of Athletes,* 9 Seton Hall J of Sports L 1 (1999); Diane Sudia & Rob Remis, *Athlete Agent Solicitation of Athlete Clients: Statutory Authorization and Prohibition,* 10 Seton Hall J of Sports L 205

(2000); Diane Sudia & Rob Remis, *Statutory Regulation of Agent Gifts to Athletes*, 10 Seton Hall J of Sport L 265 (2000); Diane Sudia & Rob Remis, *Athlete Agent Contract: Legislative Regulation*, 10 Seton Hall J of Sport L 317 (2000).

22. Ala Code, § 8-26-4.

23. *See, e.g.*, Ga Code Ann § 43-4A-10.

24. *See, e.g.*, Ala Code §§ 8-26-4, 8-26-5; Fla Stat § 468.453; Ga Code Ann §§ 43-4A-4 & 43-4A-5; Iowa Code Ann § 9A.3; Ky Rev Stat Ann §§ 164.682 (Michie 1999); La Rev Stat Ann § 4:422; Md Ann Code § 4-407; Miss Code Ann § 73-41-3; NC Gen Stat §§ 78C-72; Okla Stat Ann tit 70, § 821.62(c); Tex Rev Civ Stat Ann § 2051.101.

25. Nev Rev Stat § 597.920.

26. Cal Bus & Prof Code § 18896.

27. *See, e.g.*, Ark. Code Ann §§ 17-16-201 (Lexis 1999).

28. Cal Bus & Prof Code § 18896.

29. Conn Gen Stat §§ 20-556.

30. NC Gen Stat § 78C-72(f).

31. Ala Code § 8-26-14; Cal Lab Code § 1519; Ga Code Ann § 43-4A-13; Iowa Code Ann § 9A.6; Miss Code Ann § 73-41-9; NC Gen Stat § 78C-17(e); Okla Stat Ann tit 70, § 821.62(g); Tex Rev Civ Stat Ann art 8871, § 2(h).

32. Ga Code Ann § 43-4A-13; Fla Stat Ann § 468.453(g).

33. Ky Rev Stat Ann § 518.010(9); Mich Comp Laws Ann § 750.41 le(3)(g); Minn Stat Ann § 325E.33(b).

34. Ala Code 8-26-2(2); Cal Lab Code § 1500(b); La Rev Stat Ann § 421(A)(4), (5); NC Gen Stat § 78C-60; Okla Stat Ann tit 70, §§ 821.61(A)(4), (5).

35. Mo Ann Stat § 436.209(2).

36. *See, e.g.*, Ala Code §§ 8-26-22(b); Ark Code Ann § 17-16-205(b)(2); Cal Bus & Prof Code § 18897.63(c); Fla Stat Ann § 468.456(2)(b); Ky Rev Stat Ann § 164.683(11); NC Gen Stat § 78C-77; Or Rev Stat Ann 702.027; Tenn Code Ann § 49-7-2114(b)(2); Tex Occ Code Ann § 2051.351(A).

37. NC Gen Stat § 78C-77.

38. *See, e.g.*, Ala Code § 8-26-7(a)(11); Ark Code Ann § 17-16-205(b)(1); Cal Bus & Prof Code §18897.63(b); Colo Rev Stat Ann § 23-16-105(2)(a); Fla Stat Ann § 468.456(2)(a); Ky Rev Stat Ann § 164.683(10); Or Rev Stat Ann 702.027; Tenn Code Ann § 49-7-2114(b)(1); Tex Occ Code Ann § 2051.351(b)(1).

39. Or Rev Stat Ann 702.027.

40. Ala Code § 8-26-22(d).

41. Calif Bus & Prof Code, § 18897.5.

42. The National Association of Intercollegiate Athletics (NAIA), organized in 1940, has rules similar to those of the NCAA. Its member institutions are generally smaller schools. *See Williams v Hamilton*, 497 F Supp 641 (DNH 1980).

43. Miss Code Ann § 74-41-7(1)(c); Tex Civ Prac & Rem Code Ann § 131.002 (West Supp 1990).

44. *Kan Stat Ann* § 44-1513 (2000).

45. *Minn Stat Ann* § 325.33 (2000).

46. *Ga Code Ann* § 43-4A-16 (2000).

47. *E.g.*, Kan Stat Ann § 44-1505 (2000); NC Gen Stat § 78C-73 (2000); Ga Code Ann § 43-4A-7 (2000).

48. *See, e.g.*, Ala Code § 8-26-22 (2000); Ark Code Ann § 17-16-102 (2000); Fla Stat Ann § 468.454 (2000).

49. Colo Rev Stat Ann § 23-16-105 (2000).

50. *E.g.*, Fla Stat Ann § 468.4561 (2000); NC Gen Stat § 78C-79 (2000).

51. *E.g.*, Ga Code Ann § 43-4A-13 (2000); Cal Bus & Prof Code § 18897.87 (2000).

52. *E.g.*, Ga Code Ann § 43-4A-16 (2000); La Rev Stat Ann § 4:426 (2000).

53. 5 Pa Con Stat § 3309 (2000).

54. *E.g.*, Kan Stat Ann § 44-1511 (2000).

55. *E.g.*, Iowa Code Ann § 9A.11 (2000).

56. *E.g.*, Tenn Code Ann § 49-7-2116 (2000).

57. *E.g.*, La Rev Stat Ann § 4:433 (2000).

58. *See* Edward V. King, Jr., *Dependency Leads to Abuse*, New York Times § 8–9, col. 2 (March 5, 1989).

59. *See, e.g.*, Cal Bus & Prof Code § 18895.2(2)(a); Fla Stat Ann § 468.452(2); La Rev Stat Ann § 430; Miss Code Ann § 73-41-2 1; NC Gen Stat § 78C-2(1)(c); Okla Stat Ann tit 70, § 821.71.

60. *See, e.g.*, Ala Code § 8-26-2(2); Iowa Code Ann § 9A.2(2); Ken Rev Stat Ann § 164.680(3)(b); La Rev Stat Ann § 4:421(2); Ohio Rev Code Ann § 4771.01(B)(2); Tenn Code Ann § 49-7-2111(2).

61. *Texas Fines Former Heisman Winner Firm Under Agent Law*, NCAA News (December 27, 1989).

62. *Id.*

63. Danny Robbins, *Agent Fined, Suspended by State*, Houston Chronicle, January 19, 1996.

64. Franz Lidz & Richard O'Brien, *Seminole Justice*, Sports Illustrated, August 8, 1994.

65. Jack McCallum & Richard O'Brien, *Singled Out*, Sports Illustrated, July 25, 1994.

66. *Limogate Finally Runs Its Course*, Sun-Sentinel Ft. Lauderdale, June 23, 1999.

67. *Agent's Arrest Ordered by Judge*, Atlanta Journal and Constitution, September 1, 1999.

68. *Man Impersonates Jarvis' Agent*, News and Observer (Raleigh), May 26, 2000.

69. Chris Harry, *Attorney Pleads Out in UF Case*, Orlando Sentinel, May 25, 2000.

70. *See, e.g.*, *Taylor v Wake Forest University*, 191 SE2d 379 (NC Ct App 1972) cert. den. 192 SE 2d 197; *Begley v Corporation of Mercer University*, 367 F Supp 908 (E D Tenn 1973); Derek Quinn Jones, Note, *Educating Misguided Student Athletes: An Application of Contract Theory*, 85 Columbia L Rev 96 (1985). *See also* Woods & Mills, 40 Alabama L Rev 141 (cited in note 19).

71. Scott Edelman, *Colleges Can Take Action Against Agents*, New York Times, (October 15, 1995).

72. *Id.*

73. *Id.*

74. Rob Remis, *The Art of Being a Sports Agent in More Than One State: Analysis of Registration and Reporting Requirements and Development of A Model Strategy*, 8 Seton Hall J of Sport L 419, 449 (1998). These panels are also permitted to advise student athletes regarding professional careers; provide information to assist athletes in obtaining a loan for purchasing insurance to guard against a disabling injury; and review a proposed contract with a professional team. *Id.*

75. *Id.*

76. Diane Sudia & Rob Remis, *The History Behind Athlete Agent Regulation and the "Slam Dunking of Statutory Hurdles,"* 8 Villanova Sports & Ent L 67, 88 (2001).

77. *Id.* at 67, 85.

78. *Id.* at 67, 86. For a thorough discussion of vagueness concerns with athlete agent laws, see Rob Remis & Diane Sudia, *Escaping Athlete Agent Statutory Regulation: Loopholes and Constitutional Defectiveness Based on Tri-Parte Classification of Athletes,* 9 Seton Hall J of Sport L 1 (1999).

79. Gary Kohn, *Sports Agents Representing Professional Athletes: Being Certified Means. Never Having to Say You're Qualified,* Ent and Sports Lawyer 6, no. 3 (Winter 1988): 17.

80. *City of Oakland v Oakland Raiders,* 174 Cal App 3d 414 (1985). For a thorough discussion of the related preemption and federalism issue as well as the use of the supremacy clause, see Paul Wolfson, *Preemption and Federalism: The Missing Link,* Hastings Constitutional L Quarterly 69 (Fall 1988). *See* also *Partee v San Diego Chargers Football Co.,* 34 Cal App 3d 378, 194 *Cal Rptr* 367, 668 P2d 674 (1983), which reaches a similar decision in holding that the NFL requires nationally uniform regulation and that it would be unnecessarily burdened if state antitrust laws applied.

81. *Walters, Alabama Settle Dispute over Signings,* Sports Industry News 156, (May 20, 1988).

82. Craig Neff, *Soft Time,* Sports Illustrated 13 (May 23, 1988).

83. *Agent Conviction Thrown Out by Alabama Appeals Panel,* Sports Industry News 5 (January 6, 1989). *Abernethy v State,* 545 So 2d 185 (Ala Ct App 1988).

Chapter 12. A Uniform Approach

1. Robert N. Davis, *Exploring the Contours of Agent Regulation: The Uniform Athlete Agents Act,* 8 Villanova Sports & Ent L J 1 (2001) (providing a detailed discussion of the legislative history of the act).

2. There are currently more than 140 uniform laws. See Directory of Uniform Acts and Codes, U.L.A. (1989 West Supp.).

3. *See, e.g.,* Uniform Arbitration Act, Explanation, 7 U.L.A. IV (1985).

4. Davis, *Exploring the Contours,* at 3 (cited in note 1) (quoting NCCUSL's 1999–2000 Refernce Book). The National Conference of Commisioners on Uniform State Laws was organized in 1892. The objective of the conference is to promote uniformity in state law on all subjects where the states agree uniformity is desirable.

5. The majority of states provide the governor or legislature with express legislative authority to appoint an average of four commissioners for three-year terms.

6. Davis, *Exploring the Contours* at 3 (cited in note 1).

7. *Id.* at 5 (quoting letter from Richard C. Hite, Chairman, Study Committee, to Study Committee Members (July 23, 1996) (on file with author)).

8. *Id.* at 4.

9. *Id.* at 5 (quoting letter from Bion Gregory, President, NCCUSL, to Richard C. Hite, Chairman, Study Committee (June 14, 1996) (on file with author).

10. *Id.* at 5–6 (quoting letter from Richard C. Hite, Chairman, Study Committee, to Study Committee Members (July 23, 1996) (on file with author)).

11. *Id.* at 6.

12. *Id.*

13. *Prefatory Note,* Uniform Athlete Agents Act 6 (2000) [hereinafter UAAA].

14. Legislative Fact Sheet. The National Conference of Commissioners on Uniform State Laws website, <http://www.law.upenn.edu/bll/ulc/ulc_fname.htm> (visited March 12, 2002).

15. *Id.* at 5–6.

16. *Id.* at 6.

17. § 2 (2), UAAA.

18. *Prefatory Note,* UAAA.

19. *Prefatory Note,* UAAA.

20. § 5, UAAA.

21. *Prefatory Note,* UAAA.

22. Davis, *Exploring the Contours* at 9 (cited in note 1).

23. § 9, UAAA.

24. Davis, *Exploring the Contours* at 13 (cited in note 1).

25. § 5 (b), UAAA.

26. § 4 (c), UAAA.

27. *Prefatory Note,* UAAA.

28. § 10 (6)(c), UAAA.

29. § 10 (6)(d), UAAA.

30. *Prefatory Note,* UAAA.

31. § 11 (a) & (b).

32. *Prefatory Note,* UAAA.

33. § 13, UAAA.

34. § 14, UAAA.

35. § 15, UAAA.

36. *Prefatory Note,* UAAA.

37. § 16, cmt, UAAA.

38. § 17, UAAA.

39. Phillip J. Closius, *Hell Hath No Fury Like a Fan Scorned: State Regulation of Sports Agents,* 30 U Tol L Rev 511, 520 (1999).

40. Diane Sudia & Rob Remis, *Athlete Agent Legislation in the New Millennium: State Statutes and the Uniform Athlete Agents Act,* 11 Seton Hall J of Sport L 263, 279 (2001)

41. *Prefatory Note,* UAAA.

42. Davis, *Exploring the Contours* at 17 (cited in note 1).

43. Diane Sudia & Rob Remis, *The History Behind Athlete Agent Regulation and the "Slam Dunking of Statutory Hurdles,"* 8 Villanova Sports & Ent L J 67, 91 (2001).

Chapter 13. Conclusion

1. Rodney K. Smith & Robert D. Walker, *From Inequity to Opportunity: Keeping the Promises Made to Big-Time Intercollegiate Student Athletes,* 1 Nevada L J 160, 166 (2001).

2. *Id.* at 187–92.

3. *Id.* at 167.

4. Kenneth L. Shropshire, *The Erosion of the NCAA Amateurism Model,* Antitrust 46 (Spring 2000).

5. A fine summary of these possible legal impediments may be found in Smith & Walker, *From Inequity to Opportunity* at 166 (cited in note 1).

6. NCAA, *Division I Amateurism Deregulation Proposal* 2 (2002).

7. *Id.* at 1.

8. *Id.* at 5.

9. *Id.* at 6.

10. *Id.*

11. *Id.* at 7.

12. *Id.* at 8.

13. *Id.* at 8.

14. Gary T. Brown, *Board Task Force Creates Guidelines for Reform*, NCAA News 1, A8 (January 21, 2002).

15. *Division I Amateurism Deregulation Proposal* 10 (cited in note 6).

16. *Id.*

17. See David Pickle, *Experience-Based Amateurism Model Presented to Division II Membership*, NCAA News C1 (January 17, 2000).

18. Title IX of the Civil Rights Act of 1964, as amended by the Education Amendments of 1972.

19. Daniel Feigen, *Green with Envy: Athletes Earn College and NCAA Money, But What's in It for Them?* Houston Chronicle 1 (March 31, 1991).

20. Even these, if at a fixed level, could be subject to antitrust scrutiny. For a discussion of those potential issues, see *Sports and Antitrust: Should College Students Be Paid to Play?* 65 Notre Dame L Rev 206 (1990) and Note, *Sherman Act Invalidation of NCAA Amateurism Rules,* 105 Harvard L Rev 1299 (1992).

21. Mike Freeman, *Pro Football: Players Union Taking Steps to Exert More Control over Agents,* New York Times § 8, p. 5 (March 10, 2002).

22. *Id.*

23. *Id.*

24. Dan Moldea, Interference: *How Organized Crime Influences Professional Football* at 409 (William Morrow, 1989)

25. *Valukas Warns Mafia May Invade College Sports, Agents' Ranks,* Sports Industry News 125 (April 28, 1989).

26. For studies on the problems generally, see Richard Lapchick and John B. Slaughter, eds., *The Rules of the Game: Ethics in College Sports* (Macmillan for the American Council on Education, 1989), and Rick Telander, *The Hundred Yard Lie: The Corruption of College Football and What We Can Do to Stop It* (Simon & Schuster, 1989).

27. Ted Tinling, *Tinling: Sixty Years in Tennis* at 61 (Sidgwick & Jackson, 1983).

Index

Acknowledgments

A number of people were helpful directly and indirectly in researching this book. An incomplete list includes Allen Saunderson, Wendi Huntley, Ray Anderson, Stanley King, Craig Fenech, Charles Grantham, Michael Jackson, Edward V. King, Jr., Pam Lester, Ash Narayan, Roger Noll, Jeff Orleans, Phil dePiciotto, Reginald Wilkes, Wayne Wilson, Michael Siegel, Greg Smith, Bill Strickland, John Carlos, André Colona, Reginald Turner, Scott Rosner, and Kevin Young. Invaluable research assistance was provided by Jason Buchanan, Kim Chainey, Tiffany Fujioka, Nicole King, Nancy Ladson, Jeffrey Lepchenske, Roslyn Levine, Paul McNamara, Henry Moniz, Kelly Motycka, Michael Rivera, Melissa Shingles, and Sankar Suryanarayan. Important research assistance and writing was provided in Chapter 3, "Consolidation," by Marc Chodock, a one-time student of Professor Shropshire's.

This book is a collaboration of two men who followed similar yet different paths from inner-city Southern League schools in Los Angeles (Professor Shropshire at Dorsey and Professor Davis at Washington) to Stanford University to law school, private practice, and then the academy. We observed each other's work from afar as we both pursued sports in scholarship. The names looked curiously familiar but it was years before we contacted each other. This work constitutes our second collaboration in the area of sports law and business, the first being *A Modern Sports Law Anthology*.

Professor Shropshire would like to thank Kellen Winslow for an expensive, firsthand exposure to the business. Expensive but fun and informative.

We would both particularly like to thank our families for being supportive on yet another project. For Tim, that's wife Ida and daughter Adia. For Kenneth, it's Diane and their children, Theresa and Sam.